Mastering Jenkins

Configure and extend Jenkins to architect, build, and automate efficient software delivery pipelines

Jonathan McAllister

[PACKT] open source*
PUBLISHING   community experience distilled

BIRMINGHAM - MUMBAI

Mastering Jenkins

First published: October 2015

Production reference: 1211015

Published by Packt Publishing Ltd.
Livery Place
35 Livery Street
Birmingham B3 2PB, UK.

ISBN 978-1-84719-752-8

www.packtpub.com

Credits

Author
Jonathan McAllister

Reviewers
Thomas Dao

Takafumi Ikeda

Stefan Lapers

Riddhi M. Sharma

Donald Simpson

Commissioning Editor
Amarabha Banerjee

Acquisition Editor
Vinay Argekar

Content Development Editor
Amey Varangaonkar

Technical Editor
Siddhesh Patil

Copy Editors
Sonia Mathur

Karuna Narayanan

Project Coordinator
Nidhi Joshi

Proofreader
Safis Editing

Indexer
Mariammal Chettiyar

Graphics
Disha Haria

Production Coordinator
Conidon Miranda

Cover Work
Conidon Miranda

Cover Image
Stephanie McAllister

Foreword

Agile practices are gaining influence within diverse companies worldwide, yet not without a cultural and technological tension between delivery teams and various groups within their organizations.

This tension is partly born of a natural instinct to reject new ideas, but more importantly due to a disbelief that these practices will live up to their claim of delivering business value at a faster rate with better quality.

Although this book is not entirely focused on project management per se, it does lay the foundation for the success of modern product development by creating the case for Continuous Build, Integration, Delivery, and Deployment solutions.

Continuous practices help ensure that the software is being compiled and tested properly and is always in a deployable state, not only on the developer's workstation. Continuous integration will ensure that the different subsystems function correctly according to the expectations set in code and by the business. Continuous delivery ensures that the artefacts created in the previous steps can be reused and deployed to higher environments to showcase the product to its stakeholders, whereas continuous deployment pushes these artefacts to production for quick assessment of a hypothesis.

Creating a delivery pipeline is at the core of our ability to develop business value with a cadence that is desired by product owners. This is achieved thanks to something we never had the luxury of having previously: the ability to fail fast because we could not hope for anything better than being able to quickly test a hypothesis by deploying it, assessing its impact, and reverting or pivoting when misguided or misinformed about our market conditions.

Producing software in this manner cannot be achieved without automation. This provides a safety net for developers as they adapt or refactor code; it scales the regression test cases as the product evolves and grows and, perhaps as importantly, describes and executes server provisioning, configuration, and the deployment of its applications.

A product's success is based on fast feedback, whether good or bad, and this book details the practical ways of using Jenkins, its plugins, and ecosystem to assure fast feedback for architects, developers, testers, the product's stakeholders, and by extension, its customers.

It is therefore essential to master the pipeline architecture and automation in order to give businesses the tools that shorten the time between concept to cash, in addition to creating low-ceremony deployments as part of the standard software development lifecycle.

Taken holistically, this book will not only teach you about deployment pipelines using Jenkins, but will also prepare you for the cultural change to DevOps, which will improve your product development methods even further.

Itamar Hassin

Thought Leader and Project Lead, ThoughtWorks

About the Author

Jonathan McAllister has been creating software and automation since he was a child. However professionally he leverages 10 years of experience in software development, test, and delivery practices. During his career, he has architected and implemented software build, test, and delivery solutions for cutting-edge technology organizations across diverse technology stacks. Jonathon has most recenltly been focusing on build pipelines, continuous integration, continuous delivery, microservice architecture, process, and the implementation of highly scalable automation solutions for some of the industry's most notable companies, including Microsoft, Merck, and Logitech.

His focus is entirely on designing scalable software build, delivery, and test pipelines in an effort to streamline releases through standardization and help develop strategies that can elevate revenue through modern continuous practices.

As a successful entrepreneur, writer, and business consultant, Jonathan has had the unique opportunity to oversee and implement efficient delivery pipelines at organizations of varying technologies, stacks, and cultures.

Riddhi contributed to the technical content in *Chapter 5, Advanced Automated Testing*, specifically in relation to the integration of MSTest with Jenkins. We would like to thank him for his efforts in this area.

About the Reviewers

Thomas Dao has worked in the IT industry for over two decades. His domains include Unix administration, Build/Release, Java/Android development, and so on.

Takafumi Ikeda works as a sales engineer at GitHub. Before joining GitHub, he worked as a scrum master and a DevOps for many projects. Takafumi is also the author of a book that focused on DevOps. This book received an award in the Japanese market in 2014, and was also translated into Chinese and Korean and published in the Asian market. He has made several presentations as a speaker at several technical conferences in Japan and other Asian countries.

Stefan Lapers started his career almost 20 years ago as an IT support engineer. Thereafter, he quickly grew into Linux/Unix system engineering and software development.

Over the years, he accumulated experience in deploying and maintaining hosted application solutions while working for reputed customers such as MTV, TMF, and many others. In recent years, he was involved in multiple development projects and their delivery as a service on the Internet.

He enjoys spending his spare time with his family and in building and flying remote-controlled helicopters.

Riddhi M. Sharma is a senior software engineer and a technology enthusiast at Physicians Interactive. She holds extensive experience that encompasses multiple areas of technology, such as Cloud, Agile (Continuous Integration/Delivery), and software development. Riddhi is also focused on digital marketing research/strategy and growth hacking and has expertise in Salesforce's exact target marketing platform. He loves to explore product ideas, connect to the community at technical events, and speak on emerging technologies.

I would like to thank Jonathan McAllister for his passion and valuable contribution to the Jenkins community with his excellent book called *Mastering Jenkins*. I would also like to thank the entire Packt team for their great efforts on this book and high standards of work.

Donald Simpson is an information technology consultant based in Scotland, UK. He specializes in helping organizations improve the quality, and reduce the cost, of software development through build automation. Donald has also designed and implemented continuous integration solutions for a broad range of companies and agile projects. He can be reached at www.donaldsimpson.co.uk.

www.PacktPub.com

Support files, eBooks, discount offers, and more

For support files and downloads related to your book, please visit www.PacktPub.com.

Did you know that Packt offers eBook versions of every book published, with PDF and ePub files available? You can upgrade to the eBook version at www.PacktPub.com and as a print book customer, you are entitled to a discount on the eBook copy. Get in touch with us at service@packtpub.com for more details.

At www.PacktPub.com, you can also read a collection of free technical articles, sign up for a range of free newsletters and receive exclusive discounts and offers on Packt books and eBooks.

https://www2.packtpub.com/books/subscription/packtlib

Do you need instant solutions to your IT questions? PacktLib is Packt's online digital book library. Here, you can search, access, and read Packt's entire library of books.

Why subscribe?

- Fully searchable across every book published by Packt
- Copy and paste, print, and bookmark content
- On demand and accessible via a web browser

Free access for Packt account holders

If you have an account with Packt at www.PacktPub.com, you can use this to access PacktLib today and view 9 entirely free books. Simply use your login credentials for immediate access.

To my wife Stephanie who dared me to dream and reach for the stars. May she come to know that she is the only star I'll ever need. To my children Adrian, Bryce, Caden and Devin who have taught me the meaning and the purpose of my existence.

Table of Contents

Preface

Jenkins is a highly acclaimed award-winning build and automation orchestration solution. It represents the cumulative efforts of hundreds of open-source developers, quality assurance engineers, and DevOps personnel worldwide. What makes this solution uniquely innovative is it is continuously updated, improved upon, and supported by this cohesively vibrant open-source community. It is through this open-source development effort that Jenkins has remained in the forefront of Continuous Integration, and Continuous Delivery practices.

The Jenkins platform bridges engineering disciplines, quality assurance landscapes, and business interests in an effort to connect traditionally isolated factions and transform them into cohesive engineering teams. Over the years it has vaulted in popularity and gained notoriety as an industry standard tool. Through its extensibility and collaboration initiatives its adoption rate has grown exponentially and now touts well over 100K installations worldwide.

I was formally introduced to Jenkins in 2008 when it was still Hudson. It was during this era that Hudson was just beginning to gain momentum by engineering groups outside of the Java development community. The software configuration management team I worked for was looking to implement a standardized architecture and delivery service solution across a large number of diversely acquired technology stacks. This began our quest to solidify a set of standards in build and delivery that could be applied across these diverse technology stacks and scale.

These experiences provided me with a pretty solid understanding of continuous integration, continuous delivery, build pipelines, automated testing, and the capabilities of Jenkins. By 2012 we were able to scale our implementations across a multitude of technology stacks of varying size and scope. All of these experiences would eventually culminate in me writing this book.

What this book covers

This book represents the amalgamation of a decade's worth of professional research, development, and automation engineering at numerous organizations with diverse technology disciplines. I wrote this book in an effort to provide a practical implementation guide for continuous integration, continuous delivery, and continuous deployment. With this book, my objective was to provide readers with some of the tools they will need while architecting, evangelizing, and implementing complete end-to-end build pipeline solutions at organizations of varying sizes and engineering topologies.

Chapter 1, Setup and Configuration of Jenkins, aims to teach reader how to manage instances of Jenkins of any size or scale. This is not an easy feat because Jenkins is highly diverse and supports almost any platform. You will learn about the initial setup, backup strategies, configuration techniques, best practices, and how to horizontally scale and properly manage the service.

Chapter 2, Distributed Builds – Master/Slave Mode, provides you with a complete guide on how to set up distributed build solutions and slave agents. This is a critical implementation and helps you understand when Jenkins needs to expand and support larger audiences and more diverse technology stacks.

In *Chapter 3, Creating Views and Jobs in Jenkins,* and *Chapter 4, Managing Views and Jobs in Jenkins,* we aim at documenting the knobs and dials that Jenkins provides on the dashboard, and the contained views and jobs. This is fundamental Jenkins knowledge and the goal here is to provide a solid understanding of the Jenkins platform.

Chapter 5, Advanced Automated Testing, talks about how to improve quality assurance efficiency. It teaches you how to architect and implement automated testing solutions that provide business value. This is crucial to any continuous solution because the pipeline must remain efficient and free of bottlenecks. Implementing automated testing is always a gentle balancing act. There is a trade-off between the time spent executing test automation and ensuring the rapid velocity of delivery.

Automated deployments are a cornerstone of continuous practices and build pipelines. *Chapter 6, Software Deployments and Delivery,* discusses how to implement scalable automated deployment jobs in Jenkins. This includes upstream and downstream jobs and how to manage them through naming conventions. In this chapter, we will discover some tips and tricks aimed at helping to keep deployments nimble and releases efficient.

Chapter 7, Build Pipelines, introduces the concept of a build pipeline and teaches you how to develop and scale them. Build pipelines are a foundational requirement of continuous delivery and continuous deployment. This chapter has been written in an effort to provide you with a set of scalable practices that can be applied across a multitude of technology stacks.

Chapter 8, Continuous Practices, defines continuous integration, continuous delivery, and continuous deployment. It provides a practice implementation guide for each. Jenkins has evolved and extended dramatically and now supports a complete array of continuous practices. This chapter aims to convey a set of defined implementation approaches to continuous integration, continuous delivery, and continuous deployment with examples for each. Jenkins integrates extraordinarily well with hundreds of diverse technologies.

Chapter 9, Integrating Jenkins with Other Technologies, introduces some of the more exciting automation technologies, such as Docker, Ansible, Selenium, Artifactory, and Jira. This chapter shows you how to interconnect them through Jenkins. The ability to extend Jenkins through its plugin architecture is one of the primary reasons that it has become so popular.

Chapter 10, Extending Jenkins, aims at writing a set of basic how-to articles. It describes how to begin to write plugins, how to extend Jenkins with extension points, and how to manipulate the Jenkins system even further.

I hope you will embark on a journey with me in discovering Jenkins, mastering the concepts that surround build pipelines and implementing automation at scale. Writing a book is something I have dreamed of doing for many years. I hope that you will gain as much in reading the book as I have gained by writing it.

What you need for this book

An existing installation of Jenkins is recommended (but not needed). Beyond that, we have provided examples in the following programming languages:

- Ruby v1.93
- Java
- C# (via MSBuild)
- JavaScript
- Bash/Dash + Expect
- Ansible YAML

Who this book is for

This book is intended for novice and intermediate-level Jenkins enthusiasts who are in a unique position to implement and evangelize continuous integration practices, continuous delivery solutions, and as a result build pipelines.

Conventions

In this book, you will find a number of styles of text that distinguish between different kinds of information. Here are some examples of these styles, and an explanation of their meaning.

Code words in text are shown as follows: "For example if the Jenkins system is configured to utilize a context path of `http://localhost:8080/jenkins`"

A block of code is set as follows:

```
<arguments>-Xrs -Xmx512m -Dhudson.lifecycle=hudson.lifecycle.
WindowsServiceLifecycle -jar "%BASE%\jenkins.war" --httpPort=8080</
arguments>
```

Any command-line input or output is written as follows:

```
$Jenkins-Mirror>sudo su - root
$Jenkins-Mirror>cat /tmp/id_rsa.pub >> ~/.ssh/authorized_keys
```

New terms and **important words** are shown in bold. Words that you see on the screen, in menus or dialog boxes for example, appear in the text like this: "Click on the **Recovery** tab as shown"

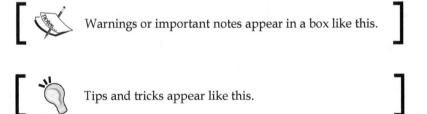

Warnings or important notes appear in a box like this.

Tips and tricks appear like this.

Reader feedback

Feedback from our readers is always welcome. Let us know what you think about this book—what you liked or may have disliked. Reader feedback is important for us to develop titles that you really get the most out of.

To send us general feedback, simply send an e-mail to feedback@packtpub.com, and mention the book title via the subject of your message.

If there is a topic that you have expertise in and you are interested in either writing or contributing to a book, see our author guide on www.packtpub.com/authors.

Customer support

Now that you are the proud owner of a Packt book, we have a number of things to help you to get the most from your purchase.

Downloading the example code

You can download the example code files for all Packt books you have purchased from your account at http://www.packtpub.com. If you purchased this book elsewhere, you can visit http://www.packtpub.com/support and register to have the files e-mailed directly to you.

Errata

Although we have taken every care to ensure the accuracy of our content, mistakes do happen. If you find a mistake in one of our books—maybe a mistake in the text or the code—we would be grateful if you would report this to us. By doing so, you can save other readers from frustration and help us improve subsequent versions of this book. If you find any errata, please report them by visiting http://www.packtpub.com/submit-errata, selecting your book, clicking on the **errata submission form** link, and entering the details of your errata. Once your errata are verified, your submission will be accepted and the errata will be uploaded on our website, or added to any list of existing errata, under the Errata section of that title. Any existing errata can be viewed by selecting your title from http://www.packtpub.com/support.

Piracy

Piracy of copyright material on the Internet is an ongoing problem across all media. At Packt, we take the protection of our copyright and licenses very seriously. If you come across any illegal copies of our works, in any form, on the Internet, please provide us with the location address or website name immediately so that we can pursue a remedy.

Please contact us at `copyright@packtpub.com` with a link to the suspected pirated material.

We appreciate your help in protecting our authors, and our ability to bring you valuable content.

The Website

When this book, I decided it would be valuable to set up a website dedicated to supporting its readers. Please feel free to visit and drop me a line with any comments or questions. The URL is provided below:

`http://www.masteringjenkins.com/`

Questions

You can contact us on our Mastering Jenkins website at or you can submit questions to the publisher at `questions@packtpub.com` if you are having a problem with any aspect of the book, and we will do our best to address it.

1
Setup and Configuration of Jenkins

Welcome to *Mastering Jenkins*. In this book, we will journey into the world of build pipelines, automated testing, product delivery, and automation. Together we will discover innovative ways to integrate Jenkins into the last mile of software development, while furthering our knowledge of modern software engineering and delivery practices. We will also discover scalable solutions that will help us catch defects faster and deliver reliable software releases at higher velocities.

Our quest to master Jenkins will take us on an adventure in software engineering, quality assurance, operations, architecture, and business process. These diverse engineering and business disciplines uniquely tie together in software delivery pipelines. By thought leading an organization and evangelizing good software development practices, we can implement diversely scalable pipelines across any number of technology stacks. As a result, an organization can outpace and outmaneuver its competition.

Sprinkled throughout the pages of this book, you will discover some Zen proverbs, which will be used to enlighten our journey. In literary works and historical texts, Zen proverbs can be found in books that date back as early as the Tang dynasty [618–907 AD]. During this period, Zen proverbs and Koans were widely adopted by Buddhist monks as a way of promoting enlightenment through critical thinking and self-discovery. These were further used as a way of teaching patience, persistence, and enlightenment.

> *"If you are planning for a year, sow rice. If you are planning for a decade, plant a tree. If you are planning for a lifetime, educate people." -- A Chinese Proverb*

This proverb instills values of planning, forethought, and education. These values are key components to engineering, and encourage a plan for future sustainability. In Jenkins, we can apply this concept to the architecture of software delivery pipelines. When advocating for any cross-discipline collaborative cross-discipline practices we will need to evangelize good architecture, plan the implementation properly, define conventions, build a scalable solution, and then educate the user base. By doing this, we can prevent most long-term Jenkins management nightmares by making it easier to navigate and maintain. Due to the highly configurable nature of Jenkins, and the various moving parts of the SDLC structuring the system carefully and organizing it should be a constant consideration.

In this chapter, we will begin our journey by discovering proven Jenkins management techniques that can help us provide a stable and scalable Jenkins experience. Together we will learn to adjust Jenkins to fit unique organizational requirements and provide better performance and fewer maintenance headaches. Let's begin!

In this chapter, our focus will be on the following topics:

- The Jenkins platform architecture
- Jenkins on Microsoft Windows
- Configuring the JVM and Java arguments
- Jenkins on Linux and Unix
- Running Jenkins behind an NGINX reverse proxy
- Running Jenkins behind an Apache reverse proxy
- Creating and managing Jenkins backups
- Setting up a Jenkins mirror
- Jenkins on Mac OSX
- The Jenkins LTS release line
- Jenkins XML configuration files

The Jenkins platform architecture and configuration techniques

Jenkins, as you are probably aware, was built using Java. It's cross platform and supports a wide variety of engineering patterns and technologies. It can effectively support organizations of all sizes. Jenkins offers endless automation possibilities and even has a vibrant plugin ecosystem.

In this section, we will cover configuration techniques aimed at advancing our knowledge of the Jenkins architecture. Together, we will lay a foundation for reliable automation and future scalability by learning how to configure the Jenkins main operating environment.

Jenkins offers a cross-platform user experience by running on a **Java Virtual Machine (JVM)**. A JVM is a powerful virtualization technology used to execute Java bytecode instructions, and provides a consistent software platform regardless of the host OS.

The Jenkins community has created native installation packages for Microsoft Windows, Mac OS X, Linux, and Unix. If Jenkins is not already installed (this book assumes it is), it's highly recommended that you use one of the community-provided packages if possible. If a native package is not available, Jenkins an most likely still be configured to run, providing that the host operating system supports any of the following web architectures:

- Apache Tomcat v5.0+
- JBoss Application Server 4.2+
- IBM WebSphere 7.0.0.7+
- WebLogic

It's recommended that you install Jenkins as a system service. There are many available options to accomplish this task on the most popular OS platforms. Additionally, it's important to automatically launch Jenkins during the boot-up phase of the machine.

Jenkins on Microsoft Windows

The initial installation of Jenkins on Microsoft Windows is straightforward. The Microsoft Windows Jenkins MSI package comes complete with the **Java Runtime Environment (JRE)** prerequisite and Microsoft .NET 2.0 framework. This bundling provides a seamless Jenkins installation experience, and alleviates the need for any external prerequisite software installations.

By using the MSI installation package, the Jenkins installation wizards will automatically install itself as a Windows service. By installing Jenkins as a Microsoft Windows service it will become easier to manage and control. Windows services provide an easy way to specify what the system should do when Jenkins crashes.

Once Jenkins has been installed we will want to verify that Jenkins has properly been installed and configured as a Windows service. To do this we will need to open the **Services** area in the **Control Panel** and locate the entry for Jenkins. To navigate to the Windows services management area, go to **Start-> Control Panel -> Administrative Tools -> Services**.

If Jenkins is installed properly as a Windows service, we will see an entry for it listed in the Windows **Services** panel, as shown in the following screenshot:

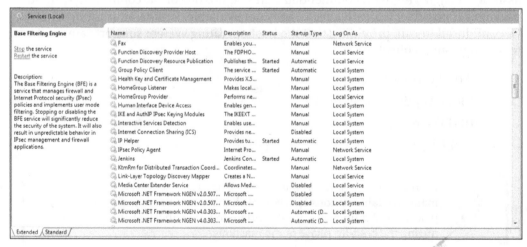

Figure 1-1: The Windows Services panel

The Windows service properties dialog displays the available options for Windows services. From this screen, we can modify how the service is started, what user account the service runs under, and even manage how Microsoft Windows recovers the Jenkins service if it encounters any problems.

To open the Windows service properties panel for Jenkins, double-click on the **Jenkins** entry on the main Windows **Services** panel. Windows will then display the **Jenkins Properties** dialog, as shown here:

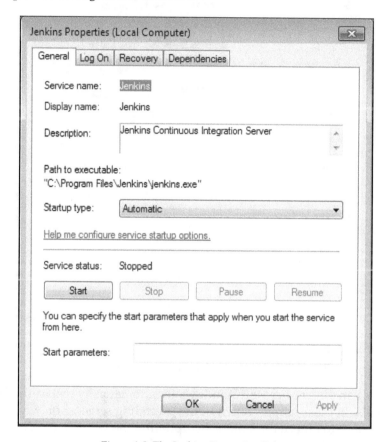

Figure 1-2: The Jenkins Properties dialog

Let's make Jenkins more fault tolerant. To do this, we need to modify the Jenkins Windows service definition and implement a more reliable way for our Jenkins service to recover from failure. Click on the **Recovery** tab, as shown here:

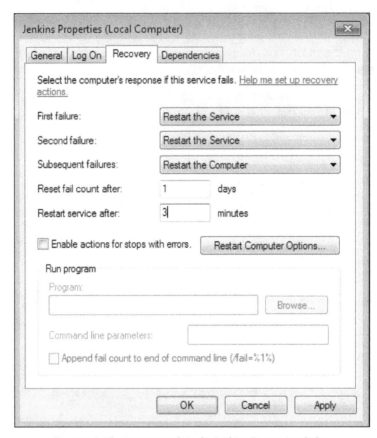

Figure 1-3: The Recovery tab in the Jenkins Properties dialog

From here, we can direct Microsoft Windows to automatically restart the Jenkins service if it fails. In the example shown in the preceding screenshot, we have implemented fault tolerance for Jenkins by updating the fields in the dialog.

To proceed update your Jenkins service to reflect the above implementation. Click on **Apply** and restart the Jenkins service.

Configuring the JVM and Java arguments–port, JRE, and memory

Java `web-ui` applications, including Jenkins, run on port 8080. To change this listening port, we need to modify the Java startup configuration file.

In Microsoft Windows, we can customize all of the Java JVM options by modifying the `Jenkins.xml` configuration file. The primary Jenkins configuration file can be found at `$JENKINS_HOME/jenkins.xml`.

On Microsoft Windows, the `$JENKINS_HOME` directory and primary XML configuration file can usually be found in one of the following locations:

- `C:\Program Files\Jenkins\jenkins.xml`
- `C:\Program Files (x86)\Jenkins\jenkins.xml`

The primary XML configuration file contains a number of settings and options that pertain to the JVM. One of these settings is the listening port. Let's proceed in changing the listening port. We will walk through these steps together.

1. Edit the primary XML configuration file in a text editor and locate the `<arguments>` node. An example of the argument node is shown here:

    ```
    <!-- if you'd like to run Jenkins with a specific version of Java,
    specify a full path to java.exe.
        The following value assumes that you have java in your PATH.
    -->
        <executable>%BASE%\jre\bin\java</executable>
        <arguments>-Xrs -Xmx256m -Dhudson.lifecycle=hudson.
    lifecycle.WindowsServiceLifecycle -jar "%BASE%\jenkins.war"
    --httpPort=8080</arguments>
    ```

2. Change the value for `-httpPort` and save the configuration file.

3. Restart the Jenkins service and verify that Jenkins is running on the preferred port.

 When customizing the Jenkins listener port, it is a requirement that the port Jenkins binds to is not in use by another service (including IIS, Apache, and so on).

Now that we have completed the adjustments to the listening port, let's take a look at some of the other available JVM options.

A default Jenkins installation is allocated 256 MB of memory. The initial memory allocated is sufficient for basic operations. As a Jenkins instance grows and becomes more complex it will inevitably run out of memory. Before we start to see build failures related to Java heap space, or PermGen memory we should allocate additional memory to Java and Jenkins.

Java v1.7, and earlier, uses permanent generation memory and maximum permanent generation memory allocations. With the advent of Java v1.8, Oracle has replaced the permanent generation memory options with metaspace memory options. This has added a bit of confusion surrounding how to properly manage memory in Java. To better understand the JVM and its memory knobs, let's take a look at the following table. It describes what each of the available memory options:

Setting Name	Example Argument	Description
Initial heap size	`-Xms = 512`	Sets the initial Java heap size
Maximum heap size	`-Xmx = 1024m`	Sets the max Java heap size
Initial permanent generation memory	`-XX:PermSize = 512m`	Sets the initial available permanent generation memory
Maximum permanent generation memory	`-XX:MaxPermSize = 1024m`	Sets the highest amount of PermGen memory that can be allocates
Maximum metaspace	`-XX:MaxMetaspaceSize = 1024m`	Sets the max metaspace amount (similar to PermGen but dynamic by default)

Java memory arguments and descriptions for Windows

Allocating too little memory may cause Jenkins and Java to throw memory errors. However, allocating too much memory will degrade the operating system's performance. It is important to adjust these settings carefully, and find a balance suitable for the target system. These settings will need to be customized to fit your specific hardware and operating system configuration. Here is an example to increase the maximum heap size:

```
<arguments>-Xrs –Xmx512m -Dhudson.lifecycle=hudson.lifecycle.
WindowsServiceLifecycle -jar "%BASE%\jenkins.war" --httpPort=8080</
arguments>
```

While customizing the Java options, there are a number of things to keep in mind. Here are a few tips and notes on allocating memory to Microsoft Windows and Java:

- Microsoft Windows has a required overhead for the OS. Be sure to leave enough RAM available for the OS to function properly (more than 128MB).

- The larger the initial heap and/or maximum heap memory size, the larger the permanent generation memory allocation will need to be. This is because the permanent generation memory stores data about the contents of the heap.

- The metaspace switch is *only* available in Java v1.8 or higher versions.

- The permanent generation memory has been deprecated and removed in Java v1.8.

- The memory values you specify must be a multiple of 1,024 and greater than 1 MB.

Jenkins on Linux and UNIX

Jenkins offers a wide spectrum of support for the Linux and Unix operating systems. Its cross-platform capabilities have made it a very popular automation tool. The Jenkins community has created native installation packages for most Linux and Unix distributions. Currently, there are installation packages available for the following Linux and Unix flavors:

- Ubuntu/Debian
- Red Hat/Fedora/CentOS
- OpenSUSE
- FreeBSD
- Solaris/OpenIndiana
- Gentoo
- Docker

The easiest way to install Jenkins on a Linux or Unix system is to use a standard package manager, such as YUM, OpenCSW, IPS, or Aptitude. For the purpose of brevity, we will focus primarily on CentOS (YUM) and Debian oriented (APT) distributions.

Configuring the JVM

On Linux and Unix hosts, configuring the JVM memory parameters involves modifying the service scripts that initialize the Jenkins daemon. For Debian/Ubuntu systems, the file you will need to modify is usually located in `/etc/default/Jenkins`.

For CentOS-based systems, the file you will need to modify is usually located in `/etc/sysconfig/Jenkins`.

Regardless of the operating system, the setting that lets us adjust the JVM options is the `'JAVA_ARGS='` property.

With the advent of Java 1.8, as mentioned earlier, there are some new and deprecated memory settings. The definitions of available memory options are described in table below:

Title	Example Arg	Description
Initial heap size	`-Xms = 512`	Sets the initial Java heap size
Maximum heap size	`-Xmx = 1024m`	Sets the max Java heap size
Initial permanent generation memory	`-XX:PermSize = 512m`	Sets the initial available permanent generation memory
Maximum permanent generation memory	`-XX:MaxPermSize = 1024m`	Sets the highest amount of PermGen memory that can allocated
Maximum metaspace	`-XX:MaxMetaspaceSize = 1024m`	Sets the max metaspace amount (similar to PermGen, but dynamic by default)

Java memory arguments and descriptions for Linux (same as Windows)

Adjusting the memory setting for Java in Linux is simply a matter of adapting the `JAVA_ARGS=` property to contain the correct switches. An example of how to change the initial heap size property is shown here:

```
JAVA_ARGS=-Xmx=512m
```

Once you have completed the modifications to fit your hardware configuration, you will need to restart the Jenkins service to make it take effect.

Memory allocation tip

The larger the initial heap and/or maximum heap memory size, the larger the permanent generation memory allocation will need to be. This is because the *permanent generation* memory stores data about the contents of the heap. These memory settings are designed to let you customize the JVM environment that Jenkins operates in.

Running Jenkins behind an NGINX reverse proxy

One of the newer web server solutions to take the Internet by storm is NGinX (pronounced Engine X). Developed in 2004 under the supervision of Igor Sysoev, NGINX was created to facilitate scalability and the load-balancing requirements of high-traffic web sites. Since its inception, this tool has gained wide acceptance and notoriety. Let's look at how to apply a reverse proxy to Jenkins. This can be accomplished in a straightforward manner. Let's take a few minutes to look at how to achieve this.

If NGINX has not already been installed on the target system, the first step will be to install it. NGINX can easily be installed onto an Ubuntu/Debian or CentOS-based system using the following terminal commands:

```
CENTOS#> yum install nginx
DEBIAN#> apt-get install nginx
```

Upon completing the installation of the NGINX web server, verify that the installation was successful by executing the `nginx -v` command. This will display the version information for the NGINX web server on the terminal and provide us with the assurance that it is installed properly.

Now that the NGINX web server has been installed onto the target system, the system will need to be configured to act as a reverse proxy for the Jenkins JVM. To accomplish this, simply update the `nginx` configuration files to contain a proxy pass. The configuration files for `nginx` on Ubuntu can be found in the following location:

```
/etc/nginx/sites-enabled/default
```

An example (provided at `http://www.jenkins-ci.org`) of a Jenkins proxy pass entry with Jenkins running under a subdomain (`Jenkins.domain.com`) is provided below.

```
server {
    listen 80;
    server_name jenkins.domain.com;
    return 301 https://$host$request_uri;
}

server {

    listen 80;
    server_name jenkins.domain.com;

    location / {
```

```
        proxy_set_header        Host $host;
        proxy_set_header        X-Real-IP $remote_addr;
        proxy_set_header        X-Forwarded-For $proxy_add_x_forwarded_
for;
        proxy_set_header        X-Forwarded-Proto $scheme;

        # Fix the "It appears that your reverse proxy set up is broken"
error.
        proxy_pass              http://127.0.0.1:8080;
        proxy_read_timeout      90;

        proxy_redirect          http://127.0.0.1:8080 https://jenkins.
domain.com;
    }
  }
```

Once the configuration file has been updated, save the file to the disk, and restart nginx with the following command:

```
#>sudo service nginx restart
```

For the Jenkins UI and the NGINX reverse proxy to properly integrate, the context paths of Jenkins and the NGINX subdirectory must match. For example, if the Jenkins system is configured to use a context path of http://localhost:8080/jenkins, the proxy pass context defined in the web server's configuration file must also reflect the /Jenkins suffix.

To set the context path for Jenkins, add the --prefix= entry to the JENKINS_ARGS= property. An example of this configuration entry is provided below.

```
--prefix=/Jenkins
--prefix=/somecontextpathhere
```

The JENKINS_ARGS configuration line is located inside the Jenkins startup bash/dash script. This file is typically found in one of the following locations on the filesystem (dependent on the Linux distribution):

/etc/default/Jenkins

/etc/sysconfig/Jenkins (line 151)

Once everything has been configured, restart the NGINX and Jenkins services to finalize the implementation of the reverse proxy redirect solution.

After this has been completed, navigate from a web browser to your Jenkins URL on port 80, and verify that the Jenkins UI behaves properly.

Running Jenkins behind an Apache reverse proxy

The Apache HTTP Server Project (referred to as Apache) was first released to the public in April 1995. Apache represents a cornerstone of the Internet and is highly acclaimed. Since its initial release, Apache has become one of the most widely adopted web server platforms around the world. Apache thrives to this day, and has a vast array of modules that extend its functionality.

Running Jenkins on a nonstandard web port is a limitation that you may wish to address. It requires users to specify the port as part of the URL, which can become a hassle to manage. To address this concern, it's useful to run Jenkins behind an Apache proxy. Apache provides an extensive set of features that can benefit Jenkins users. Some benefits of this solution include:

- Running Jenkins on port 80 (privileged port workaround)
- Adding SSL support for your Jenkins instance
- Running Jenkins from a different context, either /Jenkins or /ci
- Running Jenkins side by side with other web apps, http://jenkins.foo.com

On Linux and Unix hosts, all TCP and UDP ports lower than 1024 are considered privileged. A privileged port is one where the services exposed are running under a privileged user account (typically, root). Running Jenkins as root is considered dangerous and is, therefore, not recommended. The prescribed user account under which the Jenkins service executes is *jenkins*.

The privileged port restriction can create a bit of a problem for Jenkins administrators. We may want Jenkins to be accessible on standard web port 80, but still want to run it under the Jenkins user account. By running Jenkins behind Apache, we can address this issue while still adhering to best practices.

One possible solution is to run Jenkins behind Apache and use mod_proxy to internally redirect traffic. This solution will allow us to get Jenkins to respond to requests on a privileged port without executing it as the root user, or changing its port configuration.

Apache's mod_proxy operates by forwarding incoming TCP/UDP port 80 requests to Jenkins on port 8080. Any responses from Jenkins are forwarded back to port 80. This creates a seamless experience for web users, while allowing Jenkins to remain on its original port.

To configure Jenkins to use Apache's `mod_proxy` module, we will need a basic installation of the Apache web server (`http://www.apache.org`). If Apache is not already installed on your system, you can use the standard package manager for your Linux or Unix distribution to install it. Here are some example terminal commands to install Apache on Linux:

- Debian/Ubuntu

```
$> sudo apt-get update
$> sudo apt-get install apache2
```

  Installs Apache2 in -> `/etc/apache2`

- CentOS/Fedora

```
$> sudo yum install httpd
```

  Installs Apache2 in -> `/etc/httpd`

Once Apache is installed on the host, we will need to ensure that `mod_proxy` is installed and loaded also.

On RHEL-/CentOS-based systems, `mod_proxy` is typically installed at the same time as Apache. For Debian-based systems, you may need to install the Apache `mod_proxy` module specifically. You can look at your Apache `modules` folder on your system to see whether the `mod_proxy.so` and `mod_proxy_http.so` files are present.

To ensure mod_proxy is operating properly we need to ensure that Apache loads the `mod_proxy.so` and `mod_proxy_http.so` modules when Apache initializes. Apache's configuration file is usually `httpd.conf` or `apache2.conf`, depending on your system. Let's open up the Apache configuration file in an editor (*vi*, *nano*, and so on) and ensure that we have the proper `LoadModule` directives.

Next we will want to direct Apache to load our `mod_proxy` modules. The proper Apache configuration lines are provided below.

```
LoadModule proxy_module modules/mod_proxy.so
LoadModule proxy_http_module modules/mod_proxy_http.so
```

 If the preceding lines do not exist (or are commented out) in your Apache configuration file, you will need to add them or uncomment them.

Once the `LoadModule` changes to the Apache configuration file have been completed, we will need to configure the port 80 `VirtualHost` XML block and create a reverse proxy. An example of an Apache virtual host entry for a Jenkins instance and proxy running on port `80` is provided below.

```
<VirtualHost *:80>
ServerAdmin  webmaster@localhost
ProxyRequests       Off
ProxyPreserveHost On
AllowEncodedSlashes On

    <Proxy *>
        Order deny,allow
        Allow from all
    </Proxy>

    ProxyPass          /  http://localhost:8080/ nocanon
    ProxyPassReverse   /  http://localhost:8080/
</VirtualHost>
```

Now that the virtual host configuration entries have been added, save the configuration file to disk and restart Apache. Depending on the distribution, the commands necessary to restart Apache may vary slightly. Examples for CentOS and Debian are provided here:

- CentOS:

    ```
    $> sudo service httpd restart
    ```

- Debian/Ubuntu:

    ```
    $> sudo service apache2 restart
    ```

 If this is a root level (/) proxy pass, make sure you have a tailing slash in your `ProxyPass` and `ProxyPassReverse` directives.

For the Jenkins UI and the Apache reverse proxy to properly integrate, the context paths of Jenkins and the Apache subdirectory must match. For example, if the Jenkins system is configured to utilize a context path of `http://localhost:8080/jenkins`, the proxy pass context defined in the Apache configuration file must also reflect the `/Jenkins` suffix.

To set the context path for Jenkins, add the `--prefix=` entry to the `JENKINS_ARGS=` property. An example of this configuration entry is provided below.

```
--prefix=/Jenkins
--prefix=/somecontextpathhere
```

The `JENKINS_ARGS` configuration line is located inside the Jenkins startup bash/dash script. This file is typically found in one of the following locations on the filesystem that houses Jenkins (depending on your Linux distribution):

`/etc/default/Jenkins`

`/etc/sysconfig/Jenkins (line 151)`

Once everything has been configured, restart the Apache one more time as well as the Jenkins service to finalize the implementation of the reverse proxy solution. To verify everything is functioning properly navigate from a web browser to your Jenkins URL on port 80 and verify that the Jenkins UI behaves as expected.

Disaster recovery in Jenkins

Operating a Jenkins master from a single machine inherently creates a **Single Point of Failure (SPOF)**. If the Jenkins master was lost for any reason, rebuilding it could be time consuming and may not be very easy. If the Jenkins master is lost or destroyed, there may be a crippling impact on your organization's ability to build, test, or release. Let's address this and create a disaster-recovery plan for Jenkins to ensure a high level of availability and quick turnaround time for any failures that may occur.

Jenkins snapshot backups

Snapshot backups of the `$JENKINS_HOME` directory can provide a level of fault tolerance, and offer an effective solution for system-wide backups. There are a number of Jenkins plugins that can effectively assist us in creating snapshot backups. The most popular backup plugins include BackUp, thinBackup, and SCM Sync configuration. You will need to choose the one that best suits your specific needs.

All of the above listed plugins are available from the Jenkins **Manage Plugins** screen. You can access this area by opening Jenkins, logging in as an administrator, and then going to **Jenkins -> Manage Jenkins -> Manage Plugins -> Available** plugins.

The following screenshot shows some of the available backup plugins on the Jenkins **Manage Plugins** screen:

Figure 1-4: The Manage Jenkins screen

Installing any of the available backup plugins (or any plugin for that matter) can be accomplished by simply marking the appropriate checkbox and clicking on the **Download now and install after restart** button.

Once the plugin has been installed, it is highly recommended that you read any usage instructions and documentation. A direct link to the documentation for all Jenkins plugins can be found at `https://wiki.jenkins-ci.org/display/ JENKINS/Plugins`.

Downloading the example code

You can download the example code files for all Packt books you have purchased from your account at `http://www.packtpub.com`. If you purchased this book elsewhere, you can visit `http://www.packtpub. com/support` and register to have the files e-mailed directly to you.

Setting up a Jenkins mirror – rsync

If resources are available, another disaster-recovery option might be to set up a Jenkins mirror. A Jenkins mirror replicates a primary Jenkins instance in real time onto another host. This way, if there is an outage on the primary Jenkins instance, we can simply alternate traffic over to the mirror.

To implement a Jenkins mirror, we can use *rsync* to create a synchronized duplicate of the $JENKINS_HOME directory structure; this includes synchronizing all content, configuration files, and data onto our mirror. The Jenkins master can then be swapped with the mirror if there is a failure, or even if the primary instance is undergoing maintenance that requires downtime.

To begin the implementation of a Jenkins mirroring solution, we will need two systems with matching configurations (OS, disk, RAM, and so on). The first system will have Jenkins installed and may already be in production use. This system will be referred to as the *Jenkins-Primary*.

The second system will need to be preconfigured with a basic installation of Jenkins (which will be replaced later). This system will be referred to as the *Jenkins-Mirror*. Once Jenkins is installed on the Jenkins-Mirror, we will need to shut down the Jenkins service.

Shutting down the Jenkins service can be accomplished by executing the following command:

```
$> sudo service jenkins stop
```

Our next step in creating a Jenkins mirroring solution is to install the rsync and openssh-clients packages on both hosts (primary and mirror). Rsync is a widely utilized file and folder synchronization tool that replicates files, folders, and data across devices. It has the ability to synchronize entire folder structures or just the deltas. This makes it an optimal tool for our implementation of the Jenkins mirroring solution. The openssh-clients package works in tandem with rsync and enables rsync to perform its synchronization tasks over the SSH protocol. Let's take a minute to get these installed on the Jenkins primary and mirror systems.

To install rsync and OpenSSH ,execute the following commands for your target OS:

- RHEL/CentOS:

  ```
  $> sudo yum install rsync
  $> sudo yum install openssh-clients
  ```

- Debian/Ubuntu:

```
$> sudo apt-get install rsync
$> sudo apt-get install openssh-clients
```

Once `rsync` has been installed, let's verify that it is operating properly. Execute the following commands in the command-line terminal:

```
$> which rsync
$> rsync --version
```

If everything is functioning correctly, RSYNC will return an output similar to the examples provided here (for both primary and mirror):

- Jenkins-Mirror:

```
[root@jenkinsmirror jenkins]# which rsync
/usr/bin/rsync
[root@jenkinsmirror jenkins]# rsync --version
rsync  version 3.0.6  protocol version 30
Copyright (C) 1996-2009 by Andrew Tridgell, Wayne Davison, and
others.
```

- Jenkins-Primary:

```
[root@jenkinsprimary jenkins]# which rsync
/usr/bin/rsync
[root@jenkinsprimary jenkins]# rsync --version
rsync  version 3.0.6  protocol version 30
Copyright (C) 1996-2009 by Andrew Tridgell, Wayne Davison, and
others.
```

Now that we have verified that the necessary packages are installed, it is time to perform an initial pull of the $JENKINS_HOME directory from the *Jenkins-Primary* server over to the Jenkins-Mirror. To accomplish this, we need to use the command `sudo` to access the `root` user account on the Jenkins-Mirror, and have `rsync` fetch the contents from the Jenkins-Primary.

Enter the following commands into the terminal on the Jenkins-Mirror (replace `jenkinsprimary` in the following command with your Jenkins-Primary IP address):

```
$> sudo su - Jenkins
$> sudo rsync -avuh --delete -e ssh root@jenkinsprimary:/var/lib/
jenkins/* /var/lib/jenkins
```

The initial pull of the $JENKINS_HOME directory and its contents may take some time, depending on the size and network connection speed. Upon completion, you should see something similar to the following message in your terminal:

sent 3.55M bytes received 77.70G bytes 15.78M bytes/sec

total size is 79.64G speedup is 1.02

Once rsync has completed, we need to verify that the initial transfer was successful by starting the Jenkins service on the Jenkins-Mirror. We should inspect it to make sure it looks identical to the Jenkins-Primary server. Enter the following commands into the command line terminal to fire up Jenkins on the Jenkins-Mirror:

```
$> sudo service jenkins start
```

Once the initial pull of the $JENKINS_HOME directory has been verified, we need to implement SSH key-based authentication so that we can execute our rsync commands without password prompts and manual intervention.

To get SSH key-based authentication implemented we will need to create SSH keys and share them across our server solutions. This includes the Jenkins-Primary and Jenkins-Mirror hosts.

It is important to mention that this step may not be necessary if your host already has the RSA or DSA keys generated for the root user account.

To connect from Jenkins-Primary to Jenkins-Mirror with SSH-key based authentication, use the following commands:

```
$Jenkins-Primary>sudo su - root
$Jenkins-Primary>ssh-keygen -t rsa
$Jenkins-Primary>scp ~/.ssh/id_rsa.pub root@jenkins-mirror:/tmp/
$Jenkins-Mirror>sudo su - root
$Jenkins-Mirror>cat /tmp/id_rsa.pub >> ~/.ssh/authorized_keys
```

To connect from Jenkins-Mirror to Jenkins-Primary with SSH-key based authentication, use the following commands:

```
$Jenkins-Mirror>sudo su - root
$Jenkins-Mirror>ssh-keygen -t rsa
$Jenkins-Mirror>scp ~/.ssh/id_rsa.pub root@jenkins-primary:/tmp/
$Jenkins-Primary>sudo su - root
$Jenkins-Primary>cat /tmp/id_rsa.pub >> ~/.ssh/authorized_keys
```

Once the SSH keys are generated, we need to create a line item in the `authorized_` `keys` file to implement SSH-keybased authentication. An example of the line item in the `authorized_keys` file is shown below.

```
ssh-rsa AAAAB3NzaC1yc2EAAAABIwAAAQEA/QIL17A1XSjDLZVqf49F0Y785Foq4
A6UaBAaVQApB0yyOXVIwqu2H035nI4zDlhymgii6zfHeylHgKrjJyS2MLoiO0pFo4
XEFo2UNoy8CXKPJR+Sf9WeWjSvvoX3OE0YTfiFDMb29MvIc+bfUKRoAPeCqj4s81
Vf/v3f3JteT7ExQAN22AjUNceiIr2bxLbr7I8bMdN4886gtXYFPAtkQ3YXe1S
Wb3xlYDtL8jtAl39Cw5FSCkQM5ToLYsk95+0DAAfNAeUx/sWYVrKU+AvrkMran
JdmOa86vEnuhqOaGD3r2y+AVuLGid1r3Mcg7VrJBs0oKlj4OH9vNZF68x
CQdw== root@example.com
```

Once this step has been completed successfully, we should have the proper prerequisites in place to connect bidirectionally via SSH without being prompted for a password.

Let's test this functionality by executing the following commands on both the `Jenkins-Primary` and `Jenkins-Mirror` hosts:

`$Jenkins-Mirror>ssh root@jenkins-primary`

`$Jenkins-Primary>ssh root@jenkins-mirror`

Once the SSH key authentication has been verified, we will need to implement our synchronization solution on a schedule. Once the authentication has been verified, we will need to implement our syncing on a scheduled basis for this we will use the CRON tab. Finally, we can configure our CRON tab to execute `rsync`. This will enable the Jenkins-Mirror to automatically retrieve the filesystem deltas (once every 30 minutes). To achieve this, we need to open the crontab on the mirror (crontab -e) and add a directive, like the one shown here:

```
*/30 * * * * /usr/bin/rsync -avuh --delete -e ssh root@
jenkinsprimary:/var/lib/jenkins/* /var/lib/jenkins
```

Once the crontab entry has been input and saved, we should see data transferred from the Jenkins-Primary server to Jenkins-Mirror every 30 minutes.

 It is highly recommended that the $JENKINS_HOME folder contents be committed to source control, in addition to the mirroring option provided earlier. This will ensure that changes to the jobs are tracked and recoverable on the mirror if they were to be corrupted for any reason.

Jenkins on Mac OS X

For Mac OS X users, the Jenkins community provides a native PKG installer. This installer has a similar guided installation wizard as the Microsoft Windows one, and allows us to specify the traditional installation details. For users who wish to alter the Jenkins listening port or memory options, some command-line magic will be required.

To alter the Jenkins listening port, we need to explicitly define the port in the following properties file:

```
/Applications/Jenkins/winstone.properties
```

To accomplish this we will need to create the `winstone.properties` file if it does not already exist on our host, and detail the `httpPort` parameter inside it. An example of how to set `httpPort` in the `winstone.properties` file is shown here:

```
httpPort=80
```

Once created, the `winstone.properties` file will automatically load and override the default Jenkins port with the one specified within.

The `winstone.properties` file is not limited to simply altering the Jenkins listening port. There are other options available for customization as well. These options include `logfile`, `httpListenAddress`, and more. To obtain a complete list of the available override options, you can run the following commands from your OS X terminal:

```
cd /Applications/Jenkins
java -jar Jenkins.war --help
```

The JVM runtime memory settings (Heap memory, PermGen, and so on) are stored in a standard properties file format (`org.jenkins-ci.plist`). The launch daemon retrieves the values stored in this properties file. If no such file exists, the system will use the built-in defaults. On Mac OS X, this `plist` file will typically reside in the following location:

```
/Library/Preferences/org.jenkins-ci.plist
```

Adjusting the Java memory options for Jenkins involves modifying the appropriate property entries inside the `org.jenkins-ci.plist` file. To modify this file, we can use the OS X `defaults` command. This command allows us to read and write entries in the `plist` file without fear of corruption or improper formatting. A few example descriptions and use cases for this command are detailed in the sections below.

To view all settings in the `plist` file, execute the following command in the command-line terminal:

```
sudo defaults read /Library/Preferences/org.jenkins-ci
```

The output of the preceding command will look like this:

```
{
    heapSize = 512m;
    minHeapSize = 256m;
    minPermGen = 256m;
    permGen = 512m;
    tmpdir = "/Users/Shared/Jenkins/tmp";
}
```

To retrieve the value of the `heapSize` setting from the `plist` file, execute the following command in the command-line terminal:

```
sudo defaults read /Library/Preferences/org.jenkins-ci heapSize
```

The output of the preceeding command will look like this:

```
512m
```

To set the value of the `heapSize` setting in the `plist` file, execute following command in the command-line terminal:

```
sudo defaults write /Library/Preferences/org.jenkins-ci heapSize 1024m
```

If any alterations are made to the `org.jenkins-ci.plist` file, make sure you restart Jenkins for them to take effect. To restart Jenkins from the OS X command line terminal enter the following commands in the terminal:

```
sudo launchctl unload /Library/LaunchDaemons/org.jenkins-ci.plist
sudo launchctl load /Library/LaunchDaemons/org.jenkins-ci.plist
```

The Jenkins LTS release line

The Jenkins community recognizes that installing an edge release may be risky, and upgrading weekly (the default option) may pose a bit of an overhead in maintenance. For the more conservative users, the Jenkins **Long-Term Support (LTS)** release may be a more viable option. The Jenkins LTS release is delivered once every 12 weeks (instead of every week) and is selected by community vote. The Jenkins LTS release represents a community-voted selection of the most stable Jenkins release within the past 12 weeks.

In this section of *Mastering Jenkins*, you will learn about the Jenkins LTS release and understand how to convert an existing edge Jenkins installation over to the LTS release line. The Jenkins platform features a streamlined upgrade process, and typically provides all upgrades through the Jenkins UI. To convert a Jenkins installation over to the LTS line, there are two options available:

- Uninstall and replace the existing latest and greatest installation with the LTS package (immediate, but nuclear, option)
- Convert an existing installation and point it to the LTS update URL (waits for the next LTS release)

This section will focus on converting an existing installation over to the LTS release line. We can do this by pointing our Jenkins instance to the LTS update URL. This is because uninstalling and reinstalling the Jenkins platform is a straightforward process and is already documented in a number of places.

To migrate our Jenkins installation to the LTS release line, we will need to modify `hudson.model.UpdateCenter.xml`, located in `$JENKINS_HOME`, to point our Jenkins instance to the LTS release update center URL. The `Hudson.model.UpdateCenter.xml` file is what Jenkins uses to determine where it should look for updates to the system. The contents of this XML file are shown here:

```xml
<?xml version='1.0' encoding='UTF-8'?>
<sites>
  <site>
    <id>default</id>
    <url>http://updates.jenkins-ci.org/stable/update-center.json</url>
  </site>
</sites>
```

As you may have guessed already, the node in the XML that we will need to alter is the `<url>` node. The Jenkins LTS release has its own update center URL. Let's replace the existing update center URL with the one shown here:

```
http://updates.jenkins-ci.org/stable/update-center.json
```

Once the file is modified and saved, we need to restart the Jenkins service to complete the switchover to the LTS release line for all future updates.

 The LTS release comes out every 12 weeks. We will need to wait for this cycle to complete before our Jenkins instance is completely switched over.

The Jenkins LTS release is also available as a Docker container. This means that if the target setup is new, we can leverage the LTS Docker container (if desired) to perform the duties of the Jenkins master. Details on the Jenkins official LTS Docker container can be found at the following URL:

`http://jenkins-ci.org/content/official-jenkins-lts-docker-image`

Jenkins XML configuration files

Configuration data in Jenkins is persisted to disk via XML files. These XML files contain information describing how the Jenkins instance will behave. Understanding how Jenkins implements configuration XML files and manages the data they contain can prove to be valuable in debugging issues and keeping the system stable.

In Jenkins, persistent configuration data is serialized into XML and subsequently written to disk. The primary Jenkins subsystem serializes its data into `config.xml` files. These `config.xml` files govern the overall Jenkins system and describe how Jenkins will behave upon startup. The primary `config.xml` configuration file can be found in the following location:

`$JENKINS_HOME/config.xml`

An example of this configuration file is provided here (taken from an Apple OS X installation of Jenkins):

```
<?xml version='1.0' encoding='UTF-8'?>
<hudson>
  <disabledAdministrativeMonitors/>
  <version>1.0</version>
  <numExecutors>2</numExecutors>
  <mode>NORMAL</mode>
  <useSecurity>true</useSecurity>
  <authorizationStrategy class="hudson.security.AuthorizationStrategy
$Unsecured"/>
  <securityRealm class="hudson.security.SecurityRealm$None"/>
  <disableRememberMe>false</disableRememberMe>
  <projectNamingStrategy class="jenkins.model.ProjectNamingStrategy$De
faultProjectNamingStrategy"/>
  <workspaceDir>${ITEM_ROOTDIR}/workspace</workspaceDir>
  <buildsDir>${ITEM_ROOTDIR}/builds</buildsDir>
  <markupFormatter class="hudson.markup.EscapedMarkupFormatter"/>
  <jdks/>
  <viewsTabBar class="hudson.views.DefaultViewsTabBar"/>
  <myViewsTabBar class="hudson.views.DefaultMyViewsTabBar"/>
  <clouds/>
```

```
  <slaves>
    <slave>
      <name>Windows 2012</name>
      <description></description>
      <remoteFS></remoteFS>
      <numExecutors>1</numExecutors>
      <mode>NORMAL</mode>
      <retentionStrategy class="hudson.slaves.
RetentionStrategy$Always"/>
      <launcher class="hudson.plugins.sshslaves.SSHLauncher"
plugin="ssh-slaves@1.9">
        <host></host>
        <port>22</port>
        <credentialsId>0bb868e0-2cd6-4ab2-9781-a373d914cb85</
credentialsId>
        <maxNumRetries>0</maxNumRetries>
        <retryWaitTime>0</retryWaitTime>
      </launcher>
      <label>Windows Build Pool</label>
      <nodeProperties/>
      <userId>anonymous</userId>
    </slave>
  </slaves>
  <scmCheckoutRetryCount>0</scmCheckoutRetryCount>
  <views>
    <hudson.model.AllView>
      <owner class="hudson" reference="../../.."/>

    <name>All</name>
      <filterExecutors>false</filterExecutors>
      <filterQueue>false</filterQueue>
      <properties class="hudson.model.View$PropertyList"/>
    </hudson.model.AllView>
    <listView>
      <owner class="hudson" reference="../../.."/>
      <name>Build.TestApp</name>
      <filterExecutors>false</filterExecutors>
      <filterQueue>false</filterQueue>
      <properties class="hudson.model.View$PropertyList"/>
      <jobNames>
        <comparator class="hudson.util.CaseInsensitiveComparator"/>
      </jobNames>
      <jobFilters/>
      <columns>
```

```
        <hudson.views.StatusColumn/>
        <hudson.views.WeatherColumn/>
        <hudson.views.JobColumn/>
        <hudson.views.LastSuccessColumn/>
        <hudson.views.LastFailureColumn/>
        <hudson.views.LastDurationColumn/>
        <hudson.views.BuildButtonColumn/>
      </columns>
      <recurse>false</recurse>
    </listView>
  </views>
  <primaryView>All</primaryView>
  <slaveAgentPort>0</slaveAgentPort>
  <label></label>
  <nodeProperties/>
  <globalNodeProperties/>
</hudson>
```

As we can see, the nodes defined in the XML file provide configuration definitions for the overall Jenkins system. The nodes govern the overall behavior of the Jenkins system. Some of the configuration highlights include:

- Number of executors on the master
- Workspace folder definitions
- Security authorization strategy
- Master/slave definitions
- View definitions (the tabs on the main Jenkins dashboard)
- Slave agent ports

The second configuration XML we will investigate is dedicated to Jenkins jobs. These configuration files are located in $JENKINS_HOME/jobs/<JOBNAME>/config.xml. Each config.xml file belongs to a unique job defined in Jenkins. An XML DOM derived from the *JenkinsExample* job is provided here:

```
<?xml version='1.0' encoding='UTF-8'?>
<project>
  <actions/>
  <description></description>
  <keepDependencies>false</keepDependencies>
  <properties/>
  <scm class="hudson.scm.NullSCM"/>
  <canRoam>true</canRoam>
  <disabled>false</disabled>
```

```
   <blockBuildWhenDownstreamBuilding>false</
blockBuildWhenDownstreamBuilding>
   <blockBuildWhenUpstreamBuilding>false</
blockBuildWhenUpstreamBuilding>
   <triggers/>
   <concurrentBuild>false</concurrentBuild>
   <builders/>
   <publishers/>
   <buildWrappers/>
</project>
```

As we can see from the sample `config.xml` provided, the `Project` XML DOM contains persistent data about a given job, its build steps, and any related automation. This includes information related to SCM solutions, `triggers`, `builders`, `publishers`, `buildWrappers`, and more.

 It is highly recommended that all Jenkins configuration files are committed to source control. This will ensure that changes and history are preserved properly. This solution will also provide the ability to revert changes to a Jenkins job when needed.

Summary

In this chapter, we have focused on techniques that taught us how to create and manage a Jenkins instance. This represents the foundation for automation. By mastering these configuration solutions, you have learned ways in which you can make your Jenkins system stable and scalable. In this chapter, we have discussed port changes, memory management, backups, LTS release migration, RSYNC mirroring, and configuration data.

From here, we will move on to discover the power of Jenkins slave agents, complete job management, UI administration, and much more. As we progress through our journey, we will delve into the exciting features Jenkins provides, and begin leveraging Jenkins to automate additional aspects of the SDLC.

Distributed Builds – Master/ Slave Mode

A basic Jenkins installation operates as a standalone entity. A single Jenkins master can be responsible for source control polling, LDAP authentication, job execution, test report parsing, and more. As the role Jenkins plays in an organization expands, we may be asked to provide support for additional build environments, automated test execution solutions, configuration management solutions, and even deployments. To extend Jenkins and support these types of additional responsibilities, Jenkins features an elegant distributed build solution. This feature can be leveraged to help offload some of the work and to position Jenkins as a scalable, cross-platform solution.

> *"If you always give, you will always have."*
>
> *– Chinese proverb*

Distributed builds in Jenkins are supported by slave agent services running on unique devices, which coins the term master and slave mode. The master/slave mode architecture can assist us in scaling Jenkins from a single, overworked *master* instance to a load-balanced distributed build pool. The master/slave mode solution enables the Jenkins administrator to connect additional devices (of many kinds) to the master instance and uniquely tie job executions to the connected slaves.

In this chapter of *Mastering Jenkins*, we will discover how to scale our Jenkins installation and scale it to support additional hardware and operating system configurations. The topics that we will cover in this chapter will include:

- The Jenkins master/slave architecture
- How to create slave nodes in the user interface
- Understanding slave agent launch mechanisms
- Slave label, grouping, and load balancing
- Useful slave agent-related Jenkins plugins

After completing this chapter, we will have a solid grasp of how to evolve a simple Jenkins installation into a scalable distributed master and slave solution.

Understanding the master and slave architecture

A standalone Jenkins instance can grow fairly quickly into a disk-munching, CPU-eating monster. To prevent this from happening, we can scale Jenkins by implementing a *slave* node architecture, which can help us offload some of the responsibilities of the master Jenkins instance. Let's clarify this concept. A Jenkins slave node is simply a device configured to act as an automation executor on behalf of the master. The Jenkins master simply represents the base installation of Jenkins. The master will continue to perform basic operations and serve the user interface, while the slaves do the heavy lifting.

This distributed computing model will allow the Jenkins master to remain responsive to users, while offloading automation execution to the connected slave(s). To illustrate the concept of a master, and slave mode architecture let's look at an example. *Figure 2-1* shows a Jenkins master and three slave nodes of varying OS types:

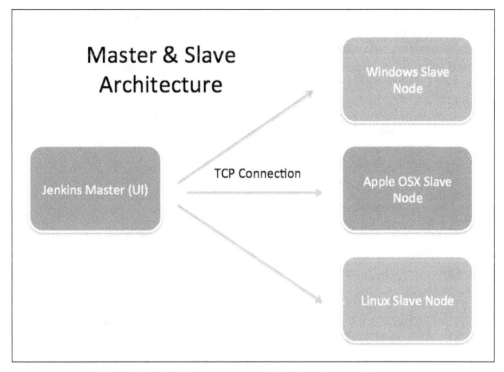

Figure 2-1: A Jenkins master connected to three slave node devices

The Jenkins slave agent can run on virtually any Java (JRE) capable device that has a network connection. This cross-platform connectivity model spans across devices of varying hardware types, processor architectures, and operating systems. This includes Windows, Mac OS X, Linux, Unix, and embedded devices. The architecture described in the preceding figure is a very simple example of a cross-platform distributed Jenkins solution. By design, this architecture can expand and contract as needed.

With all of the added capabilities that the Jenkins master and slave solution offers, it is important to know that the Jenkins master will continue its assigned responsibilities and will offload them only when specified. It is also important to know that, even after slaves are created, the Jenkins master will continue to own certain tasks that are designated solely to the master. Even when slave agents are connected to the master, the master will continue to manage some of the less resource-intensive work. Some responsibilities that are specific to the Jenkins master and cannot not be delegated to the slave nodes include:

- SCM polling (SVN, GIT, Perforce, and so on)
- Job scheduling
- LDAP authentication
- Build output, reporting, and notifications
- Job history and build logs
- Executing jobs/tasks tied to the master

This may seem a bit confusing, but it doesn't need to be. To help clarify let's illustrate the architecture in better detail. *Figure 2-2* shows a Jenkins master and slave architecture with a set of diagrams depicting the responsibilities of each:

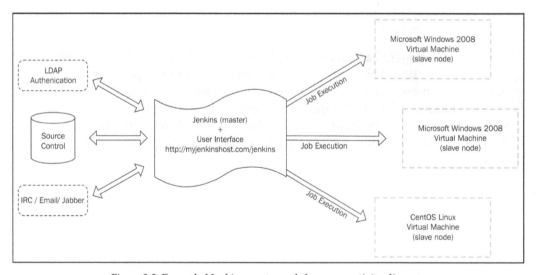

Figure 2-2: Expanded Jenkins master and slave connectivity diagram

As we can see, there will continue to be a set of core responsibilities that the Jenkins master continues to perform. Jenkins slave nodes will manage resource-intensive automation execution, while the Jenkins master will maintain the lighter tasks, such as serving the user interface, performing source control polling, and delivering notifications.

 It is important to note that, in order for the Jenkins master to offload automation to any connected slave devices, the slave nodes or jobs in Jenkins must be configured to explicitly to do so.

Creating slave nodes in the UI

In this section, we will learn how to define a new slave node through the Jenkins user interface. The Jenkins administration area provides a node management dashboard, which provides us with the ability to create new slave devices, remove old ones, and edit the ones in use. Let's jump right in and learn how to create a new slave node.

To get started, navigate to the following location:

Jenkins | Manage Jenkins | Manage Nodes | New Node

Once the screen has loaded Jenkins will present us with the new *node* basic configuration form. This basic configuration form allows us to specify some high-level configuration details about our new slave node. It lets us select either Dumb Slave or Copy Existing Node (as shown in *Figure 2-3*). The copy existing node option will only be present if we have slaves already defined in Jenkins. In our example we entered `Microsoft Windows Slave Node 01` for the node name, and selected **Dumb Slave** as the type. Once the fields have been configured click **OK** to proceed to the Detailed node configuration form.

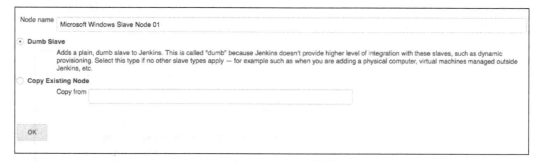

Figure 2-3: New node configuration form

The following screenshot outlines the detailed node configuration form that Jenkins presents us with. This form provides us with the ability to specify the network connection information, node labels, JVM options, and other important configuration criteria regarding our new slave node. At a minimum, we need to provide the slave node's name, description, remote root directory path, and launch method:

Figure 2-4: Detailed slave node configuration form

The information we specify on the detailed node configuration form will have a profound impact on the slave node's behavior. It is important to fully understand the fields available, their functionality, and their impact on the slave node. For edification, this table details each of the available configuration options in the detailed slave node configuration form:

Field Name	Example input	Description
Name	My Test Slave Node	A simple name for the slave node
Description	Executes on behalf of our master, as an additional worker	This field simply attaches a longer description to the node (hint IP address).

Field Name	Example input	Description
# of executors	5	Defines how many parallel jobs can run at one time on the node
Remote root directory	`C:\Jenkins\`	Defines where the slave node, its workspace, and files will live on the remote system
Labels	Windows Build	This is the label or group that the slave belongs to. We can have multiple slaves in a label to load balance
Usage	Utilize this slave node as much as possible	Controls how Jenkins utilizes this node (important for labels and groups, or general purpose jobs)
Launch method	Launch slave agents via Java Web Start	The installation, and connection method used to manage the slave node
Availability	Keep this slave online as much as possible	Describes when to enable or disable this slave node (on a schedule, on demand, or always on)
Environment variables	`PATH=/usr/bin`	Describes and preset environment variables to be propagated to the slave node.
Tool locations	`GRADLE_HOME=/home/gradle`	Describes any tool locations Jenkins will need to know about

Jenkins slaves can be configured to operate in any number of ways. Initially we will want to simply get the node up and running. We can later adjust any settings or minor configuration items to fine-tune the node. One of the key items we will need to define is the launch method.

Choosing a launch method

Jenkins true power lies in its ability to operate, and scale across OS platforms and architectures. Launching a slave node agent and attaching it to the Jenkins mater can be accomplished in a number of ways. Each method has its own use cases, benefits, and potential drawbacks. The one we select will be largely dependent on the target operating system, or environment. When creating a Jenkins slave node we will want to choose wisely. The Jenkins new slave node configuration screen provided us with the following available launch methods.

- Launch slave agents via Java Web Start (preferred)

- Launch slave agents on Unix machines via SSH

- Let Jenkins control this Windows slave as a Windows service (using DCOM and WMI is sometimes error prone)

- Launch slave via execution of command on the Master

Two of the most commonly used launch methods for slave nodes include SSH and Java Web Start. These two options are the least error-prone and offer the quickest implementation path. While these two options are the most popular, it is important to understand all of the available options in greater detail. Let's take a minute to go over them.

 Once the slave node has been created and installed, the slave operates through a small `slave.jar` file, which maintains an open bi-directional communication link to the Master. This connection mechanism is the same regardless of the launch method selected.

Slave agent via Java Web Start

The Java Web Start framework (JavaWS) is a proprietary Oracle framework, which was released in 2004 as part of the J2SE v1.4 release. For those familiar with Windows Click Once JavaWS is eerily similar. The Java Web Start framework is generally used to launch, and install Java applications directly from a web browser. The Java Web Start technology differs from a Java applet as it provides the user the capability to install a Java application onto a target machine from inside or outside of the web browser. Java applets on the other hand only reside inside of the web browser, and cannot be installed a permanent software program on the target machine.

The Jenkins development community has graciously provided an easy-to-use Java Web Start solution to assist in the installation and connection of freshly created slave nodes to the Jenkins master. Upon initialization of the Java Web Start wrapper, the Java Web Start framework will download and install a small slave agent (`slave.jar`) daemon onto the host machine. Once downloaded and installed, the `slave.jar` agent establishes a communication channel to the Jenkins master and waits for orders.

In this section of *Mastering Jenkins* we will discuss how to connect Jenkins slave nodes to a Jenkins master using the Java Web Start framework.

Prerequisites

Jenkins slave agents connected through Java Web Start require simple prerequisite setup configurations. For Java Web Start applications to function properly, it is important to ensure that Oracle Java v1.7 (as of May 2015) or newer is installed on the target slave host and is not disabled by the security settings of your preferred web browser. It is also recommended that the `javaws` command be accessible via the command-line terminal.

The Java Web Start launch option supports both a web browser and the command line. Each of these mechanisms will initialize, install, and launch the slave agent daemon. If we opt for the web browser method, we may need to pre-configure the web browser's security settings, and mime types to support it.

Each web browser has a slightly different approach to mime types, and security. To assist Oracle has graciously provided detailed instructions on how to enable Java Web Start for most popular web browsers. You can find these instructions at `https://java.com/en/download/help/enable_browser.xml`.

For Java Web Start from the command line, we will need to ensure that the `javaws` command is accessible; this often means defining the default path system variable to include the `JAVA_HOME` location. Please refer to the following Oracle documentation on Java Web Start for further information:

`https://docs.oracle.com/javase/7/docs/technotes/guides/javaws/developersguide/faq.html`

The Jenkins Java Web Start launch page

To connect a slave agent to the Jenkins master using **Java Web Start** (JavaWS), we will need to launch the Java Web Start installer. Upon initialization Java Web Start will prompt us to accept the security warning prompt, and install the slave agent daemon on the host. Once the slave agent has been installed it will proceed to automatically connect to the Jenkins master.

The launch button for Java Web Start can be found in the Jenkins user interface (administration area) via the following workflow:

Jenkins | Manage Jenkins | Manage Nodes - | <NodeName>

The JavaWS connection status screen provides the list of available launch mechanisms. From this screen, we will be able to select how to launch the slave agent:

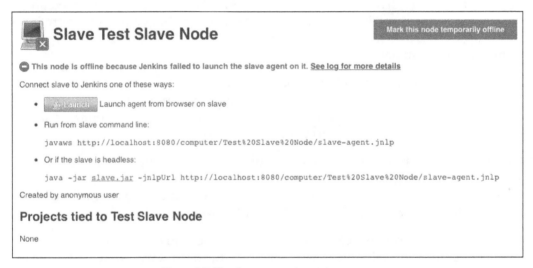

Figure 2-5: The slave connection status screen

As illustrated in the preceeding figure there are three approaches available to us to launch a slave agent. Let's take a minute to go over each of these options in detail and learn how to use them.

JavaWS via a web browser

One available option presented on the connection screen provides the ability to launch the slave agent daemon directly through a web browser. To accomplish this, we simply need to log on to the slave node (RDP, VNC, and so on), open a browser, log on to the Jenkins master, and initiate the Java Web Start launcher. While this may seem complicated, there is no need for concern. We will walk through the process step by step.

To get started, open a web browser session (on the slave node) and navigate to the Jenkins master. Then, log in as an administrator and navigate to the slave node connection status screen via the following navigation workflow:

Jenkins | Manage Jenkins | Manage Nodes | (Your Node Name)

Once the navigation to the node configuration screen has been completed, we are again presented with the Slave connection status screen (*Figure 2-5*).

Let's proceed in launching the slave agent by clicking the orange **Launch** button (with the Java symbol). This will trigger the initialization of the Java Web Start process. Once Java Web Start has initialized, follow the prompts to complete the installation, and launch the Jenkins slave agent as shown in *Figure 2-6* and *Figure 2-7*:

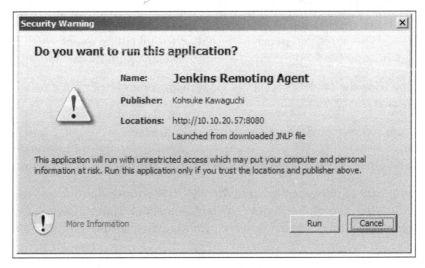

Figure 2-6: Launching the Java Web Start framework

Now that the Jenkins slave agent has launched, our friendly Jenkins concierge will greet us.

One handy feature provided by the Jenkins slave agent service for Microsoft Windows users is the ability to create a Windows service for the attached slave agent. *Figure 2-7* illustrates this installation option. This handy feature alleviates the need to trigger the Java Web Start process every time the host is rebooted.

Figure 2-7: A connected Java Web Start slave agent

Congratulations! We have now completed the initial installation of the slave agent using the web browser.

JavaWS via the command line

If a browser-based installation is not desired, we can leverage the javaws via the command line. This serves as an easy alternative for installing a Jenkins slave agent onto a target host. Lets spend a couple of minutes learning how this works.

To begin, log in to the slave device as an administrator and open a command-line terminal session.

Once the terminal is open, let's make sure Java Web Start is enabled. Input the javaws help command (javaws --help). If successful, we should be presented with a simple help screen detailing the available options for the javaws command.

Next we will want to perform the actual Java Web Start installation process. Input the command provided on the Java Web Start connection status screen (*Figure 2-7*) to begin the installation process. We have provided an example of this command below.

```
#>javaws http://<pathtojenkins>/slave-agent.jnlp
```

Upon successful launch, you will be greeted by the friendly Java Web Start installation wizard. Follow the wizard to complete the setup of the Jenkins slave node. Once complete, the Jenkins slave agent should be online and communicating with the Master.

Headless slave agents via the command line

While Jenkins offers a complete command-line solution for slaves based on Java Web Start, sometimes Java Web Start is not an option. A headless slave agent is one where Java is used to connect the Jenkins `slave.jar` daemon to the Jenkins master entirely from the command line and the Java `.jar` file without leveraging `javaws` or any intermediary launcher. This benefits those who wish to harness the command line and not be bothered by user interface prompts, security settings, and web browsers. This solution is also valuable for users who may wish to leverage the OpenJDK and Java hotspots alternatives.

To get started, we will need to ensure that Oracle Java 1.7 or OpenJDK 7 has been installed on the slave host and is accessible from the command line. We will also need to download the `slave.jar` file from the Jenkins master onto the slave. The `slave.jar` file is available as a web-accessible artifact via the Jenkins Master. This file can be downloaded at `http://<masterjenkinsurl>:8080/jnlpJars/slave.jar`.

We will want to store the downloaded `slave.jar` file in a desired location for the new Jenkins home. — for example, `C:\Jenkins\slave.jar` or `/var/lib/Jenkins/slave.jar`.

Once the `slave.jar` is in place on the slave host, open a terminal session (on the slave host), and enter the following Java command into the terminal window (replacing `Test%20Slave%20Node` with the name of your specific slave node and `localhost:8080` with the URL of your Jenkins master):

```
#> java -jar slave.jar -jnlpUrl http://localhost:8080/computer/Test%20
Slave%20Node/slave-agent.jnlp
```

If you get stuck, you can copy-and-paste the full command displayed on your slave node's connection status page in Jenkins.

Upon execution of the command, the slave agent will fire up and automatically connect to the Jenkins master. At this point, the headless Jenkins slave agent is ready for use. The detailed output from the terminal should look similar to the screenshot provided in *Figure 2-8*:

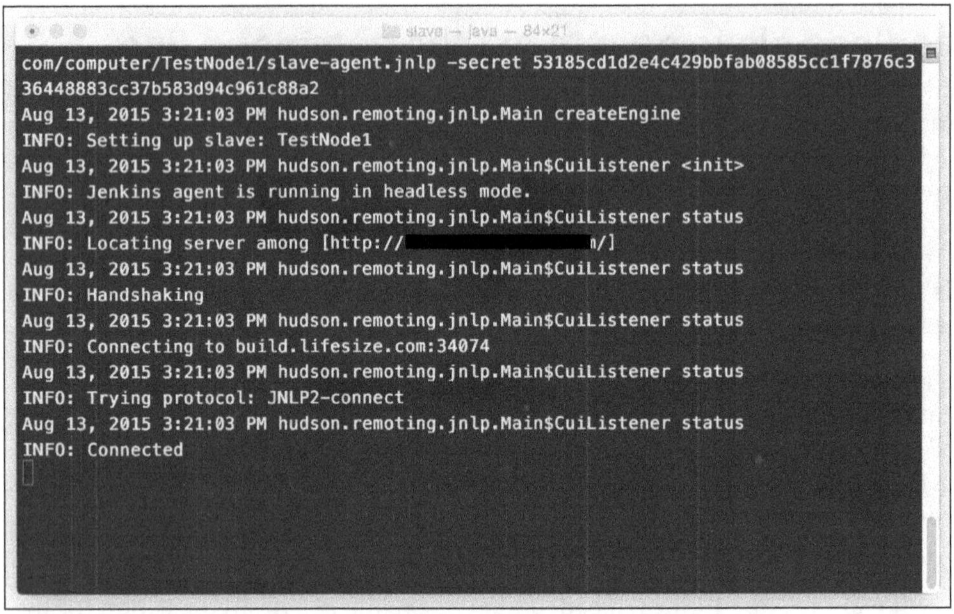

```
com/computer/TestNode1/slave-agent.jnlp -secret 53185cd1d2e4c429bbfab08585cc1f7876c3
36448883cc37b583d94c961c88a2
Aug 13, 2015 3:21:03 PM hudson.remoting.jnlp.Main createEngine
INFO: Setting up slave: TestNode1
Aug 13, 2015 3:21:03 PM hudson.remoting.jnlp.Main$CuiListener <init>
INFO: Jenkins agent is running in headless mode.
Aug 13, 2015 3:21:03 PM hudson.remoting.jnlp.Main$CuiListener status
INFO: Locating server among [http://            n/]
Aug 13, 2015 3:21:03 PM hudson.remoting.jnlp.Main$CuiListener status
INFO: Handshaking
Aug 13, 2015 3:21:03 PM hudson.remoting.jnlp.Main$CuiListener status
INFO: Connecting to build.lifesize.com:34074
Aug 13, 2015 3:21:03 PM hudson.remoting.jnlp.Main$CuiListener status
INFO: Trying protocol: JNLP2-connect
Aug 13, 2015 3:21:03 PM hudson.remoting.jnlp.Main$CuiListener status
INFO: Connected
```

Figure 2-8: Connected slave agent terminal output

Slave agents on Windows via WMI and DCOM

Over the next few pages, we will dive in and learn how to effectively create, manage, and maintain slave nodes on Microsoft Windows using the DCOM, WMI, and CIFS protocols. Before we begin the installation process for a Windows slave node using DCOM, CIFS, and WMI, it is important to define each of these technologies and their roles in the Jenkins slave node service operation.

- **DCOM**: The **Microsoft Distributed Component Object Model (DCOM)** is designed to allow software components to communicate across networked computers. The server process launcher initializes COM and DCOM servers in response to an object call.

- **WMI**: The Microsoft **Windows Management Instrumentation (WMI)** is used to automate administrative functions on a Microsoft Windows system via a script. WMI scripts can be local or triggered remotely using Windows Remote Management.

- **CIFS**: Is an acronym, which stands for Common Internet file system. It is used to share files across corporate networks or the Internet.

Implementing a Jenkins slave node using the previously described DCOM, CIFS and WMI technologies may require modifications to the Windows registry. The security implications of such modifications are not widely known, and the implementation of this type of slave service has created some trouble for Jenkins users. To address this, and make it easier for Jenkins users to get slave agents setup and running on Microsoft Windows, the Jenkins community has created a Java Web Start option. Therefore it is recommended that the Java Web Start option be utilized if this method poses any problems.

To begin configuring a WMI / DCOM based slave node we will need to first install the JAVA JRE v1.7, or later on the target host. The Java JRE or JDK can be obtained by downloading it from Oracle's website (`http://www.oracle.com`).

Next we will need to enable the DCOM service on the target Windows host. To accomplish this, open the Windows Services manager (`services.msc`) and start the **DCOM Server Process Launcher** service as shown in *Figure 2-9*:

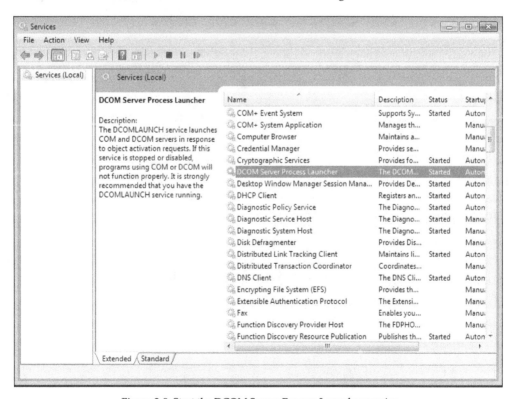

Figure 2-9: Start the DCOM Server Process Launcher service

Once the **DCOM Server Process Launcher** service has been enabled and started, we will need to also enable WMI Remoting Service, as shown in *Figure 2-10*:

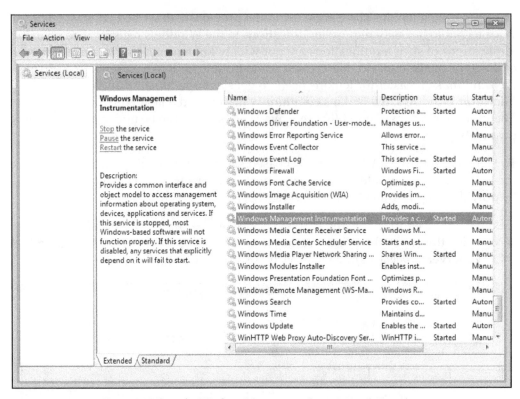

Figure 2-10: Start the Windows Management Instrumentation service.

Once the two services have been started we will need to connect the host to the Jenkins master. This is accomplished directly on the Jenkins master in the administration area. On the Jenkins administration page, navigate to **Jenkins -> Manage Jenkins -> Manage Nodes ->** <Test Slave Node> **-> Configure**. This will navigate us to our pre-created slave node.

Once we have navigated to the node configuration page we will need to configure the Jenkins master to connect to the slave host, and install the Jenkins slave agent as a Windows service. This is illustrated in *Figure 2-11*:

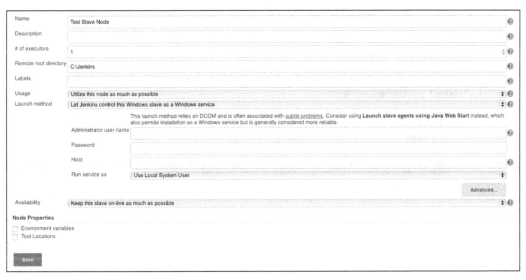

Figure 2-11: Windows DCOM slave configuration form

To configure the Windows DCOM slave, start by altering the **Launch method** and selecting **Let Jenkins control this Windows slave as a Windows service**. Once the **Launch method** drop-down has been changed, we will need to configure the following required fields, which tell Jenkins about our new slave.

- **Administrator user name**
- **Password**
- **Host** (DNS or IP address)
- **Run service as** (**Use Local System User** is the default)

Once the detailed node configuration form has been completed, click **Save** to complete the node-creation process and launch the slave service process. If everything was successful the Jenkins master will perform the following tasks.

1. Initialize the connection to the slave via DCOM and WMI.
2. Check if Java exists on the target host (install the JDK if no Java was found).
3. Copy `jenkins.exe` over to the target host.
4. Copy `Jenkins.exe.config` over to the target host.

5. Create the Jenkins slave Windows service and start it.

6. Wait for the `port.txt` file to be created (defines the port Jenkins will communicate on).

7. Connect to the Jenkins slave over the port defined in the `port.txt` file created by the slave service.

Once the node has been successfully installed and subsequently connected, the Jenkins master will list the slave as online (*Figure 2-12*).

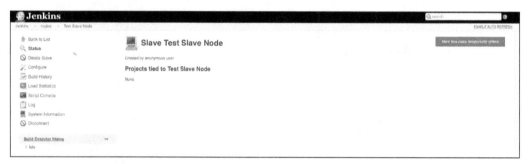

Figure 2-12: Connected slave node

Troubleshooting Windows DCOM and CIFS errors

As we discussed earlier in this chapter, the DCOM, WMI, and CIFS slave node can be error-prone. Initiating a TCP connection into a Windows host for the sole purpose of remote control will almost always require alterations to the security configuration of the target host. If the Jenkins slave agent fails to connect or initialize, we will need to debug the issue. The most obvious location to gather information about a failure is in the connection logs. To get started, navigate to **Jenkins** | **Manage Jenkins** | **Manage Nodes** | `<Your Slave Node Name>` | **Log**.

From the log viewer, we should see the error message being returned to the Jenkins master. Errors from DCOM and WMI can be generic-looking and may differ based on hardware, kernel, or Windows architecture. Let's discuss some of the common pain points and learn the associated workarounds that could possibly allow us to configure our Windows slave node using the DCOM, CIFS, and WMI launch method.

Error – access denied

This error is generic in nature but usually is the result of connectivity problems from the Jenkins master to the slave agent. Such connectivity errors may be caused by firewalls, port blocking, or security settings.

Example:

```
Connecting to 10.10.10.1
```

```
ERROR: Access is denied. See http://wiki.jenkins-ci.org/display/JENKINS/
Windows+slaves+fail+to+start+via+DCOM for more information about how to
resolve this.
```

```
org.jinterop.dcom.common.JIException: Message not found for errorCode:
0x00000005
```

Workaround 1

Possible cause: *Is Windows Firewall blocking the port?*

Sometimes, Windows firewall will block the incoming connection requests from the Jenkins master. To check if the firewall is indeed the issue, we can try the following workaround:

1. Disable the Windows Firewall service or configure it to allow inbound connections.

2. Create a Windows Firewall rule for Jenkins and set **Allow Edge Traversal**.

    Specifically, allow inbound connections through the Microsoft Windows Firewall on these ports:

    °   TCP ports 139, 445
    °   UDP ports 137, 138

3. Add the following patches to the Microsoft Windows Registry (proceed at your own risk):

    Patch 1:

    ```
    HKEY_LOCAL_MACHINE\SOFTWARE\Microsoft\Windows\CurrentVersion\
    Policies\System
    Create or modify 32-bit DWORD: LocalAccountTokenFilterPolicy
    Set the value to: 1
    ```

    Patch 2:

    ```
    Find: HKEY_CLASSES_ROOT\CLSID\ {76A64158-CB41-11D1-8B02-
    00600806D9B6}
    Right click and select 'Permissions'
    Change owner to administrators group.
    Change permissions for administrators group. Grant Full Control.
    Change owner back to TrustedInstaller (user is "NT Service\
    TrustedInstaller")
    Restart Remote Registry Service
    ```

4. Try connecting the Jenkins slave again.

 To debug this specific issue more efficiently, we can attempt a connection from the master to the slave using TCP dump. TCP dump is a tool widely used by Jenkins administrators to debug connectivity issues. Please refer to the Windows slaves troubleshooting page at at `https://wiki.jenkins-ci.org/display/JENKINS/Windows+slaves+fail+to+start+via+DCOM`.

Workaround 2

Possible cause: *Is the Microsoft Visual C++ runtime library missing?*

The Jenkins slave service may require that the Microsoft Visual C++ runtime library be installed on the system using these steps:

1. Download and install the Microsoft Visual C++ runtime library.

2. Try connecting the Jenkins slave again.

Error – no more data available

This type of error may seem generic in nature, however it is usually thrown when the Jenkins master tries to reach out to the slave node, and no communication channel can be established. The resulting error code listed will often be similar to the nondescript error displayed here.

Installing the Hudson slave service

```
No more data is available. [0x00000103]

org.jinterop.dcom.common.JIException: No more data is available.
[0x00000103]

at org.jinterop.winreg.smb.JIWinRegStub.winreg_EnumKey(JIWinRegStub.
java:390)
```

Workaround

Possible cause: *Is Microsoft Visual C++ runtime library missing?*

For the Jenkins slave service to leverage the DCOM, CIFS, and WMI protocols, it is required that the Microsoft Visual C++ 2008 runtime libraries be installed on the system. One obvious workaround is to install this package and try again. The Microsoft C++ runtime library dependency can be found at the following URL:

`http://www.microsoft.com/en-us/download/details.aspx?id=5582`

> More information is available for troubleshooting Windows slave agent connectivity issues on the Jenkins community website wiki. Please visit the following URL for more information:
>
> `https://wiki.jenkins-ci.org/display/JENKINS/Windows+sl aves+fail+to+start+via+DCOM`

Slave agents via SSH tunneling

The widely preferred approach for Jenkins slave nodes on Linux, Unix, and OS X hosts is to leverage SSH tunneling. This launch method starts by sending commands over an SSH connection, which downloads the `slave.jar` and launches the slave agent on the host. For the installation process to work, Java 1.7 or later must be installed; the slave host needs to be reachable from the master, and the account specified in Jenkins will need to have SSH logon rights for the target machine.

The SSH launch method provides a number of valuable features that make this an attractive option when connecting Jenkins slave agents to the master. These benefits include:

- More reliable connectivity and stability
- Encrypted communications
- Auto restart and reconnect functionality
- No need for slave services or `init.d` scripts

To use the SSH launch method, select **Launch slave agents on Unix machines via SSH**, SSH authorized user credentials, Host IP address, and click the SAVE button to create the new slave node. Once the slave has been saved, Jenkins will automatically attempt to connect to the slave and install the slave agent using SSH and the credentials provided. *Figure 2-13* shows an example of the configuration page for an SSH slave node:

Figure 2-13: SSH Host and Credentials Section

When configuring a new SSH slave node, the best approach for configuring authentication is to use the Jenkins credential management system. This will store the login and password information for the SSH slaves in Jenkins directly. The Jenkins credential management system allows the Jenkins administrator to manage credentials and later reuse them when executing jobs, connecting SSH slave agents, and connecting Jenkins to third-party services. To add usernames and passwords to the credentials manager, navigate to the credential management system and select add credentials in the UI:

Manage Jenkins | Manage Credentials | Add credentials

Once any credentials have been added, they will appear as available credentials in the SSH Host **Credentials** dropdown (shown in *Figure 2-13*).

Alternatively, you can elect to add the credentials for the SSH slave directly in the detailed slave configuration page via the **Add** button (also shown in *Figure 2-13*).

Upon saving the configuration for an SSH slave node, Jenkins will immediately attempt to connect to and install the slave agent service on the target host.

Detailed logs related to the connection can be viewed by clicking the  Log button on the left-hand side of the slave node status screen. If everything was successful, the logs will contain text similar to the following:

```
JNLP agent connected from /127.0.0.1
<===[JENKINS REMOTING CAPACITY]===>Slave.jar version: 2.49
This is a Unix slave
Slave successfully connected and online.
```

Administering Jenkins slaves

As Jenkins administrators it is our responsibility to monitor, and maintain the Jenkins master and slave nodes in our build farm. Jenkins features a comprehensive set of tools, and services that takes most of the guesswork out of managing a distributed Jenkins implementation. In this section we will discuss the ins and outs of maintaining a healthy Jenkins master and slave architecture.

The node administration dashboard

The Jenkins node administration page allows us to add, remove, control, and monitor the Jenkins master and any attached slave devices. *Figure 2-14* illustrates this Jenkins node administration page:

Figure 2-14: Node administration dashboard

Also featured on the slave node administration page is a detailed status and configuration side panel. The configuration panel allows the Jenkins administrator to configure warning thresholds and define new slave nodes.

Non-administrative users can view the status of slave devices by looking at the **Build Executor Status** panel.

Figure 2-15 illustrates both of these side panels in detail:

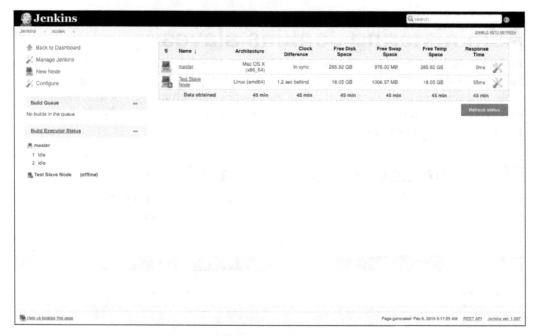

Figure 2-15: Offline slave node marked with an X

Preventative monitoring

From the slave node administration dashboard, we can see that Jenkins tracks slave node architecture, clock difference, free disk space, free swap space, free temp space, and response time. These metrics can provide insights into the overall health of the slave agents. To customize these settings, click the **Configure** button located on the left-hand side of the slave node administration dashboard. *Figure 2-16* illustrates the available options presented to us when we navigate to the preventive node monitoring configuration page:

Figure 2-16: Preventative node monitoring configuration page

As we can see from the preceding screenshot, we can set the threshold settings for connected slave nodes. Upon changing and applying any values for these thresholds, Jenkins will actively monitor the slave agents based on the updated values. If the values for a given threshold are unmet, the Jenkins master will automatically disconnect the offending slave node that specified criteria.

Managing individual slave nodes

To manage an individual slave node connected to the Jenkins master, navigate to the Jenkins slave node dashboard as shown in *Figure 2-14*. Once there, click on the name of the desired node to navigate into that target slave devices status page, as shown in *Figure 2-17*.

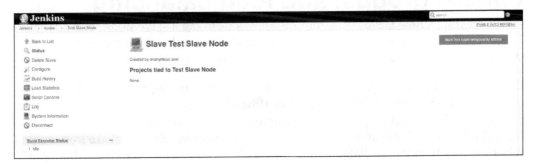

Figure 2-17: Slave node status and configuration

Once Jenkins has loaded the status page for the desired slave node, we can see that the left-hand side panel shows quite a few options. Let's define each of these options and learn what they do:

- **Back to List**: Navigates back to the node administration dashboard.

- **Status**: Navigates us back to the status page for the current selected slave node.

- **Delete Slave**: Removes the slave from the Jenkins master and severs any ties between the slave and the master.

- **Configure**: Navigates us to the detailed node configuration page.

- **Build History**: Displays a set of historical timelines of jobs that have run on this slave node.

- **Load Statistics**: Shows key metrics and resource utilization in graph form. It has three timespan view options: *Short*, *Medium,* and *Long*. These options allow us to adjust the timespan of the graph accordingly.

- **Script Console**: Jenkins features a robust built-in scripting system called Groovy. With this console, you can run arbitrary one-off scripts directly on the slave node. You will learn more about writing Groovy scripts for Jenkins later.

- **Log**: Displays in real time the connection status between the Jenkins master and the slave node. These logs can be very valuable when troubleshooting connectivity issues.

Labels, groups, and load balancing

When creating a new slave node, Jenkins allows us to tag a slave node with a label. Labels represent a way of naming one or more slaves. We leverage this labeling system to tie the execution of a job directly to one or more slave nodes.

By leveraging the labeling system described above we can begin to create very powerful load-balanced Jenkins solutions. When Jenkins discovers a job execution is pending, which is tied to a label, it will attempt to locate any available slave nodes tagged with that label that are not in use. If any nodes with that label are free Jenkins will run the job on the available node. If no nodes are available, Jenkins will queue the job for the next available node that has the specified label. *Figure 2-18* illustrates a simple label containing two Microsoft Windows slaves tagged with the label **Windows**.

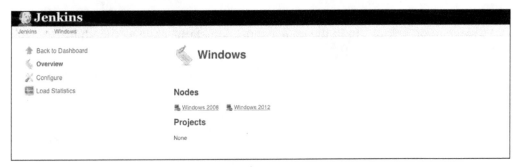

Figure 2-18: A basic Windows build pool

Attaching a slave to a group by creating a label

By labeling multiple slave nodes with the same label, we can create groups. Groups of devices can prove to be handy when offloading automation. Creating a group of slave nodes simply means that they share a common label.

Let's imitate the *Windows* example from the preceding screenshot and create a Windows group with two connected slave nodes. For the sake of brevity, we will presuppose that we already have the two Windows slaves connected to the Jenkins master. To add each of these to the Windows group, we will simply modify the detailed configuration for each node and specify **Windows** in the **Labels** field, as shown in *Figure 2-19*:

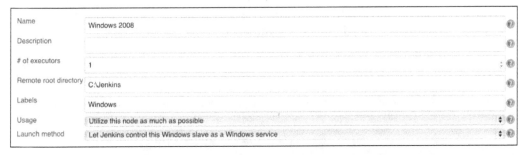

Figure 2-19: Adding a Windows label to a slave node

Once the Windows label has been added to the slave nodes, Jenkins will automatically create the group containing our two slave nodes.

Once the group has been created, Jenkins will proudly display the group (or groups) that a slave node belongs to in the node connection status page as shown in *Figure 2-20*:

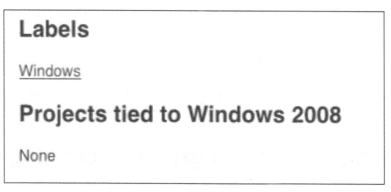

Figure 2-20: A A slave node in one group (based on a label)

Attaching a slave to many groups

Through Jenkins label and grouping system, Jenkins provides a mechanism by which jobs can run on one or many slave nodes (load balancing). For example, some automation jobs may require an x64 processor or may only build on an Ubuntu 12 system. By attaching labels to our slave nodes, the slave node group possibilities we can create are infinite. The Jenkins labelling system allows us to attach a slave node to one or many groups. Once the labels are setup, we can tie job execution of a job to one or many labels as well. To have a Jenkins slave node belong to more than one group, all we have to do is add a space in the label name. Jenkins will determine each word as a separate label, as demonstrated in *Figure 2-21*:

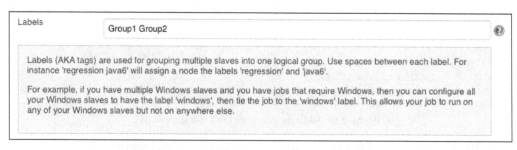

Figure 2-21: Attaching a slave node to multiple groups

After the slave node has been saved, Jenkins will recognize it as belonging to multiple groups. We can see this in action in *Figure 2-22*, which shows a slave node as a member of a **Windows** group and the **x86** group:

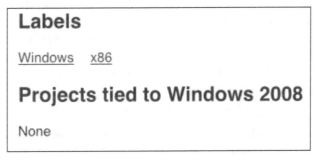

Figure 2-22: A slave node belonging to two groups

Restricting slave execution to global or tied jobs

Since the Jenkins master is also a job executor, we may wish to attach a slave as an available global executor or keep it available for tied jobs only. This allows us to offload heavy lifting to the slaves if we choose to do so. To support this, we can further adjust the way Jenkins executes jobs through the **Usage** dropdown in the detailed node configuration page for a given slave device. The usage dropdown options are described in *Figure 2-23:*

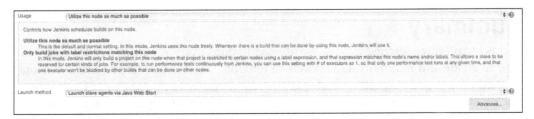

Figure 2-23: Usage dropdown in the detailed configuration form

As we can see we can make our slave a *General* executor (always available for job execution), or keep it out of the general execution pool, and restrict it to tied job requests only. The sky is the limit. In our examples we discussed only a few simple connectivity options, however this system can potentially scale to hundreds or even thousands of slave nodes and a highly adaptable architecture. It is up to you to determine how big you want to make your specific slave node implementation. Just start simple, and plan it well.

Jenkins plugins that support distributed builds

Since its initial inception, the Jenkins community has furthered the build out of the master/slave architecture by implementing a number of plugins, which provide connectivity to popular cloud technology stacks. The master/slave architecture has been extended to provide direct integration with Amazon EC2, Microsoft Windows Azure, ElasticBox, and more. When creating a master/slave solution, and deciding on architecture, it is prudent to check for plugins that can extend your implementation and make it more robust.

At the time of writing this book, some of the more notable master/slave distributed build extension plugins for Jenkins include:

- Amazon EC2 plugin
- Microsoft Azure
- Swarm
- Docker plugin
- Hadoop plugin
- CloudBees Cloud Connector plugin
- Selenium plugin
- vSphere Cloud plugin

Summary

In this chapter, we learned how a distributed Jenkins system works. We learned how to create and maintain slave nodes in Jenkins. We also developed our skills and learned how to scale our slave nodes to fit a development organization of any size. The master/slave node concept is really one of Jenkins shining points, it's a true distributed computing platform, and can be leveraged to create some really awesome solutions.

In the next chapter, we will begin to dissect views and Jenkins jobs. Together, we will begin to leverage the automation capabilities of this powerful platform.

3
Creating Views and Jobs in Jenkins

At the heart of the Jenkins platform is the main dashboard, tab based views, and build jobs. In this chapter of *Mastering Jenkins*, we will dive into creating and organizing jobs and views within the Jenkins system. By mastering these features, we can begin to explore some of the more advanced capabilities Jenkins provides. While reading this chapter, it is a good idea to adopt practices that assist in making your unique configuration more effective and skip over the ones that don't.

> *"Yesterday I was clever and wanted to change the world. Today I learned wisdom and only wish to change myself."* - *Rumi*

The majority of this chapter will center around understanding the Jenkins dashboard, creating views, and defining jobs

Our objective will be to completely understand these foundational principles so that we can build on them in later chapters, and take our Jenkins implementations to the next level. The topics we will cover in this chapter will include the following:

- The Jenkins user interface
- Creating custom views
- Creating Jenkins jobs

The Jenkins user interface

In Jenkins the dashboard represents the primary entry point into the Jenkins system. Upon loading Jenkins we are presented with a screen that allows us to create new jobs, schedule the execution of existing jobs, navigate into defined jobs on the system, and more. Let's drill-down into the capabilities of the main dashboard and dissect some of the functionality.

The user interface of Jenkins can be logically divided into four primary content areas: the **Header**, the **Job Table**, the **Configuration Panel**, and the **Build Queue and Executor Status Panel**. *Figure 3-1* illustrates each of these four content areas.

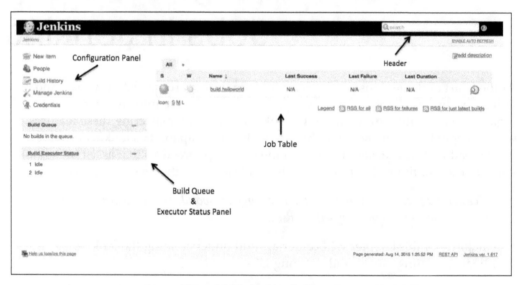

Figure 3-1: The Jenkins dashboard

As we can see from the preceding screenshot, this specific Jenkins implementation is pretty slim; it has only one job and one view defined. Your specific Jenkins instance will probably be more complex. Let's take a quick tour of each of the previously described content areas and learn about the roles they play within Jenkins.

The main header

The main header in Jenkins provides a lot of valuable functionality and information. The main header includes UI navigation breadcrumbs, an editable description link, the enable/disable auto refresh switch, and a comprehensive context search solution. Let's look at each in greater detail.

- **Breadcrumbs**: The breadcrumbs system provides a visual orientation indicator and navigation history. Each of the crumbs displayed provides a link that allows the user to navigate to specific pages within the current hierarchy quickly.

- **Edit Description**: The editable description link provides us with the ability to add descriptive text to our dashboard, view, job, or build. This can be handy for attaching notes or information that can be reviewed later.

- **Enable/Disable Auto Refresh**: The auto refresh switch will enable/disable the auto page refresh feature. This is a browser-based refresh alternative and can help alleviate the need to click the refresh button repeatedly.

- **The Context Search Box**: This is prominently displayed in the top-right corner of every page. It serves as both a text-based search solution and a quick-jump context navigation bar. *Figure 3-2* illustrates the Jenkins UI for the **Context Search** box.

Figure 3-2: Search box

The **Search** box is designed to help save time and increase efficiency when searching for content and navigating the user interface. We can leverage it as a simple search solution to locate information based on an inputted search term, or we can leverage it as a powerful quick-jump context navigation solution. Let's look at the quick jump option in greater detail.

The quick-jump navigation solution is handy for quickly navigating to specific pages and content within the Jenkins platform via keywords. Let's look at some examples of the context search feature and learn how it can be used.

Jumping to a page using the context search solution can be accomplished by simply specifying the Jenkins page. Below are three examples of this feature:

- **Job Name**: Here, we can specify the name of a job directly in the search box to immediately navigate to that project's overview page.

    ◦ **Input example**: myproject

    ◦ **Result**: Navigates the user to the project's overview page for the specified job, myproject

- **Job Name + configure**: Here, we can specify the word *configure* (with a space separator) after a job name to navigate directly to a job's configuration page.

    ◦ **Input example**: myproject configure

    ◦ **Result**: Navigates to the job configuration page for myproject

 It is important to note that the context search box is case-sensitive. This can be disabled on a per-user basis via their profile. To make the search case-insensitive, navigate to the user's profile configuration page and untick the **Case-sensitivity** checkbox.

The context search feature supports the concept of sub-contexts. This additional feature allows us to drill into subpages directly by specifying additional keywords. For example, we can tell Jenkins to automatically navigate to a specific build's console output display. We accomplish this by specifying the job name and a few additional search parameters, more specifically the build number (in numeral format) and the key word *console*. To better clarify this functionality, let's look at a simple example.

- **Job Name + build number + console**: Here, we can specify the keyword *console* in conjunction with the build number and job name to navigate directly to the console output log for a given build.

    ◦ **Input example**: myproject 1234 console

    ◦ **Result**: Navigates the user to the console output for build 1234 on the Jenkins job, myproject

The search solution also has the ability to understand pointer-based input parameters, including *last build, last stable build, last failed build,* and so on. This allows the Jenkins user to navigate to information quickly without the need to research individual data points.

The configuration panel

The configuration panel in Jenkins is always located in the top-left corner just below the header. Upon entry into the Jenkins platform, the configuration panel provides initial top-level configuration options. Each subpage within Jenkins will have its own configuration panel options and context-specific configuration knobs. For example, if we are on a job status page, the configuration panel will look much different than if we are on the main dashboard. The next screenshot illustrates the main dashboard configuration panel and the stock configuration items available:

Figure 3-3: The top-level Jenkins configuration panel

We can see from the preceding screenshot that there are a number of available configuration options on the configuration panel. Let's take a look at the default items presented in the configuration panel on the main Jenkins dashboard. These represent the entry point into the Jenkins system:

- **New item**: This option is used to create new Jenkins jobs.
- **People**: This option navigates to the user configuration dashboard where user accounts can be viewed or modified.
- **Build history**: This option navigates to a dashboard that represents a view of the build jobs the system has executed, their statuses, and their trends.
- **Manage Jenkins**: This is the entry point into the administration area of Jenkins. The administration area of Jenkins provides a plethora of configuration options and settings, which can be adjusted to suit individual requirements.
- **Credentials**: This option navigates to the **Credentials** dashboard. The **Credentials** dashboard offers the ability to create, remove, update, and delete user account credentials. The Jenkins system can use these for configuration and automation tasks.

The job table

The job table in Jenkins illustrates the jobs defined within the Jenkins system along with some basic status information. As our Jenkins implementation matures, the number of jobs will inevitably expand. This will make keeping the system maintainable increasingly important. To help organize a growing list of jobs, views (tabs) can be created and configured to display subsets of the jobs defined within the Jenkins system.

Implementing a structured approach to creating jobs and views in Jenkins can help keep things organized and easier to maintain. It is a wise idea to settle on a naming convention for the defined jobs in the Jenkins system and enforce this. This can help us avoid a chaotic implementation and prevent confusion. By creating and enforcing a naming convention for our jobs, we can automatically filter the contents of a view by regular expressions or definitions. *Figure 3-4* shows an illustration of a Jenkins job table with three jobs: a build job, a deployment job, and a smoke test job.

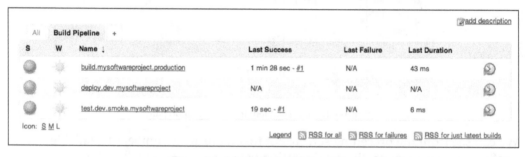

Figure 3-4: A basic view with three jobs

From the preceding screenshot, we can quickly visualize the health of our jobs. We can also see when they last succeeded and how long they took to execute.

Organizing jobs by pipeline step and name

One of my favorite organizational methods is to name the jobs by category and project name prefixes. I will typically prefix the job name with the role it's going to play in the build and delivery pipeline, and project name. Here is an example:

`build.myproject`: This prefix delineates a build/compile job for `myproject`

`test.myproject`: This prefix describes a job designed to execute smoke tests

`monitor.envname`: This prefix describes a job designed to monitor an environment's health

`deploy.envname.myproject`: This prefix describes a job that will perform a deployment to an environment

`provision.envname`: This prefix describes a job that will run a `chef`, `puppet`, `cfengine`, or `ansible script` to provision an environment (in preparation for deployment)

Now that we have an understanding of the purpose of the job table, let's take a moment to drill into the job table and understand the default columns.

- **Status of the last build**: This details the most recent status of the job. Jenkins defaults to red for failure, blue for success, and yellow for unstable.

- **Weather report**: This shows the aggregated report of recent builds.

- **Name**: This is the name of the job. This can be optionally sorted by clicking on the **Name** label.

- **Last success**: This describes how long ago the last successful execution of this job was.

- **Last failure**: This describes how long ago the last failure of the build job was.

- **Last duration**: This describes the run time length of the most recent execution of the build job.

- **Table footer**: This contains the RSS feeds and the footer of the jobs table, links to the **Legend**, and associated RSS feed. It is situated just below the job-listing table in the user interface.

- **Legend**: This link navigates us to a graphical legend that displays all relevant icons on the dashboard and their respective definitions.

If green and red are more desirable than the traditional blue, you might consider using the *Green Balls* plugin as an alternative solution. This plugin can be found by searching the available plugins provided by the Jenkins plugin center.

RSS feeds

Just below the jobs table on the Jenkins dashboard resides a set of RSS feed links. RSS feeds provide a fluid data source, which streams up-to-the-minute details about jobs, and statuses in Jenkins. These details include job status, recently executed jobs, and more. The following screenshot illustrates the RSS feed links provided by Jenkins via the main dashboard:

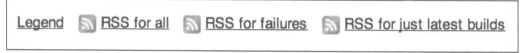

Figure 3-5: RSS feed links

As we can easily see from the preceding screenshot, Jenkins provides a handy RSS feed icon next to each available RSS feed. This makes identifying RSS feeds easier as we dive into the subsystems of the Jenkins platform.

Understanding RSS feeds in Jenkins is an important learning exercise as there are a number of useful additions to the Jenkins platform that make use of these RSS feeds. Let's take a minute to see what data streams each of the RSS feeds provides on the main Jenkins dashboard:

- **RSS for all**: This is a simple RSS feed describing all jobs and their statuses
- **RSS for failures**: This is an RSS feed describing all jobs with a *failed* status
- **RSS for just latest builds**: This is an RSS fee describing the most recently executed jobs

Using the RSS feeds available within Jenkins, we can subscribe our favorite RSS feed reader to these feeds or connect them to a build notification program. Build notification programs are available for most popular operating systems and can help us keep an eye on the Jenkins system without the need to constantly reload the Jenkins user interface. In case you're curious about build notification programs, see the following list of some of the available build notification programs and their respective links.

- Mac/OS X—Jenkins notifier for Mac OS X at `https://wiki.jenkins-ci.org/display/JENKINS/Jenkins+Notifier+for+Mac+OS+X`

- Windows—Desktop notifier for Jenkins at `https://wiki.jenkins-ci.org/display/JENKINS/Desktop+Notifier+for+Jenkins`

- Android mobile—Hudson monitor for Android at `https://wiki.jenkins-ci.org/display/JENKINS/Hudson+Monitor+for+Android`

- iOS Mobile—Jenkins notifier, which is available on the App Store

 A complete list of the available integration technologies and tools can be found at `https://wiki.jenkins-ci.org/display/JENKINS/Use+Jenkins` (under the **Tools** section).

The Jenkins build queue and executor status panel

The build queue and executor status panel provides us with visibility into current job executions and queued automations on the Jenkins system. This is a handy solution for determining the current load on the Jenkins system and can help us keep jobs from hanging or getting stuck in the queue. The next screenshot illustrates the **Build Queue** and **Build Executor Status** panels:

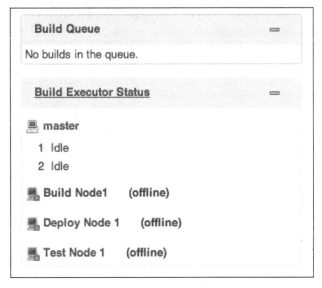

Figure 3-6: The Build Queue and Build Executor Status panels

By clicking on the **Build Executor Status** link located on the top of the **Build Executor Status** panel, Jenkins will navigate us directly to the slave node dashboard, which lists the master Jenkins executor and any defined slave nodes.

By clicking on any of the listed executor node names inside the **Build Executor Status** panel, Jenkins will navigate us to the status of that respective device.

The **Build Queue** section displays jobs that have been triggered for execution, but do not have an available executor. Jobs listed in the queue can be clicked on directly. By clicking on a queued item, Jenkins will navigate us back to the originating Jenkins job that triggered its addition to the queue.

For jobs we would like to cancel (either queued or running), we can click on **X**, which is prominently displayed next to each item in the table.

Jobs in Jenkins

To facilitate the creation of new jobs, the Jenkins platform provides a handy **New Item** menu link on the main Jenkins dashboard. This link represents the entry point into job creation. In this section of *Mastering Jenkins*, we will learn the various job types we can create in Jenkins and what makes each project type unique.

Upon clicking on the **New Item** link from the main dashboard, Jenkins will navigate us to the basic job configuration page where we can define the name of the job and select the appropriate project type. This screenshot illustrates the basic job configuration page we just described:

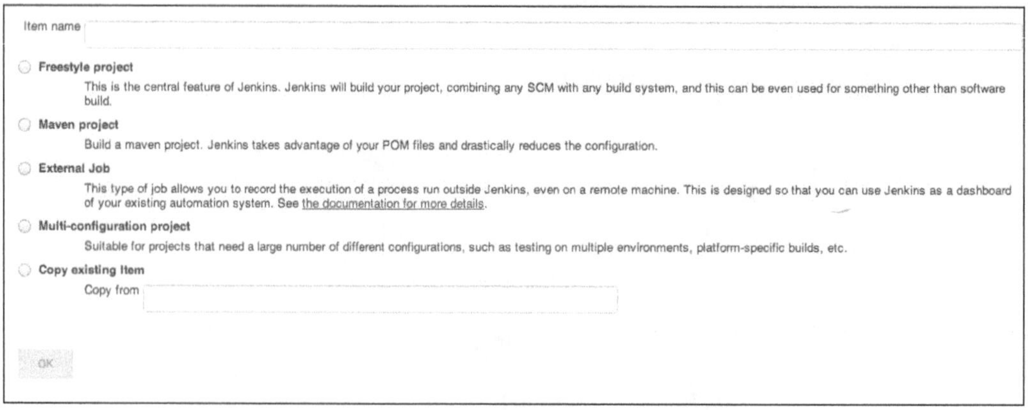

Item name

○ **Freestyle project**
This is the central feature of Jenkins. Jenkins will build your project, combining any SCM with any build system, and this can be even used for something other than software build.

○ **Maven project**
Build a maven project. Jenkins takes advantage of your POM files and drastically reduces the configuration.

○ **External Job**
This type of job allows you to record the execution of a process run outside Jenkins, even on a remote machine. This is designed so that you can use Jenkins as a dashboard of your existing automation system. See the documentation for more details.

○ **Multi-configuration project**
Suitable for projects that need a large number of different configurations, such as testing on multiple environments, platform-specific builds, etc.

○ **Copy existing Item**
Copy from

OK

Figure 3-7: New item basic configuration page

Each of the options presented in the new item basic configuration page represents a unique type. The selection made on this page will have a profound impact on how the job will function. Let's discuss each of the available job types and learn about the individual options prescribed for each job:

- **Freestyle project**: This provides the ability to create a completely custom job that can behave in any way we choose.

- **Maven project**: This is designed specifically for JAVA Maven projects. It utilizes **Production and Operations Management Society (POMS)** and provides an easy to use interface for execution of Maven targets.

- **Multiconfiguration project**: This is designed for projects that have multiple configurations (x86, x64, and so on). It allows you to specify a single job with multiple output types.

- **Copy existing job**: This allows the user to duplicate the contents of an existing job and alter the name.

- **External job**: This allows the user to trigger and monitor an external Jenkins job. This external job type is particularly handy when there are multiple Jenkins instances (for example, a development Jenkins instance and a production Jenkins instance) that are responsible for production deployments.

> For each of the job types, Jenkins provides a detailed job-configuration page, which allows us to define and customize the functionality of the job. Some of the configuration options described in the freestyle project type are common to all job types. For the sake of brevity, the job types described after the freestyle project job type detail only the customization options that are unique to that project type.

Freestyle projects in Jenkins

The freestyle project is the most commonly utilized job type in Jenkins. This job type contains a number of configuration options, and buttons, which we can use to define, and execute automation steps. Let's discuss how to implement a freestyle project in Jenkins.

To create a freestyle project type in Jenkins, toggle the **Freestyle project** option on the basic job configuration page and specify a unique job name. Upon inputting these details into Jenkins, we can click on the **OK** button to continue. Jenkins will then navigate us to the detailed job configuration page, as shown in *Figure 3-8a* and *Figure 3-8b*.

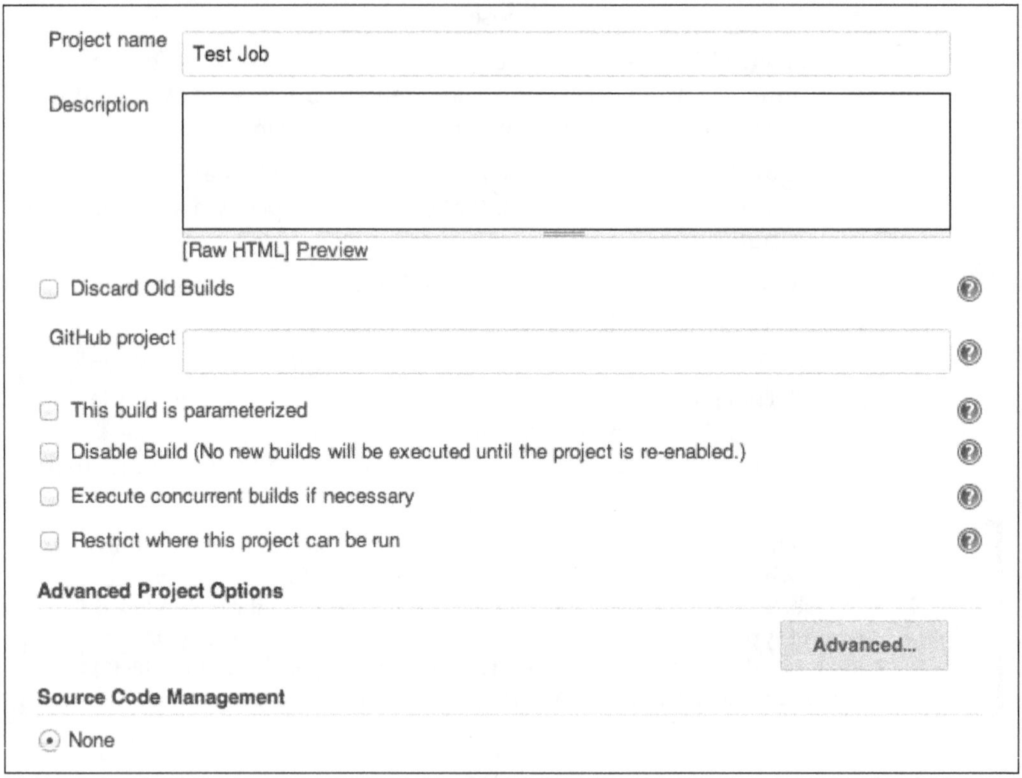

Figure 3-8a: A detailed job configuration page

Figure 3-8b illustrates the lower portion of the detailed job configuration page, with a sample **Execute shell** build step:

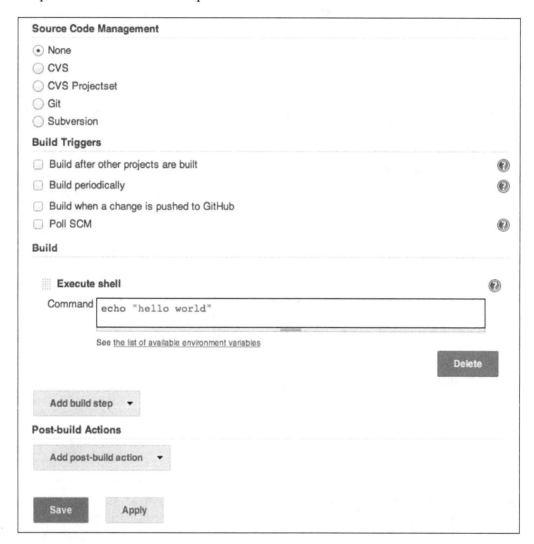

Figure 3-8b: Lower portion of detailed job configuration page

The detailed job configuration page provides a configurable user interface where we can specify and manage a job's information, source control modules, and automation steps. At first glance, this page may look a bit daunting; however if we look a bit more closely, we can see that the configuration options presented are organized by category. These categories are described below.

- **Project details**: This provides a basic set of options that define the general properties of the job in Jenkins
- **Advanced project options**: These are advanced options that can be tweaked to customize the behavior of your job in Jenkins
- **Source code management**: This defines configurations related to source control (many options)
- **Build triggers**: This section defines upstream jobs, build scheduling (CRON), and continuous integration options (SCM polling)
- **Build steps**: These include automation steps to execute as part of the build
- **Post-build actions**: These include any steps to execute once the build has completed

Jenkins adheres to a job lifecycle process. The job execution lifecycle is a set of governing phases a job will pass through prior to and during its execution. The defined phases in the job execution life cycle include the following.

1. Polling.
2. Pre SCM.
3. SCM.
4. Pre build.
5. Build steps.
6. Post build.

The preceding phases we just described represent automation execution segments, organized by functionality. These help us determine the order our automation will run in. Additionally, when it is time to extend Jenkins through the use of plugins, groovy scripts, or related additions, understanding these life cycle steps will prove crucial.

When creating a Jenkins job, it is equally important to completely understand the various categories and available configuration options available. Let's break down the freestyle project to better understand its capabilities.

Project options

The project information section contains detailed information about the present job. The options available within the project information section includes critical descriptive information, definitions of where the job will run, what input parameters the job requires for execution, and how the job will be listed on the Jenkins dashboard. It is important to explore the options available in this section in detail and completely understand the configurations available to us. The following table describes a brief overview of each of the available configuration options presented in the top most section of the detailed job configuration page:

Field	Input type	REQ.	Description
Project name	Text	YES	This is the name that will be used by Jenkins to describe the job. This name is also used upon execution to define the WORKSPACE folder the job will use to store any temporary files during its run.
Description	Text box	NO	This is an optional description for the job. This information will be displayed just below the project name on the job's status page.
Discard old builds	Toggle	NO	This is the frequency at which build history is pruned. These logs can grow significantly. It is wise to set this option to a reasonable time frame.
This build is parameterized	Toggle + choice	NO	This option lets you create input parameters for the job. The input parameters specified will be passed into any automation steps as environment variables.
Disable build	Toggle	NO	This disables the job until the checkbox is not ticked.
Execute concurrent builds if necessary	Toggle	NO	This allows for parallel builds to run on multiple executors if they are available (load balancing).
Restrict where this project can be run	Toggle + Text field	NO	This allows you to specify a label or executor that the job will run on. This feature is highly useful to create a build farm of multiple architectures or platforms.

Defining build parameters

One of the most notable configurations available in the job configuration page is the **This build is parameterized** checkbox. This option allows us to add and define the input parameter criteria for the job. These parameters will then be passed into the jobs executing automation as environment variables. To better illustrate this concept, *Figure 3-9* illustrates a sample build job configured with parameters that prompt for job specific information prior to execution. The inputs defined in our example include compiler flags, build mode, and build notes (however, it could be any bit of useful information):

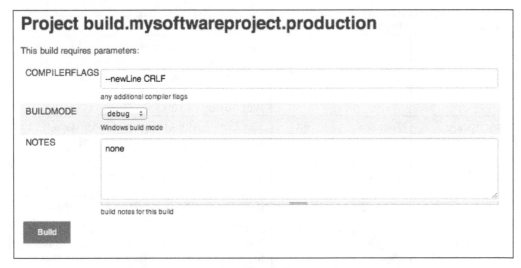

Figure 3-9: Running a Jenkins job with the required parameter inputs

Build parameters can be of varying types, and are specified in the job's configuration page. To illustrate this *Figure 3-10* shows the job configuration implementation from the backend configuration perspective.

Figure 3-10: Defining a Jenkins job with the required parameter inputs

Jenkins provides a number of parameter types out-of-the-box. These parameter types define the input fields that will be displayed to the user when the **Build Now** button is clicked. The following input options are built into Jenkins as available parameter types.

- Boolean parameter
- CVS symbolic name parameter
- Choice parameter
- Credentials parameter
- File parameter
- Password parameter
- Run parameter
- String parameter
- Text parameter

Advanced project options

The **Advanced project** options configuration section in the detailed job configuration page allows us to specify advanced configuration items for our Jenkins jobs. These are reserved for more advanced users and are very useful. It would be wise to explore this section in detail as it contains configuration options for upstream and downstream job execution (which is discussed in greater depth in *Chapter 7, Build Pipelines*) as well as CI quiet period wait times, and more. The description information for each of these available options is provided below.

Field Name	Input Type	REQ.	Description
Quiet period	Check box + Text field	NO	This option can prevent Jenkins from prematurely attempting a build when a checkin hasn't been completed or is done in multiple checkin steps. See the help icon in Jenkins for additional use cases.
Retry count	Check box + Text field	NO	The source control checkout retry count option will tell Jenkins to retry a failed checkout of the source code x number of times before giving up.
Block build when upstream project is building	Check box	NO	This option tells Jenkins to wait until any upstream-dependent jobs that are running have completed prior to executing this job.
Block build when downstream project is building	Check box	NO	This option tells Jenkins to wait until any downstream-dependent jobs have completed prior to reporting the status of this job.
Use a custom workspace	Text box	NO	This text box allows you to specify a custom workspace folder name for the job.
Keep the build logs of dependencies	Check box	NO	This check box prevents Jenkins from log rotating any dependent jobs logs.

Source code management

The source code management section of the detailed job configuration page describes the mechanism Jenkins will utilize when retrieving source code content from a source control management system. This section of the detailed job configuration page presents us with a number of available options we can choose from to define our source control retrieval mechanism, and regulate the granularity of the pull. Jenkins will present us with the following choices, which we can select from to define our source control solution:

- **None**: No source checkout required.
- **CVS (Concurrent Versioning System)**: One of the first widely adopted source control systems. It has since evolved into more modern version control strategies, such as SVN.
- **SVN (Subversion)**: This is recognized as one of the most popular source control systems in use today.

The Jenkins platform, by default, features source control modules for CVS and SVN. To add support for Git, Perforce, Mercurial, and other modern source control systems we will need to install the appropriate plugin to support it. As a result of the comprehensive nature of source control management, this section will primarily focus on SVN and Git since these are the most popular systems in use today. Let's spend a few minutes looking at how to utilize SVN and Git in Jenkins.

Source control via SVN

- **Repository URL**: This is the URL for the SVN repository you would like to attach to the Jenkins job. This URL requires an http or https prefix. The URL can contain subfolders as required, for example, `http://svn.myorg.com/myrepo/trunk/asf/ant/`. If additional checkout modules are required by your Jenkins job, you can click on the **Add more locations...** button to specify additional SVN locations.
- **Local module directory (optional)**: This field allows you to specify the local checkout subdirectory relative to the job's workspace.
- **Repository depth**: This specifies the shallow checkout option in Jenkins. This option allows you to restrict Jenkins from utilizing full recursion when checking out a source tree. The default option is **Infinity**.

- **Ignore externals**: This option is used by Jenkins to prevent SVN from checking out attached external modules that are connected to the SVN source location.

- **Checkout strategy**: This option allows you to specify how Jenkins will perform the checkout of the source tree. More specifically, it allows you to select from one of the following options:

    ° Use `svn update` as much as possible

    ° Always checkout a fresh copy

    ° Emulate clean checkout by first deleting unversioned/ignored files, then update using `svn update` (one of the best ways to handle large source trees)

    ° Use `svn update` as much as possible, with `svn revert` before update

- **Repository browser**: This specifies which SVN repository browser to link the job to. The Jenkins platform supports Assembla, CollabNet, FishEye, ViewSVN, and many more.

Advanced SVN options

The SVN module in Jenkins supports highly configurable filters, which can be applied to polling and checkouts in SVN. These filters allow you to ignore checkins with specific commit messages, include checkins with specific folder structures, exclude the triggering of the job based on checkins by a specific usernames, and more. If you're looking to filter your job trigger based on a specific file or include a specific folder, this area should have the option you're looking for.

Source control via Git–requires the Git plugin

Git is a modern distributed version control solution that is increasingly becoming popular. To support Git in Jenkins, we will at a minimum need to install the Git plugin onto our Jenkins system. These options require the Git plugin and include the following:

- **Repository URL**: This is the URL of the Git repository to clone. If more than one repository is required, you could use the respective **Add Repository** button to define additional repositories.

- **Branches to build**: This set of fields allows you to specify one or more branches to checkout as part of the initial pull from the repository. The default is master.

- **Repository browser**: This specifies the default repository browser to use for this Git repository. Jenkins supports `AssemblaWeb`, `Kiln`, `TFS`, `github-web`, and many more.

One of the more popular Git development patterns is to leverage short-lived feature branches, coupled with a pull request to facilitate code reviews and integration. The Jenkins community has created a pull request builder plugin to facilitate this exact workflow and provide continuous build support. The plugin can be found at `https://wiki.jenkins-ci.org/display/JENKINS/GitHub+pull+request+builder+plugin`.

Additional behaviors

The additional behaviors buttons in the Git source control management area contains a plethora of additional functionality we can leverage to gain more granular control over the Git clone and checkout process. It is highly recommended that you explore this area in detail as each option has features that can aid in obtaining the perfect checkout and clone results for your organization's source control implementation.

Build triggers

Build triggers are events fired that result in the execution of a build job. The build triggers section of the detailed job configuration page provides us with the ability to specify criteria Jenkins will listen for. The configurations made to the build triggers section of the detailed job configuration page will define the specifics of the events that Jenkins will use to trigger the execution of the job. Some examples of common build triggers include:

- SCM changes (polling or push)
- Upstream job completion
- Timer scheduling
- Manual scheduling of a build (build button)

Beyond the basic build triggers listed earlier, the Jenkins community has provided a number of additional plugins that can also be leveraged to trigger the execution of a job. Here are some of the more popular plugins:

- Parameterized trigger plugin
- Trigger/call builds on other projects
- Promoted builds plugin
- URL trigger plugin
- RabbitMQ trigger plugin

Build steps

Build steps in Jenkins define the automation and sequences that will occur during the run of a job. Upon executing a job, Jenkins will execute the defined build steps specified within the build steps section in the same order in which they are listed. Let's take a look at some automation steps we can define in the detailed job configuration page:

- **Execute Windows batch command**: This build step will allow you to input MS-DOS batch-compliant commands. Upon execution Jenkins will convert the inputted text into a .bat file and execute it on the target executor (master/slave etc.).

- **Execute shell**: This build step will allow you to input a set of Unix shell bash commands or bash script code. Upon execution Jenkins will convert the inputted text to a shell-compliant script and execute it on the target executor (master/slave etc.).

- **Invoke Ant**: Jenkins provides tight coupling with Java technologies, such as Ant. By implementing this build step, you can tell Jenkins to call a specific Ant target within an Ant build script. Upon execution Jenkins will initiate Ant (defined in the main Jenkins configuration area) and call your specified target.

- **Invoke top-level Maven targets**: Jenkins' close integration with Maven is equally as comprehensive as its integration with Ant. Using this build step you can target a specific Maven lifecycle task.

Additional build steps can be made available via the vast array of plugins available for Jenkins. For example, Ruby scripts can be executed via the Ruby plugin, whereas MSBuild is supported via the MSBuild plugin.

Post-build actions

Post-build actions in Jenkins execute upon completion of the primary build steps. Post-build actions are handy for notification and tasks that are not necessarily dependent upon successful completion of each build step executed. Some examples of post-build steps are:

- Archive the artifacts
- Build other projects
- Publish the JUnit test result report
- Publish JavaDoc
- Notifications

Additional post-build steps may become available as you install plugins and customize your Jenkins instance. If you need a task to execute regardless of the overall build status (successful, failed and so on) the post-build action section is the preferred area to work in.

Maven projects

The Jenkins platform integrates very tightly with Java projects. Jenkins supports Maven 2/3 POMS directly out of the box and even offers a Maven project type (for creating build jobs specific to Maven) and primary configuration options in the master setup area, where we can specify the default Maven installation location the jobs will use.

By utilizing the Maven project job type in Jenkins, we can compile source code, execute tests, incorporate dependencies, and much more. Let's learn how to harness the tight integration with Maven and Jenkins. To get started, let's walk through the Maven job project type in Jenkins and discover some of the special integration features.

When implementing the Maven job type, there are a number of obvious Maven-specific features that will give us a notable advantage over the standard freestyle project type. These include:

- Automatic parsing of POM project files
- Coupling of the Maven run to Jenkins with automatic determination and execution of the subsequent steps
- Automatic determination of dependencies between projects

To begin, create a new Jenkins job using the **New Item** link on the main dashboard, and select **Maven** as the project type. This is shown in *Figure 3-11*.

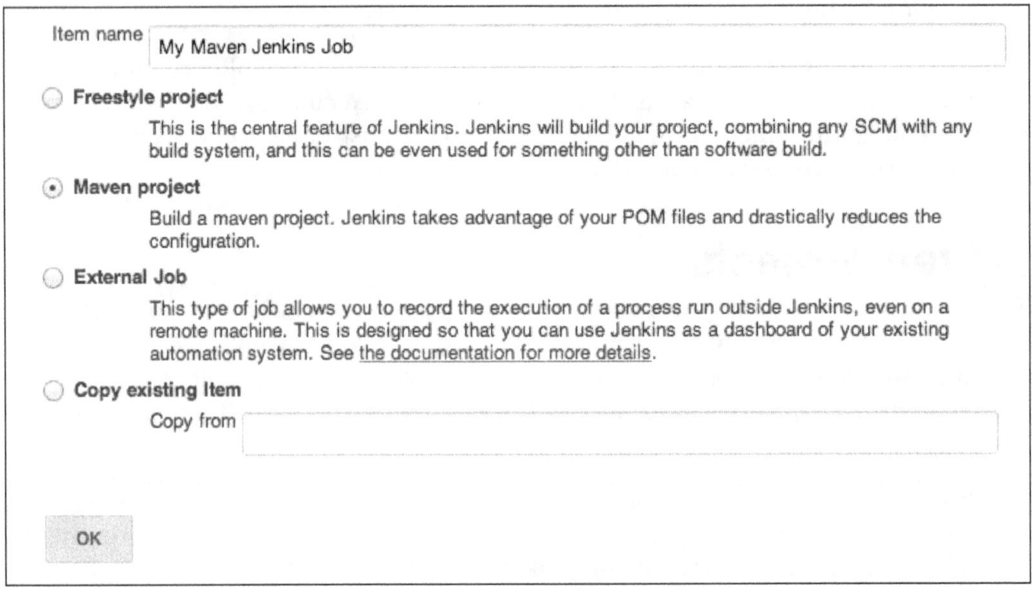

| Item name | My Maven Jenkins Job |

○ **Freestyle project**

This is the central feature of Jenkins. Jenkins will build your project, combining any SCM with any build system, and this can be even used for something other than software build.

⊙ **Maven project**

Build a maven project. Jenkins takes advantage of your POM files and drastically reduces the configuration.

○ **External Job**

This type of job allows you to record the execution of a process run outside Jenkins, even on a remote machine. This is designed so that you can use Jenkins as a dashboard of your existing automation system. See the documentation for more details.

○ **Copy existing Item**

Copy from

OK

Figure 3-11: A basic job configuration page (Maven selected)

Upon clicking on **OK,** Jenkins will navigate us over to the detailed project configuration page. Once Jenkins has loaded the detailed job configuration page for our Maven project, we are presented with a number of configuration options, which are again divided into sections. The configuration sections for a Maven project in Jenkins are strikingly similar to the ones available for the freestyle project type, but with some notable differences.

Build triggers

The build triggers section of the detailed job configuration page contains one notable Maven specific option:

- **Build whenever a snapshot dependency is built**: This checkbox tells Jenkins to automatically trigger a build for this job if another job contains a reference in its POM to the artifacts produced by this job

Build step

The Maven project type in Jenkins features one Maven-specific build step. This build step features the ability to execute Maven and specify the relevant Maven project options and goals. Let's take a look at the Maven build step and some of its available options.

- **Maven version**: To have Jenkins execute goals on a Maven project, you will need to specify any Maven installations you may have. Maven installations can be configured in the main Jenkins configuration area, which you can access by navigating to **Manage Jenkins -> Configure System**. Each Maven installation configured will be displayed in the <Maven Version> dropdown.

- **Root POM**: If preferable, we could specify a subfolder for Jenkins to search for the top-level pom.xml file. This option may be useful if your source control system contains the POM inside a subfolder or if you have multiple source control modules you are checking out from your SCM.

- **Goals and options**: This option allows you to specify the goals you would like to execute during your Maven project build, for example, *clean install*.

Advanced options

In addition to the default Maven options presented within the build step and build triggers, there are a number of advanced options that can be configured. Let's take a look at the advanced options and some of the customizations we can implement.

- **MAVEN_OPTS**: This specifies the JVM options Jenkins passes to Maven upon execution.

- **Incremental build — only build changed modules**: This option allows you to speed up your build process by only building items that have changed.

- **Disable automatic artifact archiving**: If this item is checked, Jenkins will not archive artifacts generated during the execution of this project.

- **Disable automatic site documentation artifact archiving**: By checking this box, we are effectively telling Jenkins not to archive all artifacts of a Maven site.

- **Disable automatic fingerprinting of consumed and produced artifacts**: By selecting this option, we are instructing Jenkins to not automatically determine the fingerprints for an artifact and record it.

- **Enable triggering of downstream projects**: Jenkins provides the ability to chain jobs together. This becomes highly useful for Java projects as a typical Maven project has more than one build dependency.

- **Build modules in parallel**: This enables multithreaded compilation of modules.

- **Use private Maven repository**: When selected, Jenkins will force Maven to use the `.repository` file as the local maven repository definition.

- **Resolve dependencies during POM parsing**: This option will configure the Jenkins job to automatically resolve and retrieve dependencies defined within the Maven POM file.

- **Run headless**: If a build does not require direct access to the desktop (Windows), this option can be selected to remove the desktop interaction for the process.

- **Process plugins during POM parsing**: Self-documenting.

- **Use custom workspace**: Jenkins allocates a workspace for each job. This workspace serves as the home location for source code files and artifacts during the execution of the job. Using this option, you can specify a custom workspace location on the target executor.

- **Settings file**: The `settings.xml` file is used to specify configuration for Maven. By customizing this field, we can specify an alternate location where Jenkins and Maven will look for this file.

- **Global settings file**: This dropdown allows the user to specify one of two options:

  - Use default Maven global settings
  - Global settings file on filesystem

Post-build steps

The Maven project type in Jenkins features a unique set of post-build actions. This feature supports the conditional execution of post-build steps based on specified criteria. The available options include the following:

- Run only if build succeeds
- Run only if build succeeds or is unstable
- Run regardless of build result

The integration of Jenkins with Maven is quite unique. This is because at its root Jenkins was designed to support Java development solutions. For additional information related to Jenkins and Maven please consult the Maven Project plugin wiki page located at `https://wiki.jenkins-ci.org/display/JENKINS/Maven+Project+Plugin`.

Monitoring external jobs

The Jenkins platform features a wide variety of project types and a diverse set of automation solutions. One of the lesser-known jobs that Jenkins offers allows us to monitor an outside job/process for completion. By harnessing this feature, we can tie Jenkins to other build systems, automations, or applications that reside outside the Jenkins ecosystem, and have them report back to our *monitor an external job* project in Jenkins.

Let's take a few minutes to learn how to implement a Jenkins job that monitors an external process and reports back upon completion. To begin, create a new Jenkins job using the **New Item** link on the main dashboard and specify **External Job** as the job type. Once created, you may notice there are very few detailed configuration options for this specific job type. This is because the way this job type will receive its status is by waiting for a job-specific callback from the Jenkins core.

External job types rely on the Jenkins core automation engine to execute processes from the command line and report status back to the Jenkins system. Let's consider the following command-line example excerpts provided by the Jenkins community:

- For Debian/Ubuntu:

```
$> sudo apt-get install jenkins-external-job-monitor

$> export JENKINS_HOME= http://user:pw@yourjenkinsurl/path/to/
jenkins/

$> java -jar /path/to/WEB-INF/lib/jenkins-core-*.jar "job name"
<program arg1 arg2...>
```

- For Windows:

```
C:\> SET JENKINS_HOME=http://user:pw@myserver.acme.org/path/to/
jenkins/

C:\> java -jar \path\to\WEB-INF\lib\jenkins-core-*.jar "job name"
cmd.exe /c <program arg1 arg2...>
```

In the preceding examples, the external job-monitoring project type allows us to initiate a shell command or script using the `java` command and the Jenkins core subsystems. Once the shell command has completed, Jenkins will report the status back to the job name specified via the command line. This type of solution allows users to connect Jenkins with other build solutions easily and maintain the status within the specified Job.

Multiconfiguration jobs in Jenkins – matrix jobs

A multi configuration project in Jenkins is valuable for instances where a build or automation task has multiple steps that are very similar in nature except for a few key pivot points. A multi configuration project may be useful when there are multiple input flags of a similar nature. Such projects might be based on a *Debug* or *Release* compiler flag, or a specific architecture definition (x86 or x64).

It is important to note that this type of project in Jenkins sacrifices some amount of customization that would otherwise be available in a free style project in exchange for some basic conventions. In return the user gains the ability to create an axis, and reduce redundancy across multiple jobs.

Configuration matrix

The configuration matrix is the defining feature of the multi configuration job in Jenkins. This feature allows us to specify steps within the job that would regularly be duplicated and allows us to parameterize these via an axis.

At the core of the multi configuration project in Jenkins is the user-defined axis. Using the **Add Axis** drop-down menu, we can select from the available axis types and define build slaves, label expressions, or user-defined custom options. We can consider an axis in the Jenkins multi configuration project as a pivot point and allow one job to do the work of many.

Slaves

The slave option on the **Add Axis** dropdown provides us with the ability to restrict the execution of the parallel build steps to the defined slave nodes on the Jenkins system. The displayed input is in tree-form with checkboxes that can be ticked to allocate slave node devices to the execution pool. This is illustrated in *Figure 3-12*.

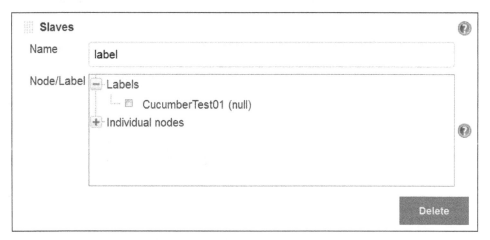

Figure 3-12: Add axis— the slaves option

Label expression

A label expression axis allows us to define slave nodes or executors directly by the group name that the job will run on. This is similar in nature to the **Restrict where this project can be run** option we discussed earlier in the *freestyle project*, but it lets the individual legs of the axis define the slave devices they will run on.

This screenshot illustrates the **Label expression** option with a label defined as WindowsSlavesGroup:

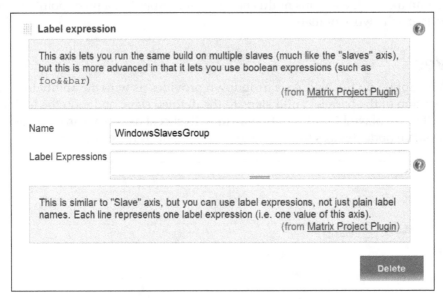

Figure 3-13: A label expression definition

User-defined axes

The user-defined axis is probably one of the most useful features of the multi-configuration job in Jenkins. This option allows us to specify a set of values and a key that will be used to iterate over a job step multiple times. To better illustrate, let's consider the following `ant` commands and see how we can make use of an axis to reduce duplication of our Jenkins jobs:

```
#>ant set-target-foo debug compile
#>ant set-target-bar debug compile
#>ant set-target-foo release compile
#>ant set-target-bar release compile
```

Instead of defining multiple build steps or jobs, we can utilize the **Add Axis** feature to call one build step multiple times with a unique parameter passed into each call. This is simply an iterator that passes in a unique value per execution. By selecting the user-defined **Axis** option from the **Add Axis** dropdown, we can specify a name (variable) and a set of whitespace values (or values separated by carriage returns) that will define the passed-in parameters.

Once the axis values have been defined, we can access them via a standard environment variable parameter in the build step, as illustrated here:

```
#>ant $target $releasetype compile
```

As we can see in our example *$release* and *$releasetype* contain the pre-defined axis variables we described via our white space values above.

It may take some experimentation to get multi-configuration jobs defined and working properly in a manner that is suitable for your specific needs. Once inputted and configured properly, multi-configuration jobs can become an invaluable tool within your Jenkins arsenal.

Creating views

Views in Jenkins allow us to organize jobs and content into tabbed categories, which are displayed on the main dashboard. As a Jenkins instance expands, it is logical to create associated views for appropriate groups and categories. For example it may be a good idea to create a *Build* view, which displays build-specific jobs within it. Let's spend a few minutes discovering how to implement a new view within Jenkins and learn ways to filter its content.

To implement a new view, there is a tab icon with a plus sign located on the main Jenkins dashboard, as illustrated in *Figure 3-14*:

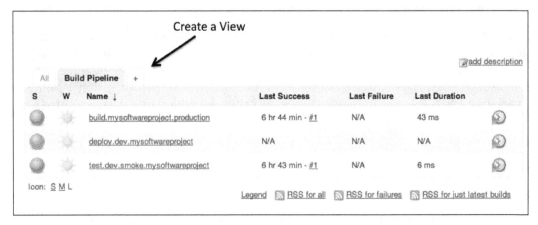

Figure 3-14: Creating a new view

Upon clicking on the **+** tab, Jenkins will navigate us to the basic view configuration page. From this page, we will need to specify a name and view type for our new view. The default view type available in Jenkins is the **List view**. This view type contains a list of jobs. Additional view types may become available if/when any plugins that support creating additional view types are installed onto the Jenkins system. For now we will stick to the **List view** view type. Once the view type has been defined, click on **OK** to proceed to the detailed view configuration page, which is illustrated in *Figure 3-15*.

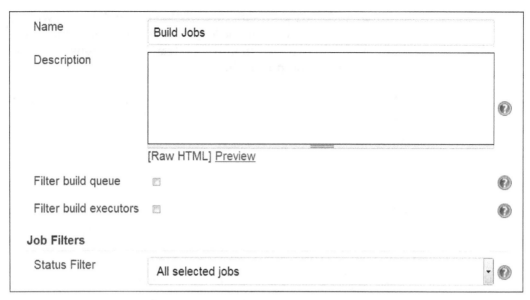

Figure 3-15: A detailed view configuration sample page

The detailed view configuration page contains a number of options that we can use to customize the look, feel, and content of the view. To better understand the switches and knobs available, let's walk through each of the sections displayed within the detailed view configuration page:

- **Basic Details**: The **Basic Details** section of the detailed view configuration page contains fields that define the header content of the view (name and description), as well as some basic filtering options for the jobs that can be listed (**Filter build queue** and **Filter build executors**).

- **Job Filters**: The **Job Filters** section of the detailed view configuration page contains a set of more advanced filter options, which can help narrow down the list of jobs that the tab will contain. Such items include **Status Filter**, filter by job name (check the appropriate boxes for the jobs to list), and use regular expressions.

- **Columns**: Now that we have the jobs that we want to list on the view, we may want to customize the columns in the job table. To accomplish this, there is a handy columns section that we can utilize to detail the columns that will be displayed. The available columns include:

  ○ **Status**

  ○ **Weather**

  ○ **Name**

  ○ **Last success**

  ○ **Last failure**

  ○ **Last duration**

  ○ **Build button**

Filtering jobs by regular expression

One of the more valuable features we can leverage when creating views is regular expression filtering. This solution allows us to specify a naming convention filter specification for the view. It exists in regular expression form and will cause Jenkins to filter the Jenkins jobs displayed in the view based on the match results of the regular expression entered. This screenshot illustrates the configuration field that allows us to input a regular expression filter:

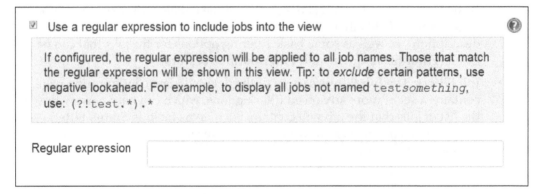

Figure 3-16: Regular expression filtering

Filtering by regular expression is quite easy. Let's look at some examples:

- `.*MyProjectName.*`: This filters Jenkins jobs in the view to include all projects that contain the text, `MyProjectName`

- `(?!MyProjectName.*).*`: This filters Jenkins jobs in the view to exclude all projects that contain the text, `MyProjectName`

- `(?![0-9].*).*`: This filters Jenkins jobs to exclude all projects containing `0-9` numerical digits

As we can see, through the implementation of regular expression filtering we can enforce naming conventions and keep our Jenkins instance organized.

Summary

In this chapter, we learned more about dashboards, views, and project types in Jenkins. We learned some valuable tools available to create them. You learned about Java properties files and understood how we can begin to leverage them to pass build data from one job to another. In the next chapter, you will learn about managing build jobs, views, and dashboards.

4
Managing Views and Jobs in Jenkins

Managing views and jobs in Jenkins is typically a responsibility assigned to the Jenkins administrator. To assist us in this responsibility, our friendly Jenkins concierge features a number of investigative tools that we can leverage to debug any issues that may arise. In this chapter, we will get acquainted with some of the features Jenkins provides to administrators. We will learn to better navigate the Jenkins user interface and also learn how to trace job failures, sleuth slave node outages, and analyze health trends.

Learning to effectively navigate and manage a Jenkins instance is a skill that will be honed over time and generally comes through the experience of doing it. Experience can teach what no teacher could have taught. Wisdom evolves through these experiences and comes from practice. As you spend more time practicing and honing your Jenkins skills, you will learn how to effectively manage a Jenkins instance of any size.

> *"Tell me, I'll forget, Show me, I may remember, But involve me and I'll understand." – Chinese Proverb*

Together, we will discover some lesser known features, and learn how to harness them to better manage the information housed in Jenkins. Additionally, we will walk through a number of tutorials on views and jobs in Jenkins, and learn how to better navigate the Jenkins platform.

To begin let's discuss the areas of focus for this chapter. This chapter will focus on the following topics:

- Managing Views in Jenkins
- Navigating a job's project page
- Drilling into a job's execution

Managing Views in Jenkins

Views are represented as tabs in the Jenkins platform on the main dashboard and are positioned at the top of the dashboard. Each tab is the manifestation of a view defined in the Jenkins system. The primary purpose of views is to display an organized subset of the jobs defined. Views can help us organize the jobs within Jenkins by category, state, or regular expression. A relatively new Jenkins installation may not require a structured organizational system but, as the number of jobs grows organically, organizing the jobs by category will become more and more important. In this section of *Mastering Jenkins*, we will learn how to manage views and discover some tips and tricks we can leverage to optimize our Jenkins installation.

Altering the default "View"

The default behavior of the Jenkins platform is to list all jobs defined in the Jenkins system on the main dashboard. The **All** tab displays every project currently defined in Jenkins in one all-encompassing list. As jobs become deprecated and projects are no longer actively developed, it is prudent to migrate projects off the primary dashboard view and onto views that are dedicated to specific categories. To better illustrate this concept, *Figure 4-1* shows a set of categorized views in Jenkins organized by job type or pipeline:

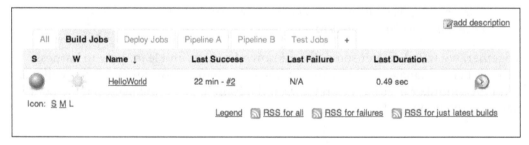

Figure 4-1: An example of categorized views in Jenkins

As we can see, creating views can help ensure that users can quickly locate the jobs that matter to them, and avoid hunting for specific jobs on the primary entry points in Jenkins.

This solution can help dramatically organize active jobs in Jenkins. While this is a step in the right direction, there could still be a problem managing a growing list of historically deprecated jobs and data. Let's learn a quick trick we can employ to help better manage historical or deprecated jobs on the Jenkins dashboard. The best way to pair down the number of jobs displayed on the main Jenkins dashboard is to create a new default view containing only the active jobs on the system. Once the new Active jobs view has been created, we will continue to allow the **All** tab to contain a complete list of jobs on the system, however Jenkins users would not need to wade through a lot of clutter to find what they are looking for. After the new default view has been implemented we could switch out the primary entry point tab that Jenkins will display, which would provide a nice clean dashboard containing ONLY the active jobs on the system.

The following screenshot illustrates an example of the approach we just discussed and uses an **Active Projects** view integrated into Jenkins as the primary entry point.

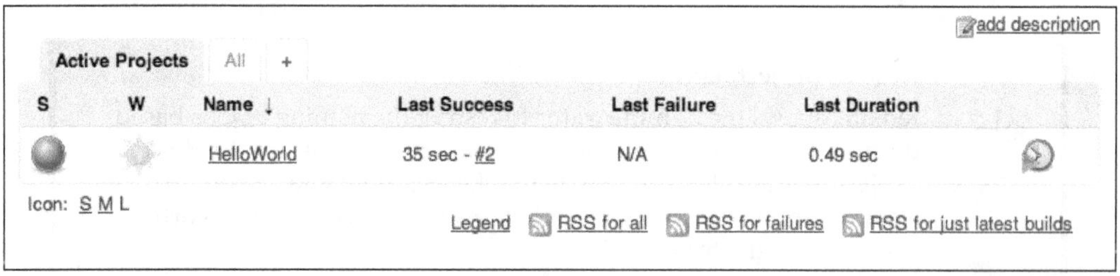

Figure 4-2: An alternate view example

Once the new **Active Projects** view has been created, we will want to set it as the default view for the Jenkins system. Jenkins provides a handy **Default view** configuration option located in the main Jenkins administration configuration page. This option will become available when more than one view exists on the system. To alter the default view, the Jenkins administrator will have to navigate to the **Jenkins -> Manage Jenkins -> Configure System** page to begin making the necessary adjustment.

Once you navigated to the primary Jenkins configuration page, we need to locate the **Default view** configuration option. This is illustrated in *Figure 4-3*:

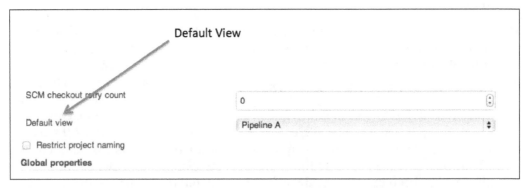

Figure 4-3: Altering the default view

Once the drop-down option has been changed, Jenkins will automatically use the selected view instead of the default **All** view when users navigate to Jenkins. This solution can help hide deprecated jobs that have become obsolete and take up valuable dashboard space.

Restrict project naming

Jenkins allows the administrator to restrict the naming of jobs based on specific patterns. To implement name restrictions use the **Restrict project naming** checkbox. By using this solution, you can enforce a set of naming conventions for Jenkins jobs. This option is worth exploring in greater depth.

Customizing the basic content of a View

As we mentioned earlier, the available views are displayed in the uppermost sections of the Jenkins dashboard and are shown as tabs. To modify the contents of a view in Jenkins, click on the desired view. Then click on the **Edit View** link from the configuration panel on the left-hand side, as shown in *Figure 4-4*:

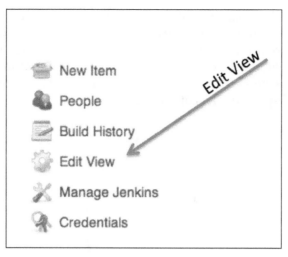

Figure 4-4: The Edit View link on the Jenkins dashboard

Upon clicking on the **Edit View** option for the selected view, Jenkins will navigate us to the detailed configuration page for that view. From this configuration page, we can customize the view and make alterations. Let's take a moment to detail out the customization options available from the **Edit View** configuration page.

The **Edit View** configuration page is divided into three primary categories. The categories include a general configuration options section, **Job Filters**, and Display Columns. Let's look at each category in greater depth.

From the general configuration section at the top, we can modify basic configuration details such as the name of the view, the description, and some basic view filter toggles, which filter the jobs displayed within the view.

The **Job Filters** section is just below the general configuration area. It provides a more granular filtering system that allows us to delineate the projects that our view will display. The most useful of these filters is probably the regular expression filtering option, which provides a unique way to select jobs that will be displayed via regular expression.

Just below the **Job Filters** section is the **Columns** section. This area allows us to alter the columns displayed in the view. The columns selected will describe the projects listed as well as the relevant status information. From this section you can define the columns displayed within the view. Adding preferred columns from the drop-down menu provided or deleting them using the **Delete** button allows us to modify which view columns are displayed. The columns available include:

- Status
- Weather
- Name
- Last success
- Last failure
- Last duration
- Last stable
- Build button

Advanced customization of a "Views" content

The Jenkins platform provides a lesser known but very powerful solution to modify the content of a view via the view's description text box. The description text box originally was designed to display a simple text description on the header of a job or view. By adjusting the Jenkins global security settings, we can configure Jenkins to support and serve rich HTML content directly in the header. This provides us with an incredible amount of control over a view's content. While this feature allows for a number of unique customizations, it is important to note that it may also create some inherent security vulnerabilities. Therefore we discourage anyone from using this solution on a public or Internet accessible Jenkins instance.

To get started, we will need to alter the security settings in Jenkins. The first step in enabling HTML content in the Jenkins description text box is to configure Jenkins to not escape raw HTML tags. To implement HTML support in descriptions, navigate as the Jenkins administrator from the main Jenkins dashboard over to the configure security area located in the Jenkins administration area. You can navigate to:

Jenkins | Manage Jenkins | Configure Global Security

Once the global security settings page has loaded, locate the **Markup Formatter** drop-down menu and select **Raw HTML** from the available options, as illustrated in *Figure 4-5*.

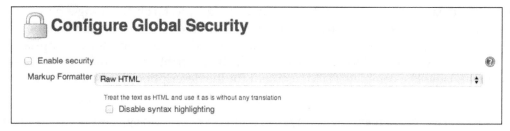

Figure 4-5: The Raw HTML option

Once the modification to the **Markup Formatter** setting has been made, click **Save** to confirm the alterations to the security configurations. At this point we should be able to add raw HTML elements to Jenkins description boxes.

Alternative: Jenkins Anything Goes plugin

If the preceding solution does not work on your specific Jenkins instance, you can consider using the *Anything Goes* plugin to accomplish the same task.

Now that the proper security settings are in place, we should be prepared to add custom HTML content in our Jenkins description boxes.

Let's begin by learning how to add a simple CPU load graph, which displays the load statistics for the Jenkins master at the top of the view. The following screenshot illustrates a set of **Load Statistics**, which will display on the main Jenkins dashboard after we have completed the proceeding tutorial:

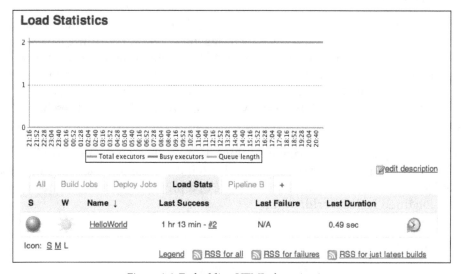

Figure 4-6: Embedding HTML charts in views

To begin the implementation of the load statistics graph start by creating a new view titled Load Stats and configure it to display all **Enabled** jobs via the **Job Filters** configuration section. Once the view has been created and displays the appropriate jobs, we will want to edit the view and modify the description to contain a simple set of HTML tags. The complete HTML content for the description is provided below.

```
<h2>Load Statistics</h2>
<img src="/computer/(master)/loadStatistics/graph?type=min&width=500&h
eight=200" type="image/svg+xml" />
```

Once the content of the description box has been set, click **Save** to complete the implementation. Once the configuration has been saved we should see a nice diagram detailing the master instance's **Load Statistics** on the **Load Stats** view.

This lesser known feature provides us with a significant amount of flexibility. It allows us to implement dramatic view customizations and can radically alter the content of the views on the Jenkins dashboard. This section only highlighted one potential customization. However, there are hundreds more possible. With embeddable HTML, the sky is the limit.

Navigating a job's project page

Now that we have a solid grasp of managing views in Jenkins, let's turn our focus over to **Jobs**. In this section, we will learn to navigate the job overview page. There are a lot of options and indicators available, and it is important to understand each of these as they can assist us in tracing issues, debugging build failures, and identifying relevant information quickly.

The job overview page contains configuration options and job execution details for the specified Jenkins job. The interface includes information regarding execution status, build history, last execution times, and SCM polling data. The optional configurations available on the left hand panel include the ability to edit jobs definitions, a button to delete the job from the Jenkins system, a recent changes link, and more. Let's look into the job overview page in greater depth and see how it works.

To navigate to a job overview page in Jenkins, simply click on the preferred job from the main Jenkins dashboard, and Jenkins will load the overview page for the specified job. *Figure 4-7* illustrates an example of a project overview interface for a freestyle job titled **HelloWorld**:

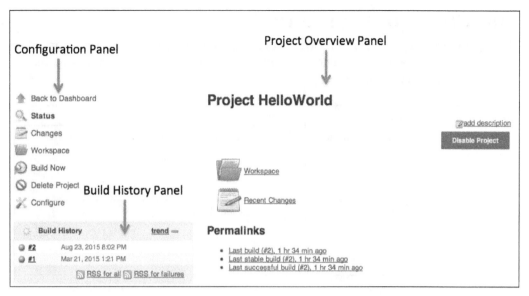

Figure 4-7: The HelloWorld project overview page

As we can see from the preceding screenshot, the job overview page contains three unique display panels. Each panel contains relevant project information related to the selected job's configuration and status.

These panels can be described as follows:

- The configuration panel (upper-left)
- The build history panel (lower-left)
- Project overview (central)

In our **HelloWorld** project, there are a number of features that allow us to trace the history and configuration details of the job. Let's take a few minutes to walk through each of the options available on this page and see what role each plays in our Jenkins ecosystem.

The Configuration panel

The Configuration panel contains job-level features that are useful for managing the configuration of a Jenkins job. The following table illustrates the options available with their respective icons and descriptions:

Icon	Title	Description
	Back to dashboard	Navigates back to the main Jenkins dashboard
	Status	Refreshes the job status page
	Changes	Navigates to the recent SCM changes page
	Workspace	Navigates to the workspace interactive browser
	Build now	Schedules a build
	Build with parameters	Schedules a build with specified parameters
	Delete project	Deletes the current project from the Jenkins system
	GitHub polling log *if SCM polling enabled	Navigates to the GitHub polling history page (this option will only be available if the GitHub plugin in Jenkins is installed and SCM polling is enabled)

	Subversion polling log *if SCM polling enabled	Navigates to the subversion polling history page. (this option will only be available if SCM polling is enabled *and* Subversion is specified as the SCM module the job will use)
	*Maven projects only — provides a list of modules	This option provides a list of modules defined in a Maven POM (Maven projects only)
	Configure	Allows the Jenkins user with the appropriate permissions to configure the job and edit the detailed job configuration information

The Build History panel

The **Build History** panel represents a visual history of builds that have taken place during the course of a job's lifetime in Jenkins. For matrix job types, this option presents a drill-down-style navigation system to navigate into the matrix axis below. Regardless of the job type, the build history can be granularly managed by a retention system that can be implemented through the log rotation configuration option, which is located in the job's detailed configuration area. This feature allows us to configure a retention policy for the job's build history by altering the log rotation option. This will tell Jenkins to automatically remove outdated or stale executions from the build history panel based on the configuration specified. (for example, 10 days or the last 30 builds).

The numerical list in the build history panel displays the most recent build executions and their associated status information (Failed/Success). The **Build History** panel serves as a primary indicator for historical status, build execution time, current execution status, and more. Let's dive deeper into the build history panel and see how it can enrich our Jenkins experience. *Figure 4-8* provided below illustrates the current **Build History** panel connected to a project defined in Jenkins:

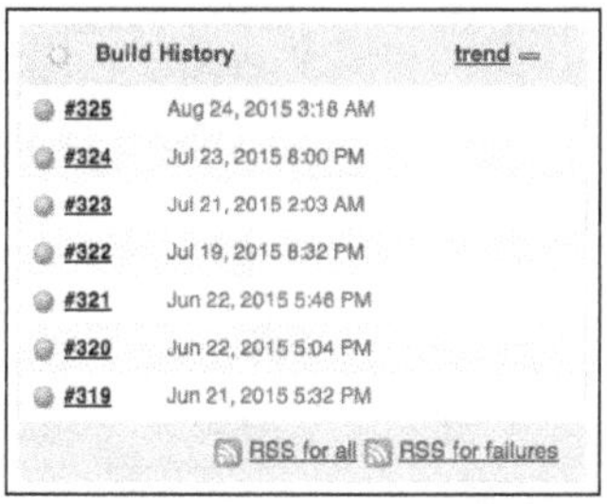

Figure 4-8: The Build History panel

The header of the **Build History** panel (illustrated in *Figure 4-9*) prominently features an icon indicator, which relays the historically calculated health of the Jenkins job as well as a trend link, which provides **trend** details related to the job.

Figure 4-9: The Build History header

The health of a Jenkins job in the build history panel is converted to a weather icon, with possible statuses, including sunny, cloudy, rainy, or stormy. This health metric is determined based on past successes and failures, which are translated into trends. For a detailed history of the job, we can click on the **trend** link on the header to navigate to a detailed timeline page which provides complete historical data related to the job. The stability of the job (in percentage form) is the metric that is leveraged to determine the health weather icon on the **Build History** panel.

Customizing each build's line entry in the history

Each execution of a job will result in an additional line being added to the build history panel. By altering a given build's description, we can embed custom data into this column. It may be wise to include useful information, such as version information, to make this panel easier to read.

Jenkins features an interactive user interface to display in real time any currently running executions of a job. An example of this is illustrated in the following screenshot:

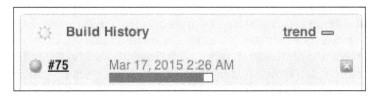

Figure 4-10: The currently running job indicator

As we can see from the preceding screenshot, the job status indicator displays a progress bar when the current job is running. The progress bar displayed estimates the job's completion time based on a calculated average of previous executions. If a job execution is in progress and another execution is scheduled, the **Build History** panel will display the queued item, as illustrated in *Figure 4-11*:

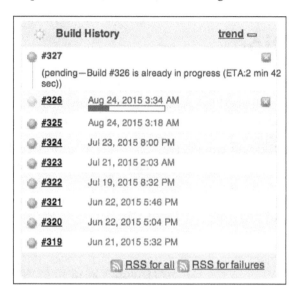

Figure 4-11: Pending job execution

We can also see from the preceding screenshot that, if the current job has an execution in progress, the **Build History** panel provides an easy way to terminate the current execution (marked by a red X). The panel also offers and efficient way to navigate directly to the console output of the presently running execution (by clicking on the status bar) where we can see the live console output contents for the running job.

The project overview – central panel

The project overview panel provides basic details about the job and its most recent executions, including:

- A link to the workspace browser (depends on the current security settings)
- A link to the SCM change log of the project
- An option to set the description
- A button to disable the project from future execution

- A few useful RSS feed links to stream pertinent data about the job
- Test automation trend graphs (if you have that configured)

This section is fairly simple in nature, but it will grow to become more and more important as we dive into individual job executions in the next section.

Job execution

When a job execution fails, the Jenkins system provides a set of comprehensive tools that can help us investigate the details of the failure. To get the most out of the Jenkins system, users will need to become familiar with the basic operations of the project status page and learn how to investigate build information efficiently.

The first step in investigating any job run failures is to understand the contents of the **Build History** panel and locate the build that requires further investigation. Failed builds are noted with a red sphere next to the associated execution, and successful executions are noted with a blue sphere (unless you are using the *greenballs* plugin). You can click on executions from the **Build History** panel to navigate to the detailed execution status page for the specified run, as shown in *Figure 4-12*:

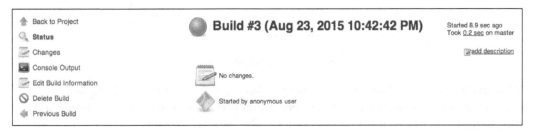

Figure 4-12: The detailed execution status page

Upon navigating to the detailed status page, there are a few panels and options that will immediately become helpful and allow us to manage and investigate the job. Specifically, these areas include:

- The job execution configuration panel (left panel)
- Status panel (center panel)
- The console output (icon and link)
- The SCM changes (icon and link)

Let's take a few minutes to learn the ins and outs of the available options on the job execution status page.

The Job Execution Configuration panel

The job execution configuration panel provides options to investigate and manage individual job runs. It contains links to see any SCM changes that went into a job run, view the console output of the job run, edit a description note pertaining to a job run, or delete the run entirely from the system. Let's take a minute to look at the individual options available in the job execution configuration panel:

Icon	Title	Description
	Back to project	Navigates back to the project status page
	Status	Refreshes the job run status page
	Changes	Navigates to the recent SCM changes page
	Console output	Navigates to the console output of the job
	Edit build information	Allows us to specify a small note about the run of the job
	Delete build	Deletes the build from the job history

The Status panel

The status panel for a given build number provides a brief overview of a job's execution. The information provided on the status panel is intended to act as a cursory overview page. It includes details surrounding the execution time of the job, details related to SCM changes (latest only), execution timings, and any descriptions provided after the build completed. The following screenshot illustrates an example of the status panel for **Build #4**:

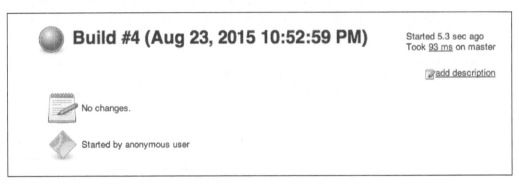

Figure 4-13: A status panel example

The Console Output

The **Console Output** will contain the complete text log of output from the execution, including any clues surrounding failure status. The following screenshot illustrates a simple example of the console output log:

Figure 4-14: Example console log output

In addition to the graphical **Console Output** log illustrated earlier, Jenkins features a plain text option, which can be useful when the console log contains special characters or has grown to larger sizes. To navigate to the plain text console output, click on the **View as plain text** link, as shown in *Figure 4-15*:

Figure 4-15: View as plain text link

Jenkins features a comprehensive SCM change log to assist us in locating any specific SCM changes applicable to a given build. To view the changes that have recently been integrated, we can utilize the **Changes** link, which is also located on the left-hand configuration panel.

Disabling failed jobs

It is usually a good idea to disable a Jenkins job once a failure has been identified. This will give you time to investigate and fix the issue (or find the person who can) without Jenkins automatically triggering additional builds while the job remains in a failed state.

Summary

In this chapter, we discovered how to manage jobs and views in Jenkins. We learned some tips and tricks to customize views and descriptive headers, and we discussed how to best investigate failed builds.

In the next chapter, we will discover advanced automated testing techniques. We will begin to learn how to integrate industry-proven testing infrastructures into our Jenkins platform.

5

Advanced Automated Testing

Advancements in information technology, and telecommunications have fueled Internet businesses worldwide. These advancements have catalyzed one of the most complex, and competitive economies in modern history. It is through this competitive marketplace that cloud computing, and **Software as a Service (SaaS)**, were born. These business ventures have vaulted from once risky endeavors into industry-proven vertical markets, with the potential for high yield returns. What's interesting about these particular vertical markets is that they are only feasible if an organization can come up with an innovative idea, and manage the costs associated with software engineering, quality assurance, delivery, and operations. In an effort to mitigate the costs involved, these business ventures typically employ strict standards, cutting-edge automation, and stringent quality control practices.

In the ongoing effort to drive efficiency, businesses are beginning to leverage adaptations of Six Sigma, Continuous Improvement, Agile, A/B Testing, and other innovative engineering process paradigms in an effort to identify value added features, increase efficiency, control research and development expenditures, improve production process, and meet customer demands effectively. While the aforementioned practices are innovative and cutting-edge, legacy software solutions can still make use of them. That being said, the implementation of innovative automated testing strategies for legacy projects is not going to happen overnight.

> *"Be not afraid of growing slowly, but instead be afraid of standing still"* – Chinese proverb

To bridge the gap between immature quality assurance initiatives and highly efficient automated solutions that provide tangible business value we will need a roadmap. Our strategic roadmap will need to combine people, process, and product with automation to provide business value, and alleviate bottlenecks.

In this chapter of *Mastering Jenkins* we will focus on automated quality assurance. We will learn how to implement automated quality initiatives via Jenkins, and discover some of the fundamental practices involved in creating scalable quality assurance solutions. More specifically the topics we will cover in this chapter will include the following:

- Quality assurance initiatives and test automation terminology
- The software development lifecycle
- Connecting product code to tests
- Baking quality into the product code
- Automated testing in Jenkins
- Unit tests in Jenkins through MSTest
- Organizing test jobs
- Distributed testing solutions

Quality assurance initiatives and test automation terminology

Quality assurance can often seem like a mystical religion that engineering pays lip service to, in an effort to appease the business and add a quality approved seal to a product. Traditional implementations of manual quality assurance initiatives often feel very abstract and repetitive. Quality assurance is simply the practice of verifying functional requirements, and identifying defects, in an effort to create and preserve market credibility. In the end poorly created software products have no credibility, and zero hopes of competing against similar products that are functional. Adopting, and implementing innovative automated quality assurance solutions, and coupling those with automated testing apparatuses, can provide significant business value. These solutions increase businesses credibility, and promote customer reliance on the software products delivered.

Automated testing further assists the business by removing the human equation from manual error-prone testing practices, reduces the man hour cost of executing test plans, and provides a living audit of the code base. When automated test systems are architected properly they have the potential to identify defects, prevent regressions, and catch performance failures prior to delivery to the end customer.

Let's consider some key questions that may come up when implementing a quality assurance initiative based on automation.

- Where will the automated tests run? What will they run against?

- Will any group of automated tests potentially clog the development or delivery pipelines or decrease efficiency? How will we address this?

- When are the automated tests going to run? As part of the build (Unit Tests)? Against the UI (Functional/Acceptance/Regression)? Are they simply basic sanity tests (Smoke)? Do the tests validate application performance (Stress)?

- Are the tests white box or black box? Do we want black box tests to run on the deployment environment? Or from another location?

- Will there be a data impact as a result of the test execution? How will the system reset?

- How long is a reasonable time for the tests to run, and still provide value? When should a test be removed from the pool?

By asking these questions we can begin to narrow down an automated quality assurance initiative into ideas and concepts, and start to think about conventions. By performing a little bit of upfront work in defining the test cases, scenarios, suites, and automated testing roles we can help ensure the future scalability of the delivered assets, and provide a comprehensive testing solution that creates business value. Now that we have a basic idea of some high-level QA considerations, let's take a minute to define some quality assurance, and automated testing terminology:

- **Unit tests**: Unit tests can be described as tests that run directly on the build machine during the build process and are designed to validate the I/O of classes, methods, objects, and functions. Properly constructed unit tests serve as a direct audit of the code base. They can assist development in identifying deprecated code segments, faulty classes and methods, and unstable software bits. The best-practice adherence to unit testing is to ensure that, if any unit tests fail to execute, the build should fail as a result. When a unit test does fail it should become an urgent task to address the failure. Constructing a unit test solution does not need to be complex. A simple setup and teardown apparatus can get us 90% of the way there. To better illustrate this, *Figure 5-1* describes a simple example of a unit test suite.

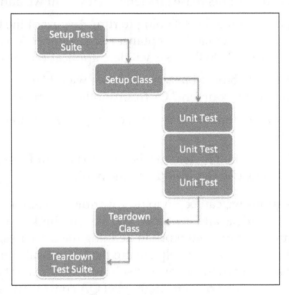

Figure 5-1: A unit test structure

- **Smoke / BVT (Build Verification tests)**: Smoke tests (more commonly known as build verification tests) validate basic operational functionality of a software project. Generally these tests attempt to identify simplistic operational failures that are catastrophic, and prevent the software from being considered viable for further testing. These sanity tests will typically execute immediately after a deployment or installation of a software project onto a centralized environment and verify that the software meets the most minimal functionality requirements. These tests are intended to be fast running, few in number, and should not be destructive to any data layers. If any of the smoke tests fail then immediate action should be taken to address the failures. *Figure 5-2* describes a very basic smoke test flow chart.

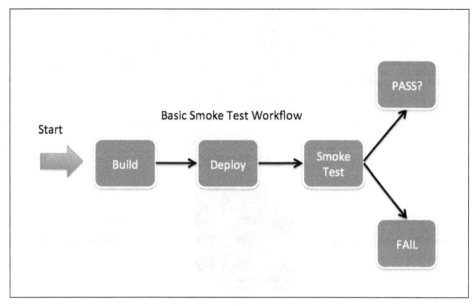

Figure 5-2: A basic smoke test workflow

- **Functional tests**: Functional (or acceptance) tests validate the operability of a software project, and ensure the implementation of the software project is in line with functional requirement specifications, and business initiatives. In a best-case scenario the same developers who write the application code will assist in writing the functional test suites. The reason developers should assist is to ensure a 1:1 match of code developed to tests created (similar in nature to test-driven development).

- **Regression tests**: Regression tests aim to reproduce defects identified by users in the field. The ultimate goal of a regression test is to automate the reproduction of a defect, and ensure that the defect does not re appear. Advanced regression testing solutions should aim to provide a system that can visually reproduce a defect for developers based on the entry of a bug tracking ticket identification number. In such a system a developer would simply enter the bug ID into the automated test case execution system, which would then illustrate the steps needed to reproduce a bug on a given environment.

- **Capacity tests**: Capacity tests are tests designed to simulate stress and load on an application suite. These tests help ensure that the software can withstand real-world use and abuse. Testing application load and stress capabilities can be accomplished via the implementation of valid use case scenarios, which are then replicated and distributed across multiple simulators.

- **Black Box tests**: Black Box tests execute from that same perspective as the end consumer of the software. They have no visibility into the internals of a software project or the system it runs on and can only see the software from the consumer's perspective. It is important to note that the consumer of a software project may be a human, a service, a process, or another automation source. *Figure 5-3* illustrates black box tests:

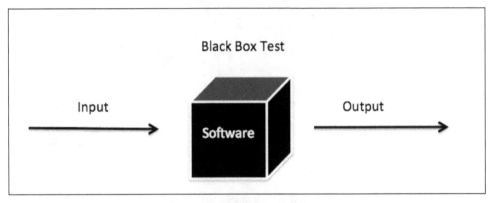

Figure 5-3: A simple black box test

- **White Box tests**: White box tests are tests that have the ability to see into the internals of a software application and can validate file structures, application process ID's, and other internally available information related to the software. White box tests may also have the ability to see into the system that the software is running on and can verify lower-level operational capabilities of the software itself. *Figure 5-4* provides a high-level overview diagram that describes white box testing:

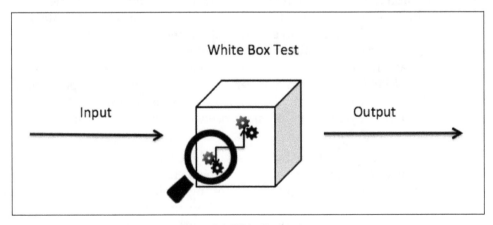

Figure 5-4: White Box testing

- **A/B testing**: Understanding customer usage and acceptance of new features within a software project has been a business hurdle for many years. A/B testing allows business interests to propose new features to end-users, collect usage data metrics through analytics, and provide feedback related to the adoption of a proposed feature. These experiment-driven testing solutions allow the business to decide through data metrics when a feature creates customer value, and when it does not, thus allowing the business to focus on features that drive revenue. More advanced implementations of A/B testing solutions allow the business to incrementally expose users to a feature hypothesis and collect real-time feedback on its adoption.

The Software Development Lifecycle

The **Software Development Lifecycle (SDLC)** can be described as the unique phases a software project journeys through from birth to release. A traditional SDLC includes planning, engineering, and test and release phases. These phases are designed to be circular in nature and future iterations of the project will inherently repeat the previously taken SDLC steps. *Figure 5-5* illustrates a traditional SDLC:

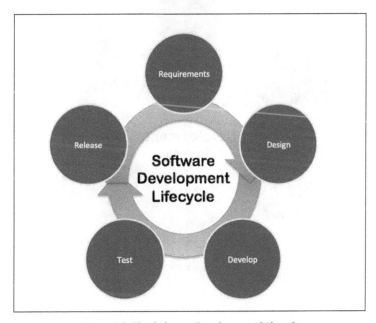

Figure 5-5: The Software Development Lifecycle

The model described earlier illustrates a traditional waterfall approach to software development. In a continuous delivery or continuous deployment model, the iterations are much smaller, and an automated pipeline will need to be carefully created to support the higher velocity of releases in conjunction with dynamic automated testing.

To support the above stated modern continuous practices the SDLC will need to be expanded to reflect the shift towards continuous integration, continuous delivery, and continuous deployment. The proposed alterations to the SDLC will aim to illustrate pre-production environments, delivery phases, and delineated test buckets. An adapted SDLC would need to appropriately reflect the process of executing an incrementally more aggressive set of test suites for each defined deployment phase in the delivery process. If all of these changes sound a bit confusing, don't worry; we are going to cover them step by step. *Figure 5-6* illustrates an example of an expanded SDLC, which can support short incremental continuous testing and deployment cycles:

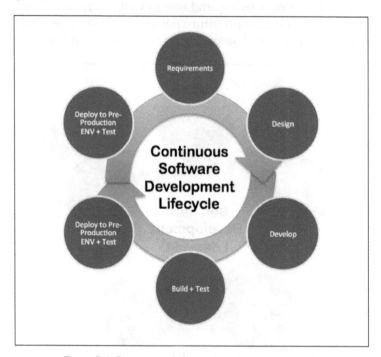

Figure 5-6: Continuous Software Development Lifecycle

The expanded SDLC illustrated earlier intends to better encapsulate a delivery pipeline. As such this enhanced SDLC model would be more viable for continuous delivery or continuous deployment and may not be suited to waterfall development. The diagram provided previously should also support an expanded or contracted SDLC (depending on organization size and maturity). The deployment and testing phases illustrated earlier can be inserted or removed as necessary to fit with an organizations logical business requirements and size.

When applying continuous integration or deployment, automated testing implementations should execute a different set of automated tests for each pre-production deployment. This is in an effort to progressively validate the quality of the software project during each subsequent phase of the SDLC. A list of progressive testing buckets is provided below.

- Unit tests
- Functional Tests
- Regression Tests
- Acceptance Tests
- Performance/Capacity Tests
- BVT/Smoke Tests (after every deployment)

Now that we have some of the basic concepts illustrated in our SDLC, and have learned how to expand it to fit with an evolving automated testing solution, let's define some best practices that can help us achieve the best results.

- When implementing automated testing solutions try to ensure that the number of technologies implemented is kept to a minimum.
- Define pre-production environments and their purpose. It is important to note that *production* doesn't have to be specific to web projects. It is simply a declaration of released status.
- Settle upon an automated deployment technology.
- Identify test buckets dedicated to each pre-production environment (functional, regression, capacity and so on).

- Create a repeatable engineering process with room for a backlog and strategy for crisis management.

- Automate everything—From build processes, to test execution, to test notification systems, deployments, and server provisioning.

- Don't allow emergencies to dictate process. Embrace failure as part of the process and create mechanisms to recover quickly.

In up coming sections we will outline some best practices around automated testing and development patterns in an effort to support continuous integration, continuous delivery, or continuous deployment. Jenkins provides great support for all of these practices and by implementing good architecture the sky is the limit.

Connecting product codes to tests

When in grade school we all learned the concepts surrounding the scientific method. It involved formulating a hypothesis, and validating our hypothesis by gathering supporting proof. As a software project matures, learning to apply the scientific method to automated testing will become increasingly important. The implementation of these principles is actually quite simple. The code change or feature represents the hypothesis and the validation of the hypothesis is the test(s) written, which prove it. In a standard **Test Driven Development** (TDD) model, tests are written prior to the code change. This is a very powerful model with very visible benefits. As powerful as TDD is it's import to mention that strict enforcement of writing tests prior to implementation can lead to arbitrary restrictions in prototyping, and may not work effectively in all cases. The important thing to adhere to is simply a consistent incremental approach to writing tests for each change committed.

Many organizations have migrated their development resources into hybrid cross-functional teams (DevOps, DevQualOps etc.) in an effort to facilitate the creation of software, encourage quality and validation, and help manage ongoing maintenance of a software solution. Test-driven development specifically purports to ensure there is functional validation of a given code hypothesis as part of the engineering process. *Figure 5-7* illustrates a basic approach to Test Driven Development with an added step of building and packaging the binary assets and tests together.

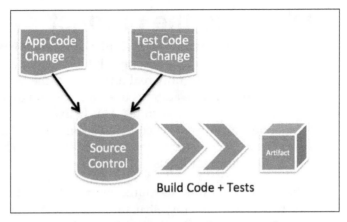

Figure 5-7: The Test Driven Development paradigm

Applying a form of Test Driven Development after implementing a clearly architected test execution system with rapid feedback loops can provide a solid foundation for a software project to grow upon. While it's no silver bullet it can help us to unify engineering, quality assurance, and operations personnel. Once adopted, the business can move to release strategically or at a preferred cadence instead of an arbitrary deadline created by engineering.

This alluring business and engineering paradigm indeed alters the day-to-day engineering culture and operating efficiency surrounding software development, test, and delivery. Each of these once segregated groups will inherently evolve and increasingly emphasize standardization and cross-discipline approaches to delivering software. As a result the organization will need to foster a collaborative approach to delivery. This means implementing standards and conventions. In turn they will be able to develop, and deliver high-quality solutions faster and outwit the competition.

The value that test-driven development provides an organization can be easily quantified. Developers will begin to think more like testers, and will aim to find new and creative ways to validate their code hypotheses. Testers will begin to think more like developers and will increasingly look for new and innovative automated approaches that can aid in their testing efforts. Initial implementations of TDD will by nature cause a short-term decrease in development cadence and feature velocity, but long term it will lead to fewer defects in the software project, and encourage a level of quality in the code created. This is often referred to as crafting code.

Baking quality into the product

Automated testing development is in many ways similar to product-based software development. The end goal of an automated testing solution is to validate the viability of another software project. The only real difference is the target audience of the solution created. Just as product code adheres to standards and quality rigor so should the respective test harnesses, and test suites. This helps ensure that test code is managed in much the same way as product code. This shift in mindset raises the software process and architectural considerations. Let's identify some best practices that should be adhered to for testing solutions.

- All test code should be committed to source control. It would be wise additionally to create a test directory structure along side the product being tested. This helps ensure that the test code is kept in lockstep version with the product code. Some software frameworks already support this convention directly. Some examples include Ruby on Rails, Java Maven, Play, and Ember.js.

- Test code may or may not be compiled: however, syntax errors should be checked during the build process and any errors should be considered valid reasons to fail the build.

- Test code should be versioned and managed in the same fashion as product code. This will help match the version of a software project to a version of the test automation. By implementing this type of solution, an organization can go back in time and see what the status of the tests were at the time of a previous release.

- Tests should be packaged alongside binary assets. When moving towards a DevOps culture the product packages typically flow from one environment to another. Adopting this process would allow the test suites to do the same.

Efficient automated test architecture

Creating automated tests can be a high value addition to any software project. When automated tests are architected carefully the automation can facilitate speedy QA cycles with minimal human intervention. When automated tests are not carefully architected they can be a huge choke point for software releases. If automated testing takes in excess of 72 hours to complete, the end results become ambiguous and the value of the automated testing solution is lost.

Organizing tests to provide business value without bottlenecking software delivery can be a balancing act. As a best practice we will want to keep in mind the cost associated with each test and understand any velocity implications to the release process. When architecting an automated test solution consider the following pyramid, which is designed to showcase a comparative proportion of tests.

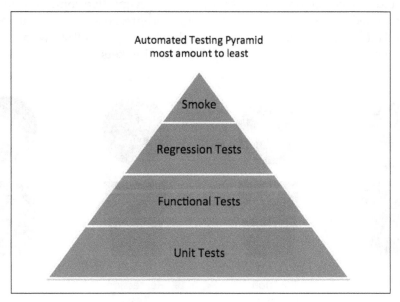

Figure 5-8: Test coverage pyramid

While the general value of automated testing is well observed throughout the software development community, the implementation details and reasoning are often conflicting. This has led to a disparate fragmentation on best practices and implementation guidelines. Regardless of the implementation specifics there are considerations to be made in relation to test decay, timely execution, and as a result a direct impact on scalability.

The best practice recommendation outlined in Continuous Delivery specifies that quality requirements should increase as the software project approaches release. The solution that best adheres to this is test buckets, which ensure that there is no duplicated execution of automated tests (except smoke). If the deployment or subsequent test execution takes too long to execute, the pipeline gets backed up and the rapid feedback loop looses its value. The preventative solution is to clearly define automated test buckets, and implement a progressive deployment and testing system. To better illustrate the concept of test buckets *Figure 5-9* shows a simple automated test pipeline with explicitly defined test buckets.

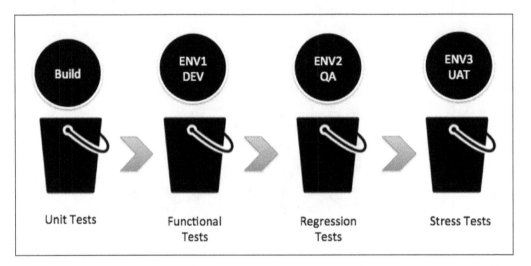

Figure 5-9: A sample test pipeline with buckets

From the above diagram we can see that the test suites are organized into test buckets, which are then executed after a software deployment to a pre-production environment. This helps prevent duplicate test runs and facilitates efficiency in executing automated tests.

 Smoke test tip

It is highly recommend that a simplistic smoke test suite be created and executed immediately after the deployment to an environment. The smoke tests will validate the viability of the environment and determine if it is worth testing further.

Now that we have a better understanding of the architecture we want to create let's dig in to some Jenkins specific implementation examples and see how we can apply our newly acquired knowledge.

Automated testing in Jenkins

The Jenkins community has developed numerous plugins that support a wide array of automated testing tools, patterns, and reporting solutions. The diverse nature of these plugins makes Jenkins an ideal automated testing tool. Each solution will have its own unique benefits and drawbacks. These should be carefully considered prior to implementing any automated solutions in Jenkins. Basic automated test reporting is a straightforward process, which Jenkins can assist us with by collating automated test reports, graphing successes and failures, and determining regressions. All of these help provide insight on the underlying quality of a software project.

One of the more common implementations surrounding automated testing is to utilize a testing technology that employs JUnit or xUnit reporting. These formats are built into Jenkins directly. Jenkins is however not limited to these report formats. Many other formats and testing solutions are available via the plugin ecosystem. To begin with, let's take a minute to look at some of the more popular solutions Jenkins supports.

- WATIR (JUnit)
- WATIN (NUnit)
- Node.JS + Grunt (xUnit)
- Ember Test (embtest xUnit)
- CPPUTest (xUnit)
- Ruby Unit Tests (CI Report gem)
- RSpec (**Behavior Driven Development (BDD)** testing framework)
- Jasmine (BDD Testing framework)
- TestNG
- QUnit

As we can see there are numerous test frameworks that provide direct support for executing automated tests and reporting the results. For a more comprehensive list please utilize the Jenkins plugin documentation located at the following URL:

```
https://wiki.jenkins-ci.org/display/JENKINS/Plugins
```

Let's dive in and learn a bit about the JUnit and xUnit formatting, which is the most popularly leveraged Jenkins reporting solution. In the next section we will learn how to execute tests and publish test reports in the JUnit and xUnit formats.

JUnit and xUnit test results are based on an XML DOM structure, which illustrates the following information in a nested XML tree format:

- Test suite(s) and respective name
- Number of tests in the suite(s)
- Number of test cases executed
- Number of test cases skipped
- Number of test cases failed
- Test execution time
- Error and exception data

The basic XML structures for these results are strikingly similar in nature and data content. Below are examples of xUnit report formats, and JUnit report formats respectively.

- xUnit:

```xml
<?xml version="1.0" encoding="UTF-8"?>
<testsuite name="myXUnitTests" tests="1" errors="1" failures="0"
skip="0">
    <testcase classname="test_suite.TestA"
            name="test_A" time="0">
        <error type="exceptions.TypeError"
message="SomeException">
        Traceback (most recent call last):
        ...
        TypeError: SomeException message
        </error>
    </testcase>
</testsuite>
```

- JUnit:

```xml
<?xml version="1.0" encoding="UTF-8"?>
<testsuites>
    <testsuite name="JUnitExampleReport" errors="0" tests="0"
failures="0" time="0" timestamp="2015-05-24 10:23:58" />
    <testsuite name=" JUnitExampleReport.constructor" errors="0"
skipped="1" tests="3" failures="1" time="0.006" timestamp="2013-
05-24T10:23:58">
        <properties>
            <property name="project.jdk.classpath" value="jdk.
classpath.1.8" />
```

```
        </properties>
        <testcase classname="JUnitExampleReport.constructor"
name="should default value to an empty string" time="0.006">
            <failure message="test failure">Assertion failed</
failure>
        </testcase>
        <testcase classname="JUnitExampleReport.constructor"
name="should default consolidate to true" time="0">
            <skipped />
        </testcase>
        <testcase classname="JUnitXmlReporter.constructor"
name="should default useDotNotation to true" time="0" />
    </testsuite>
</testsuites>
```

To facilitate data parsing and rendering of test results; Jenkins offers plugins for both xUnit and JUnit report parsing. These plugins are respectively titled:

- JUnit Plugin (comes with the Jenkins default install)
- xUnit Plugin

The JUnit Plugin comes pre-installed with the stock Jenkins setup and therefore does not need to be explicitly installed. Conversely the xUnit plugin will need to be explicitly installed prior to use (**Jenkins Administration -> Plugins**).

Once the proper plugins have been installed we will need to configure our build job to properly identify, and consume any test reports created during the execution of the tests. To do this we will need to navigate in the Jenkins UI to the preferred job and click the **Configure** link to load the detailed configuration page for the job. This screen is illustrated in *Figure 5-10*.

Figure 5-10: The Jenkins Job configuration page

The xUnit plugin provides the option to parse test report files either in the build phase OR as a post build action. This allows a bit of extra flexibility surrounding actions that may occur prior to or after the processing of the results (hint: sending email test reports to developers, or ensuring failed tests don't fail the build). To configure Jenkins to parse xUnit results during the main build process, simply add the **Process xUnit test result report** build step to the main Jenkins job configuration.

To configure Jenkins to parse either JUnit or xUnit results as a post build action, simply add a post build action step by clicking on the **Add post build Action** button at the bottom of the configuration page, as illustrated in *Figure 5-11*.

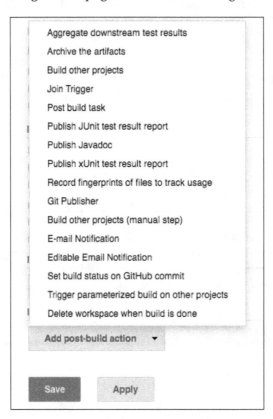

Figure 5-11: Add post-build action to publish a test report

Once the proper build or post build steps have been added we will be given the opportunity to configure various options regarding where and how Jenkins will process the results.

Figures 5-12 and *Figure 5-13* illustrate examples of the configuration panels presented to us after adding a xUnit or JUnit post build step.

Figure 5-12: Configuration options for xUnit Test report

As we can see from the above xUnit configuration screen we can configure PASS/FAIL thresholds, skipped test thresholds, and timing margins for the parsed xUnit results.

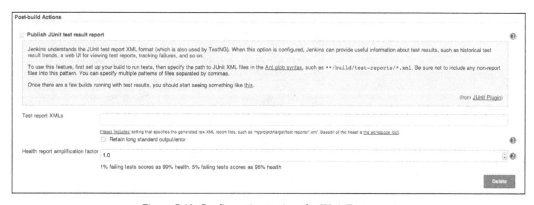

Figure 5-13: Configuration options for JUnit Test report

As we can see from the above JUnit Report parsing options, the plugin provides us with the ability to specify file search locations for our test results, and health report amplification factors. Amplification factors allow us to specify a percentage of failed tests, which we can use to gauge the health of the software project and ensure failing tests have the appropriate impact on the jobs PASS/FAIL status.

After implementing the configuration settings to implement either xUnit or JUnit parsing we will want to execute the job and verify that Jenkins is properly publishing the automated test results. After the job has been executed successfully we should see a new **Test Results** link presented to us in the middle of our Jenkins project overview page as shown in *Figure 5-14*.

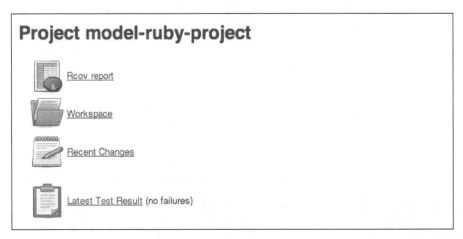

Figure 5-14: Latest Test Result overview

By clicking on the **Latest Test Result** link Jenkins will navigate us to a drilled down report of our latest test execution as shown in *Figure 5-15*:

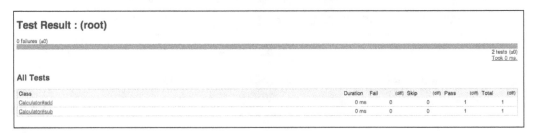

Figure 5-15: Sample test drill down

As Jenkins collates trends surrounding additional test executions it will begin to graph the results directly on the project page. This graphing widget is a hugely valuable feature. The graphs that Jenkins provides deliver a glance overview of trends related to test execution. These graphs even feature the ability to drill into the quality metrics and isolate regressions, new failures, and more. *Figure 5-16* shows an example of a test automation graph feature in Jenkins, which is green and red due to the *greenballs* plugin.

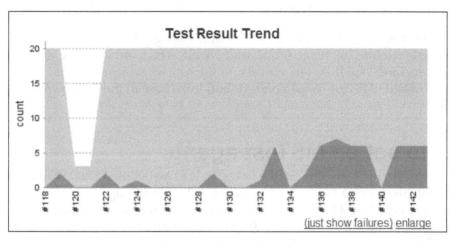

Figure 5-16: Test Result trend

Now that we have a handle on capturing automated test results and graphing the information in Jenkins using xUnit and JUnit let's spend some time discussing the finer points of MSTest and Unit tests. This will be highly valuable for Microsoft Windows and .NET users.

Unit tests in Jenkins through MSTest

As we mentioned earlier, unit testing provides developers with a formalized way to write code documentation, and encourages better coding practices. Unit testing is simply breaking down the functionality of a program into unit-testable behaviors, which can be repeatedly executed to verify the behavior of the code in response to standards, boundaries, and data inputs.

TDD, Test Driven Development or TFD, Test First Development, as we mentioned earlier, is a development technique where developers repeat a process of three activities, which are tightly interwoven.

- **Testing**: Creating automated tests
- **Coding**: Writing minimal code to just pass those tests
- **Design**: Refactoring code to improve internal implementation without changing the external contract

At the time of writing, there are numerous Unit testing frameworks available. The most notable are MSTest, JUnit, CUnit, and NUnit, which are available for .NET, JAVA, Linux, and Windows respectively. In the next section we will take a look at how to execute MSTest-based unit tests and learn how to publish the results in Jenkins.

How to set up MSTest agents

To integrate Jenkins with MSTest, the first step is to install the Visual Studio Test Agents onto the Jenkins build server, or slave. When installing test agents, it is important to note that it has to the same version of Visual Studio used on the developer workstations. To proceed, download and install the agents using any of the following links:

- Agents for Microsoft Visual Studio 2013: `http://www.microsoft.com/en-gb/download/details.aspx?id=40750`
- Agents for Microsoft Visual Studio 2015: `https://www.microsoft.com/en-us/download/details.aspx?id=48152`

Once installed `MSTest.exe` will be located in the following location on the build server:

```
C:\Program Files (x86)\Microsoft Visual Studio 12.0\Common7\IDE\MSTest.exe
```

Once installed it can be used to run tests from the command line. In the next section we will discover the basic parameters and command line entries needed to accomplish this.

Running automated tests via MSTest

The MSTest.exe program has several options available that we can use to customize the behavior of our test run. (To see a complete options/summary type MSTest /h or /?).

To run MSTest.exe, we need to specify either a test metadata file or a test container, using either the /testmetadata option or the /testcontainer option, respectively.

- The /testmetadata:[file name] option can be used only once per command, and indicates one test metadata file.

- The /testcontainer:[file name] option can be used multiple times per command, and indicates multiple test containers. It needs to include the path to the folder in which the metadata file or test container resides.

- The /category:[test category filter] option allows us to select tests that reside categories to run.

- The /resultsfile:[file name] option allows us save the test run results a specified result file.

Additionally we will need to specify on the command line the binary files that contain the tests that we want to run. Using default value (***test*.dll) we can tell the build agent to search recursively for any .DLL files that match our glob pattern of *test*.dll housed in the binaries subdirectory of the build agent's working directory. To better clarify the execution of this let's look at an example.

A example MSTest execution

The following is an example MSTest execution:

```
C:\>cd C:\Program Files (x86)\Microsoft Visual Studio 12.0\Common7\IDE

C:\Program Files (x86)\Microsoft Visual Studio 12.0\Common7\IDE>MSTest.
exe /testcontainer:"C:\Program Files (x86)\Jenkins\jobs\Build.
ExampleProj\workspace\source\ExampleProj \bin\Release\ExampleProj.Tests.
dll" /resultsfile:"C:\Program Files (x86)\Jenkins\jobs\Build.ExampleProj\
workspace\source\Build\Tests.Results.trx"
```

Running MSTests and reporting the results in Jenkins

The purpose of integrating unit tests into Jenkins is that it gives immediate feedback on the operability of the code created, provides an audit of the code base, and helps to flag potential issues and defects as early in the development cycle as possible.

The test projects defined in the Visual Studio .SLN file will compile every time the Visual studio solution is built. This means that any unit test compilation failures will also fail the build. Once the test DLLs have been built we will want to execute those in Jenkins. This will allow us to track the PASS/FAIL trends, and begin to capture code coverage metrics. In order to run the unit tests we can implement them via the following steps in Jenkins.

1. Writing an MSbuild script to execute MSTest.exe with parameters and automatically locate the pre-built test dlls:

```xml
<?xml version="1.0" encoding="utf-8"?>
<Project DefaultTargets="ExecuteMSTest" xmlns="http://schemas.
microsoft.com/developer/msbuild/2003">

    <PropertyGroup>
        <MsTestExePath>C:\Program Files (x86)\Microsoft Visual
Studio 10.0\Common7\IDE\mstest.exe</MsTestExePath>
        <MsTestResultPath>$(WORKSPACE)\MyResults.trx</
MsTestResultPath>
        <Configuration>Release</Configuration>
    </PropertyGroup>

    <Target Name="ExecuteMSTest">

        <ItemGroup>
            <MSTestAssemblies Include="$(WORKSPACE)\**\
bin\$(Configuration)\*.Test.dll"/>
        </ItemGroup>
```

```
        <PropertyGroup>
            <MsTestCommand>"$(MsTestExePath)" @
(MSTestAssemblies->'/testcontainer:"%(FullPath)"', ' ') /
resultsfile:"TestResults\Results.trx""</MsTestCommand>
        </PropertyGroup>

        <Exec Command="$(MsTestCommand)" ContinueOnError="true" />

    </Target>

</Project>
```

2. Using **Execute Windows batch command** in the Jenkins job configuration as a post-build action:

Figure 5-17: Execute Windows batch command window

Update the `batch` command to contain the below example:

```
"C:\Program Files (x86)\Microsoft Visual Studio 12.0\Common7\
IDE>MSTest.exe" /testcontainer:"C:\Program Files (x86)\Jenkins\
jobs\Build.ExampleProj\workspace\source\ExampleProj \bin\Release\
ExampleProj.Tests.dll" /resultsfile:"C:\Program Files (x86)\
Jenkins\jobs\Build.ExampleProj\workspace\Tests.Results.trx"
```

In the above example the command will execute MSTest test cases that reside inside the `ExampleProj.Tests.dll` test binary, and automatically save the test results into the Jenkins workspace.

Publishing test results in Jenkins

To integrate the MSTest results into Jenkins, we can use the MSTest plugin to map the MSTest format results to a format that Jenkins natively understands (Junit XML results). The plugin is available from the **Manage Plugins** screen (**Jenkins**, **Manage Jenkins**, **Manage Plugins**, click the **Available** tab).

After the plugin installs successfully, there is a new entry in the **Post-build Actions** section of the job configuration. Select **Publish MSTest test result report** in the **Post-build Actions** and enter the path `**/*.trx` we used above for the results output location as shown in the following figure:

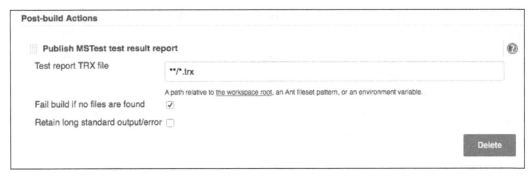

Figure 5-18: Publish MSTest test result report in Post-build Actions

When the Jenkins build job runs again, a new **Test Results** area will be displayed on the run summary screen that indicates we don't have any failing tests. Clicking the **Test Result** link for more details will navigate us to a page, that will show the test results parsed from the results file. This will include information on all of the running tests and their execution times. In addition to the test information, there will also be a new menu item on the left side named **History** for the build. Clicking on this will show historical information on the test runs, including a graph of the execution times and test counts.

Organizing test jobs

As our test implementations in Jenkins mature, we will want to ensure that the system remains organized. This will help keep things easy to navigate, and manageable for novice users. One easy way to help assist in keeping the system maintainable is to implement a naming convention for automated test jobs.

An example of how to do this is illustrated below:

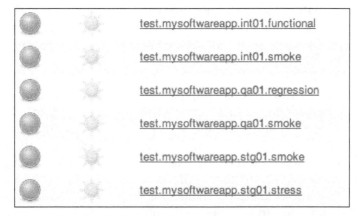

Figure 5-19: Test job naming convention based on pipeline

Upon implementing a naming convention, we can leverage views and regular expressions to display those jobs in a unified manner and enforce our naming convention. The filtering of test jobs can be configured through views and regular expressions. While keeping the naming conventions enforced will provide a level of scalability" there are always additional measures that can be taken.

Another approach is to leverage the *Categorized View* plugin, which allows us to nest jobs together and provides an easy way to group similar jobs. For more information on the Categorized View plugin please visit the following URL:

```
https://wiki.jenkins-ci.org/display/JENKINS/Categorized+Jobs+View
```

These are just some of the possible implementations that can help enable a scalable approach to software testing and delivery by using naming conventions. It is important for you to select an approach that works best for your organization.

Distributed testing solutions

Implementing simple stand-alone test jobs in Jenkins is easy; however it's not very scalable. For tests that are long-running or require a significant amount of computing resources we will want to implement a more scalable automated testing solution. Fortunately there are a several ways to accomplish this. In this section of *Mastering Jenkins* we will learn some tricks we can employ to assist us when the need arises to scale our automated testing solutions.

The Selenium Grid

One potential automated testing solution that can effectively scale and parallelize automated tests is a Selenium grid (Web Driver). The Selenium grid was conceptualized via Dan Fabulich, and Nelson Sproul (with help from Pat Lightbody) in 2005. It wasn't until 2008 however that the Selenium grid as we know it came into fruition. It was further enhanced into the Selenium WebDriver, which is the popular implementation used today. Used by popular companies such as eBay, Google, Merck, Yahoo and others, this solution can potentially handle hundreds of thousands of test executions by distributing the testing suites across a grid of connected machines. Generally Selenium is designed to provide automated testing for web applications; however it has been adapted to facilitate automated testing solutions for mobile and embedded products as well. To implement this type of solution we will need to spin up a Selenium grid. Detailed instructions on how to create and configure a Selenium grid can be found at the link below (and are provided in detail in *Chapter 9, Integrating Jenkins with Other Technologies*):

Once a grid has been set up and is operational, there are a number of ways to trigger the execution of automated tests. Some prefer to simply check out the tests from source control, while others prefer utilizing a packing method. The more scientific method is to package the automated tests along with the build output and store them in an artifact repository. By creating some automation, which packages both the compiled code and the tests, we maintain the historical testability of the packages created and released. This provides a simple way to see how the test automation functioned at the time the build was created. Additionally it allows us to go back in time and validate the build output without searching through source control or hunting down deprecated dependencies. While this is not the only solution, it is definitely one worth considering.

To execute the tests contained in a package or source control, simply create automation to fetch the package (or tests) onto the grid hub, and call the test harness. To make the solution even more scalable, we can attach the grid hub as a slave node to our Jenkins master and capture the test result output via normal methods such as Surefire reports, TestNG reports and so on. This solution is by far the most scalable. Grid nodes can be enabled on just about any machine or device with a web interface. When implementing a Selenium testing solution remember that, the more machines that are attached to the grid, the more scalable the solution.

To facilitate high availability of a Selenium grid solution there are some interesting tactics that can be proposed. One interesting proposition is to encourage personnel to attach their work machines to the Selenium grid when they are not online or in the office. This will allow a Selenium grid to expand by an order of magnitude and enable parallel test execution across the machines connected to the grid.

Parallel down-stream jobs

If a Selenium grid is not something that suits you, all is not lost. Jenkins can be configured to provide a quasi grid of its own. By coupling the Jenkins master/slave architecture with some downstream job magic we can implement a distributed testing harness.

To get started we will need the following ingredients:

- A Jenkins master instance
- At least 2 slave nodes connected to the master with the capability to execute the automated tests (Cucumber, JUnit, xUnit, CPPUnit and so on.)
- A set of automated tests with a command line option to specify a specific test suite(s) to execute
- The Jenkins *Join* plugin installed

The basic architecture we will be shooting for with this implementation is pretty simple. *Figure 5-20* describes the basic architecture for our intended solution.

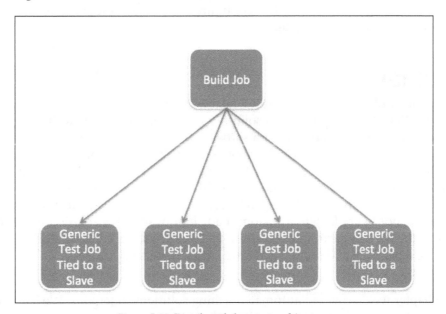

Figure 5-20: Distributed slave test architectures

The basic flow of the system will be to trigger downstream projects and pass to them the relevant details regarding which tests to execute, which environment to execute the tests against, and then collate the results in the upstream job. The magic of this solution is the ability to trigger downstream jobs simultaneously.

To implement this, simply specify each downstream job via a comma-separated list, in the top most parent job. This is defined in the job's configuration, and is added as a post-build step to trigger **Build other projects**. An example of this configuration is shown in *Figure 5-21*:

Figure 5-21: Build other projects

One the parent job has been configured properly we will next create the logical downstream jobs (each one attached to a different slave node) and have them bubble up the test reports. This can be accomplished via the *Build Flow Test Aggregator* plugin. Details of this plugin can be found at `https://wiki.jenkins-ci.org/display/JENKINS/Build+Flow+Test+Aggregator+Plugin`.

Once configured, the final step in this configuration is to test the solution and verify the results are correctly aggregated.

Summary

To begin the implementation of a truly scalable testing solution the key is standardization. This simplifies and solidifies a common set of core technologies, processes, and validation criteria for a software project. Indeed, introducing standards at an organization that has none is going to be an up-hill battle. Jenkins does provide all of the tools necessary to implement and build even the most complex systems. Even though Jenkins is highly configurable the more simplistic the implementation, the more likely it is to be successful. The key to a successful testing solution is to not to implement a custom-made highly adaptive solution but instead to remove the custom parts and substitute them with a set of conformity-driven standards, repeatable and known software engineering test processes, and automation.

In this chapter we discovered automated testing solutions in Jenkins. We learned how to create a scalable unit test solution. We covered how to implement a distributed testing apparatus and how to architect our test buckets. We even learned how to implement automated testing in MSTest, and briefly touched on A/B testing.

In the next chapter of *Mastering Jenkins* we will shift our focus over to deployments and delivery. We will learn some new and creative approaches to automating deployments and delivering our valuable software assets through the Jenkins platform.

6
Software Deployments and Delivery

As the Internet of Things increases the number of connected devices, IT operations personnel have been tasked with maintaining the existing scaled infrastructure as well as engineering new and innovative approaches to deliver software without risk. On the other side of the fence, software engineers have also been busy employing new and creative techniques to increase collaboration, control costs, and decrease production deployment failures. These two seemingly equidistant efforts have led to significant advancements in the exciting field of release engineering.

One of the more recent evolutions in release engineering combines traditionally segregated IT and development resources into hybrid cross-functional DevOps teams. DevOps-oriented teams are aimed at bridging the gap between traditional operations personnel, quality assurance engineers, and software engineers, all in an effort to employ modern, delivery practices and streamline the release of software assets. It is through these cross-functional teams that organizations have successfully implemented high-quality scalable software deployment procedures.

> *"The person who says it cannot be done, should not interrupt the person doing it"*
>
> *– Chinese proverb*

In this chapter of *Mastering Jenkins*, we will discover some of the leading trends in deployment automation. We will illustrate tactics, recipes, and tutorials that we can leverage when implementing an automated deployment solution. Our objectives for this chapter will be to cover the following topics:

- Standardizing build outputs
- Architecting a package scheme
- Implementing a **Definitive Media Library** (DML)

- Publishing assets to a DML
- Jenkins archive artifacts post-build action
- Publishing via Maven
- Publishing to Artifactory
- Pushing a Docker container
- Automated deployments
- Retrieving build artifacts and packages
- Fetching artifacts via archive the artifacts
- Fetching artifacts from artifactory
- Fetching artifacts via Maven
- Verifying package integrity
- Jenkins fingerprints
- MSBUILD via custom c# task
- Linux/Unix BASH
- Executing deployment automation
- Leveraging Jenkins slave nodes for deployment

Upon completing this chapter, we should have a solid grasp of how to architect and implement automated deployments across any number of technology stacks and disciplines in Jenkins. Irrespective of the architecture, platforms, or technology, the deployment phase of a software solution, website, embedded product, or a desktop application is arguably one of the most important phases of the software development lifecycle. The reason is simple: the deployment of a software project represents the initial experience a user will have with the software, and the path to future releases. A successful deployment signifies the beginning of business value and represents a precursory return on engineering investments.

Standardizing build outputs

The build process (especially the packaging and publishing phases) marks a foundational corner stone for automated deployments. For this reason, it is important to understand the basic lifecycle of a typical build process. The aim of the build process is generally to automate the validation of compilation quality of source-controlled assets, automate the creation of viable artifacts, and provide a software product that engineering can potentially hand to the business. While the technology stack may vary across organizations, typical build processes will follow a similar set of automation patterns. Let's look at the basic flow of a generic build process:

1. Obtain a clean copy of the source code from source control.
2. Fetch any dependencies (preferably from an artifact repository).
3. Version stamp any necessary code (may be a pre-compile or post-compile step, depending on the technology stack).
4. Compile the source code and verify syntax.
5. Execute unit tests (unit-based validation of objects, methods, and classes).
6. Collate compiled objects, binaries, or deliverables into a common output directory.
7. Create a package containing the binaries and deliverables.
8. Publish a versioned deliverable to an artifact repository.

The last two steps in the preceding process are arguably the most important ones when it comes to delivery and deployment. Properly architecting a deployable package and placing this package into an easily automatable location is paramount for deployments. The question remains though: how do we know what architecture to use for our packages? Let's dig a bit deeper.

To elaborate on what we discussed earlier, a basic build system implements a set of automated processes for a software project in an effort to not only automate the compilation of the software, but to answer some basic questions related to the code base. The questions asked and answered by the build system are as follows:

- Is the source control system accessible to the build machine and appropriate users?
- Does the code contained in source control meet basic structural standards?
- Does the source code committed to the code base compile at the time build was initiated, or does it have any obvious syntax errors?
- Is the build environment in a working state?
- Does the software pass basic unit test execution?

As we look to Jenkins and automate deployments to pre-release and production environments, we are essentially posing additional questions (our processes and automation should provide the answers provide the answers):

- Is the pre-production and production environments in a usable state?
- Does the software project install?
- Does the software project meet quality assurance standards?
- Where can engineers go to test integrated development efforts?

Leveraging automation to answer these questions can help software engineers, quality assurance resources, and management better understand the current implementation and quality of the software solution. By automating deployments of a software project to a prerelease environment, we can provide a preflight instance of an application that can be tested at any time.

Architecting and implementing an automated deployment solution in Jenkins can be a complex endeavor. Varying technology stacks (C#, C++, Java, Ruby on Rails, and so on) coupled with undefined engineering processes, can make deployment implementations virtually impossible. Standardizing the output of the build process into unified packages can help alleviate 90 percent of the complexity related to deployments. The way this is accomplished is by implementing on a set of basic standards and conventions regardless of platform, architecture, or technology stack. While this will inherently sacrifice some amount of flexibility, we will gain a set of known structures that are predictable, and can be automated against. Let's take a few minutes to learn how we can do this.

Architecting a packaging scheme

To begin to understand how to implement delivery package architecture, we need to start at the source code level. Software code (including deployment automation, tests, and related apparatuses) should be managed in the same logical source control repository that the software source code is kept in, and preferably packaged as part of the build process, to keep it in lock step release synchronization with the product. This enforces the idea that as software project's code base evolves, the deployment automation, automated testing solutions, test cases, and related infrastructure code will evolve in lockstep as well.

By storing product code, tests, and automation in the same source line in a predefined structure, we can eventually package the entire software solution's output during the build process. This allows us to create a snapshot in time, which will include a one-to-one match of binaries, deployment automation, database changes, and tests. Implementing this type of software development pattern has a number of benefits. Let's look at a few of them:

- The final deployable package will contain everything necessary to install the component or software project onto a given environment (this can make disaster recovery easier)

- The final deployable package will contain all testing apparatuses and database schema scripts needed to pass quality control gates (this makes going back in time and running tests against an older package possible)

- The software project could be easily be rolled backwards or forwards (by simply executing the automation inside a versioned package)

The following diagram shows a simple source control timeline. It describes the lockstep evolution of product code, automation, and tests with regard to packaging:

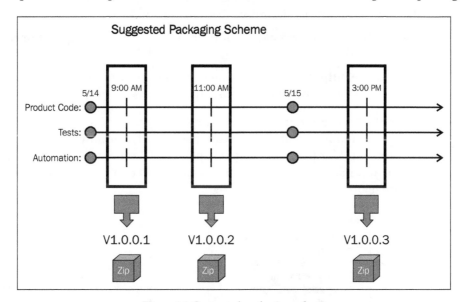

Figure 6-1: Suggested packaging scheme

One way to look at this packaging solution is to imagine a shrink-wrapped electronics product one might purchase at a big-box store. The package purchased typically includes everything needed to get up and running. This includes the product itself and instructions on how to use it. Often, you can even locate the quality control seals on the product. This proposed solution is really no different.

Build and deployment best practice

The goal of any build system should be to create a package that can be deployed repeatedly. The common phrase is *build once, deploy many*.

The packaging solution described previosly features a number of advantages over simply storing deployment automation and quality assurance test cases in segregated source control repositories. Let's look at a few of these advantages in greater detail:

- It removes the need to rebuild, reminimize, or recompile the code and tests prior to deployment

- it maintains a separation of concerns, follows continuous delivery best practices, and provides a definitive source of truth for releases

- It alleviates the error prone nature of running updated tests against previous releases or builds

- It organizes the outputs of engineering groups into a unified solution that encourages (if not enforces) collaboration

To help visualize the packaging objectives we are looking to achieve, let's look at an example of a unified standards based package. The following screenshot illustrates an example folder tree of a ZIP package, which contains the application, tests, deployment automation, and documentation. Its end contents signify a collaboratively developed deployment package:

Name	Kind	
▼ MyWebApplication-1.0.0.19.zip	Folder	
▼ app	Folder	
hellojenkins.html	HTML text	
index.html	HTML text	
▼ automation	Folder	
deploy.rb	Ruby script	
provision.rb	Ruby script	
▶ documentation	Folder	
▼ tests	Folder	
▶ functional.tests	Folder	
▶ regression.tests	Folder	
▶ smoke.tests	Folder	
▶ stress.tests	Folder	

Figure 6-2: Package contents

As we can see from the preceding example, our package's file name and format is also standardized. In our example, the final output is a ZIP with the `AppName-#.#.#.#.zip` naming convention. Your specific package implementation may vary in architecture (Zip, Tar, and so on) depending on technology stack , architecture, and convention. The final output and resulting package should be a single version-stamped deliverable, which follows the same patterns across all software projects that will have automated deployments.

Snapshots and Releases Tip

When implementing a package system, you may consider creating two or more identical packages: one for snapshots, which represents the latest build, and an additional item , which might represent the latest released version. This can be helpful when performing automated deployments and managing dependencies, as the packages could then be retrieved easily, without the need to specify a version number, and could be fetched via a simple static URL.

Strictly defined standards provide the foundation for automated deployments, automated testing, and traceability. In the end, we cannot automate what is not well defined.

Implementing a Definitive Media Library

A **Definitive Media Library** (**DML**) a term coined by ITIL and often referrerd to as a DML is recognized as a single source of truth for company software assets, dependencies, and third-party libraries. By nature a DML ensures assets are backed up, checksum verified, and managed appropriately. By implementing an artifact repository, or binary asset management system, that facilitates the aquisition of individually versioned packages, dependencies, or Docker containers, engineering id in effect organizing and showcasing software development outputs, intellectual property, and releases.

This type of solution organizes software assets in a centralized location that automation and the business can consume. An artifact management solution also provides the organization with the tools necessary to create a library of deployable entities and third-party dependencies. An additional benefit of this solution is that most modern DML solutions provide optional license-verification solutions that can help ensure that engineering is complying with applicable laws and regulations and not violating copyright rules. By leveraging an artifact management solution, the organization can better understand what they are developing and releasing.

At the time of the writing of this book, there are a number of widely available artifact management solutions. Some popular binary asset management solutions worth noting include Artifactory, Nexus, and Origin. Each of these provides an easy implementation path and asset management services. The respective links for each of these products are listed below:

- Jenkins directory (archive artifacts)

- Artifactory at `http://www.jfrog.com`

- Nexus at `http://www.sonatype.com`

- Archiva at `http://archiva.apache.org`

- Origin at `http://www.exeterstudios.com`

Coupling a binary asset management solution with Jenkins can create the foundation for a highly scalable delivery pipeline. Having the packages available through an easily automated solution, can provide a solid foundation for automated deployments. Let's spend a few minutes looking at how to publish our software assets to a DML.

Publishing assets to a DML

When publishing a package to a definitive media library, the commonly used phrase is to *deploy* it. Simply defined, it's the process by which we upload and archive packages (or dependencies) to an artifact repository. The word deploy seems like a misnomer here, since we are not really installing a software solution onto a device or system, so it may seem a bit confusing. However, it's a generally accepted term, which uniquely describes the operation we are performing. Each DML solution has its own unique ways by which artifacts are published to the DML. Let's take a look at how to implement the publishing of packages using Jenkins and other popular technologies. The DML options we will cover include the following popular artifact management solutions.

- Jenkins directly (archive artifacts)

- Jenkins Artifactory plugin (available via the Jenkins plugin ecosystem)

- Maven deploy (requires Apache Maven and Nexus, Artifactory, Archiva, and Origin)

- Docker registry (push pull or a Jenkins plugin)

Jenkins' archive the artifacts post-build action

Jenkins features an easy-to-use built-in artifact management solution. By leveraging this feature, Jenkins can capture build packages, manage digital fingerprints of binaries, facilitate downstream job deployments, manage dependencies, and more. Let's spend a few minutes walking through this unique feature and learn how it can be harnessed to store and track build artifacts.

To capture and store artifacts internally, Jenkins has a built-in file globing system, which allows us to specify a file mask that Jenkins will use to locate artifacts and archive them. This handy feature is located within the detailed job configuration page as a post-build action and is appropriately titled **Archive the artifacts**. *Figure 6-3* illustrates the **Archive the artifacts** post-build action.

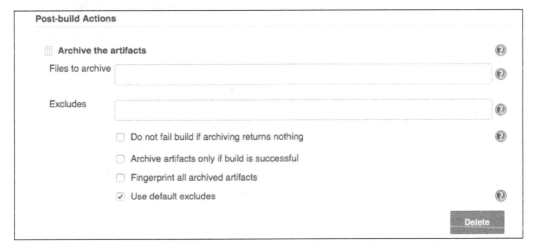

Figure 6-3: Archive the artifacts

Upon initial glance at the options available within the **Archive the Artifacts** post build action, we can see a few key configuration fields and a number of useful toggles. Let's look at each of the available options and some examples to see what they do:

Name	Example	Description
Files to archive	`folder/foo/bin/**/*.zip`	A relative workspace folder and file mask, which Jenkins will use to locate artifacts to capture and archive
Excludes	`folder/foo/bin/**/exception*.zip`	A relative workspace folder and file mask, which Jenkins will ignore when archiving

Name	Example	Description
Do not fail the build if archiving returns nothing	Check/Toggle	This allows Jenkins to ignore no files found type returns from a file mask search
Fingerprint all archived artifacts	Check	Enables Jenkins MD5 finger prints, which track the CRC integrity of the captured artifacts
Archive artifacts only if build is successful	Check	Tells Jenkins to only execute this step if the build was successful
Use default excludes	Check	Tells Jenkins to ignore common source-control files

As we can see from the preceding table, the **Archive the artifacts** solution can be quite powerful. One of the most useful options described in the preceding table is the fingerprinting system. This feature provides traceable CRC checksums for any captured artifacts and creates a verifiable chain of trust for the artifacts Jenkins archives.

Enabling log rotation for jobs that utilize archiving of artifacts

When using the **Archive the artifacts** solution provided by Jenkins, it is important to enable log rotations. This feature must be enabled on the detailed job configuration page at the top. It tells Jenkins to remove outdated builds based on a specified log rotation configuration. It will also ensure that the Jenkins disk space does not get over utilized.

Upon implementing the Archive the artifacts post-build configuration, Jenkins will (on the next build run) automatically search the project's workspace for the defined file mask and capture any files found that match the configured file mask criteria. These artifacts will then be available directly in the Jenkins UI within each build, as shown in *Figure 6-4*.

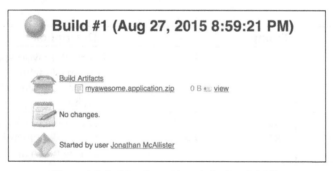

Figure 6-4: Archive the artifacts in Jenkins Job UI

When implementing the *Archive the Artifacts* post build action in conjunction with a Master and Slave node solution, any artifacts identified and archived will be automatically replicated to the Jenkins master instance. This can be very helpful when configuring downstream jobs to retrieve the artifacts that Jenkins has archived. One a set of build artifacts has been archived, they will become available for direct download. The standard pattern for the download link is `http://<JenkinsURL>/job/<JobName>/<BuildNumber>/artifact/<PATHTOFILE>/FileName.ext`.

Publishing to Artifactory

Prior to deploying a software project to an environment or system, we will need to learn how uploading or deploying a package to the artifact repository works. To better understand the architecture, let's take a look at how Jenkins can be leveraged to publish versioned artifacts to an artifact repository in Artifactory. *Figure 6-5* shows the basic upload architecture in relation to Jenkins:

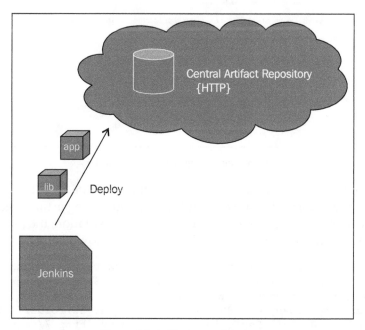

Figure 6-5: Artifactory architecture

To facilitate the architecture described above, we will need to install the Jenkins Artifactory plugin. This plugin is openly available in the plugin administration area within Jenkins.

The Jenkins Artifactory plugin operates using a file mask matching system titled **Published Artifacts,** which can be configured in the target job's detailed job-configuration page. This solution allows us to specify criteria for published artifacts. Jenkins will search for these artifacts and upload any matches found to the specified Artifactory repository. To better illustrate how to configure Jenkins to search for a file mask, *Figure 6-6* shows an example configuration page and a file mask of `*.zip` to search for within the `/Build/Artifacts` folder, which is relative to the jobs `$WORKSPACE` location.

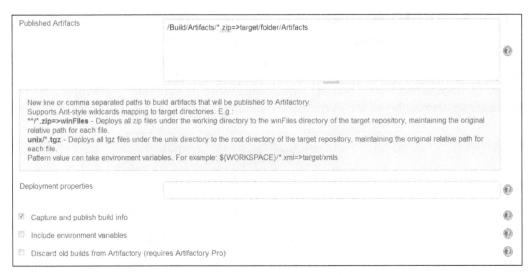

Figure 6-6: Publishing artifacts to Artifactory

A properly configured Jenkins job coupled with the integrated Artifactory plugin will create a system that automatically captures any matching artifacts and uploads them to an Artifact repository. Upon successful implementation, the job's console output logs will reflect the capturing of the artifacts as shown below.

```
For pattern: /Build/Artifacts/*.zip 2 artifacts were found Deploying
artifact: http://artifactory.mycompany.com:8080/artifactory/target/
folder/Artifacts/myPackage-1.0.0.0.zip Deploying artifact: http://
artifactory.mycompany.com:8080/artifactory/target/folder/Artifacts/
myPackage-1.0.0.0.zip Deploying build info to: http:// artifactory.
mycompany.com:8080/artifactory/api/build Archiving artifacts
```

Publishing via Maven

For Java development groups that leverage Maven, capturing build results and deploying outputs or Maven build artifacts is equally straightforward. Artifacts can be published to multiple DML solutions, including Sonatype Nexus, Apache Archiva, Exeters Origin, and others via a simple deploy target, which is embedded directly within the Maven architecture. This solution has no direct dependency on a Jenkins plugin and has no other special automation requirements. To configure Maven to *deploy* an artifact to these tools, we will need to update the Maven POM. XML file and add the distributionManagement element to the XML document. Below is an example of how to configure Maven to deploy artifacts to an artifact repository solution such as Nexus. In our example, we are running Sonatype Nexus at nexus. mycompany.com:

```
<distributionManagement>
  <repository>
     <id>deployment</id>
     <name>Company Artifacts</name>
  <url>http://nexus.mycompany.com/nexus/content/repositories/
Artifacts/</url>
  </repository>
</distributionManagement>
```

Some artifact repositories require authentication to deploy. If your artifact repository requires specific authentication to deploy, you may need to specify the following authentication data in your ~/.m2/settings.xml file. An example of how to accomplish this is provided in the XML settings document below:

```
<servers>
  <server>
    <id>deployment</id>
    <username>mydeployautheduser</username>
    <password>password123</password>
  </server>
</servers>
```

After the initial configuration and POM settings have been updated, commanding Maven to publish artifacts to the artifact repository should be as simple as calling the deploy task. Below is an example of this command:

```
$> mvn deploy
```

There are many more options available to deploy artifacts in Maven. A complete documentation set is provided at https://maven.apache.org/plugins/maven-deploy-plugin/.

Pushing a Docker container

For Docker users, the output of the build may actually be a prebaked virtualized container. This type of solution provides a unique feature-rich method to build out a completely live environment through automation. It allows development to implement and engineer the container, which is then handed directly to quality assurance to be validated. This solution ensures that an apples-to-apples analysis of an application can be done and removes any ambiguity in deployment methodologies or environment setup. For a complete and detailed documentation of the Docker container solution you can visit Docker's website at http://www.docker.com.

When Docker is in use, formalization of standards surrounding the containers, registries, build recipes, and deployment automation that manages the solution will become increasingly important. Either way, once the container has been created, leveraging Jenkins to store the container in a central registry can be accomplished fairly easily. Below is an example shell script that automates the pulling, building, and pushing of a container to a Docker registry:

```
$> docker pull ubuntu
$> docker run -I -t ubuntu /bin/bash
$> docker commit
$> docker push yourregistryurl.com/ubuntu
```

As we can see from the preceding example, containers (and their content) are managed in much the same way as the source code is. This is by design. It allows for optimal traceability of changes to the container to have a historical timeline. To accomplish this, Docker leverages a tagging solution.

When simple shell scripts are not sufficient to manage Docker containers, the Jenkins community has graciously provided a Docker build-step plugin. The Docker build-step plugin features a number of useful Docker-oriented capabilities directly within a Jenkins job. Additional information for this plugin can be found on the Jenkins community website at https://wiki.jenkins-ci.org/display/JENKINS/Docker+build+step+plugin.

Installing the Docker build-step plugin into Jenkins can be accomplished via the traditional manage plugins area located within the administration area of the Jenkins user interface.

Once the plugin has been successfully installed onto a Jenkins system, an **Execute Docker container** build step will appear within the detailed job configuration page for all Freestyle jobs. *Figure 6-7* illustrates this build step:

Figure 6-7: Execute Docker container build step

The available choices in the Docker command dropdown include the following:

- Commit changes in a specified container
- Create a new container from image
- Create an image from Docker file
- Create the exec command
- Kill container(s)
- Pull image from a repository
- Push image to a repository
- Remove container(s)
- Remove all containers
- Restart container(s)
- Start container(s)
- Stop container(s)
- Stop all containers
- Start/stop all containers created from specified image
- Start the `exec` command

Recently, Docker has gained a lot of notoriety. It is quickly becoming a preferred approach to building and serving micro-service architectures. It provides a robust solution that provides a feature-rich way to develop and deliver software and alleviates environment variances. It is important to note that at the time of the writing of this book, Docker is a strictly Linux-based virtualization solution. Docker has been in public talks with Microsoft with regards to providing a Windows implementation of the Docker container architecture, but no specific implementation has yet been delivered.

Automated deployments

Now that we have a solid understanding of how to prepare a software project for deployment by architecting a package solution and leveraging a DML, we will need to define our delivery system. The most widely accepted approach in modern software build and delivery is to apply a manufacturing assembly-line paradigm to the software-release process. This methodology is prevalent at countless software-engineering organizations and seemingly transcends any specific development paradigms, including agile, lean, or waterfall. It can also be universally applied across numerous technology stacks, including Linux, Windows, Mac, iOS, Android, Embedded, Firmware, and so on.

In an assembly-line approach to software releases, pre-built packages (or containers) flow down the assembly line, are inspected by relevant stakeholders, and are eventually handed to the business for release. Packages will traditionally start in a development environment and pass through various quality-control groups, thus incrementally exposing the risk of a bad build or defective solution. This flow eventually leads to a release. If a defect is identified while in the assembly line or a failure is discovered, the assembly line stops, and changes are implemented to rectify the failure. After a solution to a defect has been implemented, the assembly-line flow resets, and movement begins again. *Figure 6-8* illustrates the assembly-line approach to software delivery.

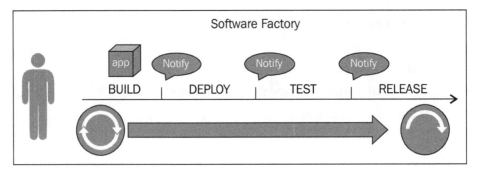

Figure 6-8: Example of a software assembly line

When implementing any automated deployment solution, deployment automation phases need to be standardized as much as possible. The goal is to create strictly adhered-to release and deployment processes and technology conventions from which automation can be created. This allows Jenkins to orchestrate the delivery aspects and perform deployments. It is important to keep in mind that we can only automate what is well defined and known about. Below is a list of basic deployment steps, which can serve as a template for creating deployment automation.

1. A Jenkins deployment job will be triggered, which will be responsible for the deployment.

2. Jenkins will need to either push the package to a targeted environment or perform the following steps on the target environment itself (via slave nodes). The deployment job will need to perform the execution of the following actions:

    ○   Identify the version of the software to be deployed

    ○   Download the versioned package from the DML

    ○   Verify the CRC fingerprints of the deployable entity

    ○   Extract the contents of the package into a temporary folder on the deployment environment.

    ○   Execute the deployment automation in the package to install the software.

    ○   Verify that the deployment was successful through basic sanity tests

3. Jenkins will need to determine whether the deployment was a success or a failure due to recognized return codes.

The assembly line approach to software releases helps ensure that appropriate stakeholders are notified of software builds that matter to them, ensure that, resources are not wasted in testing bad builds, and risk is exposed incrementally. Modern implementations of this assembly-line solution leverage digital approval processes to promote builds from one logical group to another. The first step in implementing this type of assembly-line process is to automate the retrieval of deployable entities from the DML.

In the upcoming sections of this chapter, we will walk through each of the deployment steps and learn how to implement them using Jenkins and related tools. Let's get started.

Retrieving build artifacts and packages

In order to perform a deployment of a software project onto a target system, we need access to the artifacts produced by the build job. As we mentioned earlier, artifacts come in many shapes and sizes. Some artifacts are simple libraries or dependencies, and others are complete deployment packages.

Retrieving artifacts from a DML via a deployment job can be accomplished easily. When automating the retrieval of an artifact we will need to either by leverage the **Archived Artifacts** within Jenkins directly, or utilize a third-party artifact-management software solution. The method you select is highly dependent on the architecture of your DML (which we discussed earlier). Let's look at each of the possible approaches in detail and learn how to automate the retrieval of artifacts.

Fetching artifacts via archive artifacts

When a downstream job needs to retrieve archived artifacts stored within the Jenkins system itself, Jenkins features a few options. Jobs in Jenkins provide a simple build step to copy artifacts from another project. This build step is available within the detailed job configuration page for a preferred job. *Figure 6-9* illustrates the copy artifacts build step:

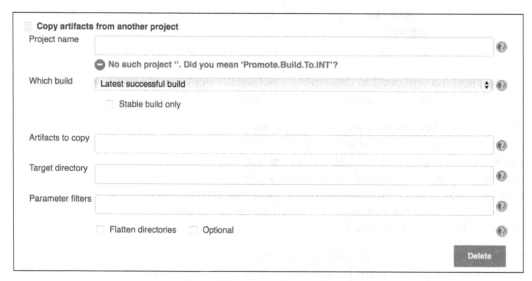

Figure 6-9: Copy artifacts build step

From the preceding illustration, we can see that there are a number of configuration options available in the copy artifacts build step. Let's spend a minute going over each of the available configuration options in greater detail. The following table describes each of the options available in detail and provides a simple example for each option:

Option Name	Example Value	Description
Project name	`build.myproject-production`	Identifies the Jenkins job name from which the build artifacts will be retrieved
Which build	Latest successful build	Provides a number of drop-down options to customize the retrieval of artifacts, for example, Latest
Artifacts to copy	`module/dist/**/*.zip`	Specifies the file mask for Jenkins to use when locating artifacts to import
Target directory	`Foo/bar/libhome/`	Specifies the relative path to the Jenkins workspace where the copied artifacts will be placed
Parameter filters	`BUILD_MODE=release`	Jobs may be filtered to select only builds matching particular parameters

After implementing the copy artifacts build step, Jenkins will automatically fetch and provide the specified artifacts in the Target directory specified. This solution offers a feature-rich yet straightforward mechanism to pull artifacts from one job over to another.

When implementing this solution on a master and slave node Jenkins system, this option is a highly scalable solution to deploy packages or dependencies to a target slave node from within Jenkins. We will discuss some tips and tricks surrounding this type of implementation further down in this chapter (leveraging slave nodes for deployment).

Fetching artifacts from Artifactory

Artifact repositories provide a scalable source of truth for build packages, dependencies, and binary libraries. An artifact-management system can be automated against easily and will typically feature an API that allows programmatic access to upload, download, and search binary assets.

The following diagram describes the basic architecture of an artifact repository and shows you how it can be leveraged to service automated deployment operations:

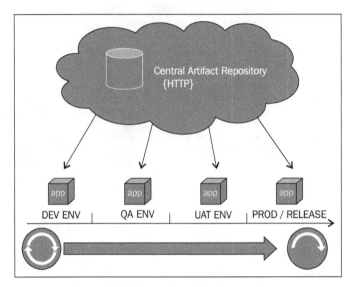

Figure 6-10: Automation of Artifact repository

Downloading packages from an Artifactory repository via automation is not a difficult exercise. To illustrate the various ways to download stored packages via automation, we have provided some basic command-line examples, which automate the fetching of packages on Linux, Windows, and Mac OSX, respectively:

Linux via WGET:

```
#> wget -O $WORKSPACE/binarypackagefoo-1.0.0.0.tar.gz http://artifacts.
mycompany.com:8081/Artifactory/simple/binarypackagefoo-1.0.0.0.tar.gz
```

Linux via CURL:

```
#> curl -o $WORKSPACE/binarypackagefoo-1.0.0.0.tar.gz -remote-name
http://artifacts.mycompany.com:8081/Artifactory/simple/binarypackagefoo-
1.0.0.0.tar.gz
```

Microsoft Windows via Powershell:

```
C:\> powershell -Command (new-object System.Net.WebClient).
DownloadFile('http://artifacts.mycompany.com:8081/Artifactory/simple/
binarypackagefoo-1.0.0.0.zip','C:\%WORKSPACE%\binarypackagefoo-
1.0.0.0.zip')
```

Windows via MSBUILD + Extension Pack:

```
<WebDownload FileName="$(WORKSPACE)\binarypackagefoo-1.0.0.0.zip"
FileUri=" shttp://artifacts.mycompany.com:8081/artifactory/simple/
binarypackagefoo-1.0.0.0.zip">
```

Mac OS X via Curl:

```
#> curl –o $WORKSPACE/binarypackagefoo-1.0.0.0.tar.gz –remote-name
http://artifacts.mycompany.com:8081/Artifactory/simple/binarypackagefoo-
1.0.0.0.tar.gz
```

Fetching artifacts via Maven

Artifact repositories also provide a scalable solution to resolve Maven dependencies. Resolving dependencies in Maven can be done via a simple update of the POM file. To better illustrate this concept, we have provided an example below:

```
<repositories>
    <repository>
        <id>central</id>
        <url>http://[host]:[port]/artifactory/libs-release</url>
        <snapshots>
            <enabled>false</enabled>
        </snapshots>
    </repository>
    <repository>
        <id>snapshots</id>
        <url>http://[host]:[port]/artifactory/libs-snapshot</url>
        <releases>
            <enabled>false</enabled>
        </releases>
    </repository>
</repositories>
<pluginRepositories>
    <pluginRepository>
        <id>central</id>
        <url>http://[host]:[port]/artifactory/plugins-release</url>
        <snapshots>
            <enabled>false</enabled>
        </snapshots>
    </pluginRepository>
    <pluginRepository>
        <id>snapshots</id>
        <url>http://[host]:[port]/artifactory/plugins-snapshot</url>
        <releases>
```

```
            <enabled>false</enabled>
        </releases>
    </pluginRepository>
</pluginRepositories>
```

In the preceding example, we simply created pointers to an Artifactory-based Maven repository. However, this type of solution will work for Archiva, Nexus, and other similar binary repository solutions.

Now that we have covered the basics on uploading and downloading binaries through a DML, let's look at the phases that will need to occur after the package has been fetched onto the target deployment system.

Verifying package integrity

The next logical step in our deployment automation is to validate the integrity of the package that was downloaded through CRC checksums. Popular DML solutions assist in this fingerprinting effort by generating MD5 and SHA1 checksum files or providing fingerprints (directly in Jenkins). These fingerprints are associated with each binary stored in the DML. Checksum files and fingerprints provide a hashed computational CRC of the binary item.

To validate the CRC of the package downloaded, we will need to compare the previously stored fingerprint-identification content against a freshly calculated one for the target binary. This can be accomplished in a straightforward manner. Coding a simple MD5 or SHA1 verification solution can be done in most popular programming languages that support MD5 or SHA1 calculations. Here are some examples of how to validate a package's integrity in Jenkins (via fingerprinting), in .NET MSBUILD for Microsoft Windows, and BASH for Linux.

Jenkins fingerprints

Jenkins automatically calculates the MD5 fingerprints (when fingerprinting is enabled via the Archive the artifacts post-build step) for internally stored artifacts. An internally stored artifact in Jenkins is simply one that was captured via the Archive the artifacts post-build action. When fingerprinting is enabled, Jenkins will automatically fingerprint all artifacts captured within a given job's execution, and their respective MD5 checksums will be available via the user interface.

After successfully fingerprinting an archived artifact, Jenkins provides a Nifty user interface option where we can view the fingerprints. This option is available by clicking on a specified build number from a Jenkins job and then clicking on the **See Fingerprints** menu option on the left-hand side. *Figure 6-11* illustrates this feature in detail:

Figure 6-11: Recorded fingerprints

An additional benefit of the Jenkins fingerprinting feature is its ability to track an artifacts usage across multiple Jenkins jobs. This can be handy to determine which jobs have consumed specific artifacts. To implement this feature, we need to configure the **Record fingerprints of files to track usage** post-build step located on the preferred detailed job configuration page. *Figure 6-12* illustrates this post-build step in action:

Figure 6-12: Record fingerprints of files to track usage

Upon implementing this post-build action; Jenkins will begin tracking any jobs that consume the captured artifacts. This traceability information will become visible via the **Recorded Fingerprints** page we described in *Figure 6-11*.

MSBUILD via custom C# task

```
<UsingTask TaskName="MD5Verification" TaskFactory="CodeTaskFactory" As
semblyFile="$(MSBuildToolsPath)\Microsoft.Build.Tasks.v4.0.dll">
  <ParameterGroup>
      <MD5PackagePath ParameterType="System.String" Required="true" />
      <MD5FileContents ParameterType="System.String" Required="true"
/>
      <MD5RequiredHASH ParameterType="System.String" Required="true"
/>
  </ParameterGroup>
  <Task>

    <Using Namespace="System.IO" />
    <Using Namespace="System.Text.RegularExpressions" />
    <Using Namespace="System.Security.Cryptography"/>
    <Using Namespace="Microsoft.Build.Framework" />
    <Code Type="Fragment" Language="cs">

                <![CDATA[


          // -- Get MD5 value for each of our items
          FileStream file = new FileStream(MD5PackagePath.ToString(),
FileMode.Open);
          String MD5Required = MD5RequiredHASH.ToString();
          MD5 md5 = new MD5CryptoServiceProvider();
          byte[] retVal = md5.ComputeHash(file);
          file.Close();

          StringBuilder MDHASH = new StringBuilder();
          for (int i = 0; i < retVal.Length; i++)
          {
            MDHASH.Append(retVal[i].ToString("x2"));
          }

          Log.LogMessage(MessageImportance.Normal, "------------------
-----------------------------------");
          Log.LogMessage(MessageImportance.Normal, "Verifying MD5
CheckSums ");
          Log.LogMessage(MessageImportance.Normal, "------------------
-----------------------------------");
```

```
        Log.LogMessage(MessageImportance.Normal, "Package Location:
"+ MD5PackagePath +" \nFresh MD5: " + MD5FileContents + "\nArtifactory
MD5: " + MDHASH + "\nUser Specified MD5:" + MD5Required);

        int MD5Compare = String.Compare(MD5FileContents.ToString(),
MDHASH.ToString());
        int MD5REQCompare = String.Compare(MD5Required.ToString(),
MDHASH.ToString());
        if ((MD5Required != null) && (((MD5REQCompare == 0) &&
(MD5Required != "OFF")) || (MD5REQCompare != 0) && (MD5Required ==
"OFF")) && (MD5Compare == 0)) {

            Log.LogMessage(MessageImportance.Normal, "MD5 Verified
Successfully");

        } else {

            Log.LogMessage(MessageImportance.High, "MD5 Verification
FAILED!");
            throw new Exception("Could not verify the MD5's the
package downloaded is corrupt.");

        }


        ]]>

    </Code>
  </Task>
</UsingTask>
```

Linux / Unix BASH script

```bash
#!/bin/bash
echo "Calculating MD5 comparisons"
if [ -z $2 ]; then
        echo "file + sum file needed"
        echo "usage: 0? "
        exit
fi

export fsum=$(cat $2)
export csum=$(md5sum $1 | awk '{print $1}')

echo "MD5 File CheckSum Value: $fsum"
```

```
echo "MD5Sum Calculated Value: $csum"

if [ "$csum" == "$fsum" ]; then
        echo "MD5 Verification Successful!";
else
      echo "MD5 Verification Failed!"
fi
```

Executing deployment automation

In the previous sections, we discovered some basic approaches to package architecture. We discussed how to implement a DML and how to leverage it to publish and retrieve packages. We also learned how to ensure package integrity via CRC checksums. Now that we have all of the precursory deployment steps in place, we will finish our deployments by executing automation to perform a deployment.

Deployment automation can come in many forms. If you're a Windows aficionado, leveraging a bash script might not work out very well. The same could be said if you're a Linux user and are attempting to use MSBuild to manage deployments. At a minimum, you will want to create the right number of Jenkins jobs to facilitate the execution of the deployment automation while keeping the system fluid. In addition, these jobs will need to properly determine the success or failure of the deployment. They should also provide the ability for them to be executed individually to deploy a specific version of the targeted software via a button click.

When implementing deployment jobs in Jenkins, we will need to be able to parse user-specified version numbers (to support out of band deployments) and act on those inputs. This is where build parameters can provide a huge amount of value. The following screenshot illustrates a basic set of parameters in a Jenkins deployment job, which will allow the user to input version number and artifact repository:

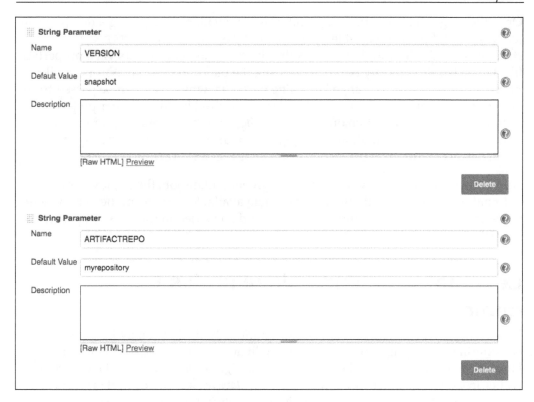

Figure 6-13: Basic set of parameters in a Jenkins deployment job

After these elements have been defined, whenever the job is executed via user input, the VERSION and ARTIFACTREPO variables will be available to the automation via environment variables. This should make fetching a specific version of a deployment package a bit easier.

When calling a deployment job via a build or otherwise *upstream* job, passing variables between jobs, such as version or artifact repository will become increasingly important. This can be accomplished via the trigger/call parameterized builds on other projects' plugin. Download and install the plugin onto your Jenkins instance. Installation details for this plugin can be found on the Jenkins wiki at `https://wiki.jenkins-ci.org/display/JENKINS/Parameterized+Trigger+Plugin`.

Once the plugin has been installed, and plugin is available, triggering a downstream Jenkins job and passing variable data, such as VERSION or ARTIFACTREPO, is straightforward. This plugin provides the ability to pass parameters via a properties file, which would typically be created during the build process. Java property files provide a unique way to mange key value pair data, which can then be passed from one job to another using the trigger/call parameterized builds on other projects plugin. For more information on properties' files and their format requirements, look at the Java documentation at http://docs.oracle.com/cd/E23095_01/ Platform.93/ATGProgGuide/html/s0204propertiesfileformat01.html.

Upon initialization of a downstream deployment Jenkins job, the deployment automation should have all the necessary data available to perform the deployment , either from values defined upon execution, or data passed in through properties file or otherwise.

Leveraging Jenkins slave nodes for deployment

When a deployment environment is not significantly sizable, it may be worth considering leveraging Jenkins slaves to facilitate automated deployments onto target systems. We discussed the setup and configuration of Jenkins slave systems earlier in *Chapter 2, Distributed Builds – Master/Slave Mode*. However, it is worth exploring this solution for automated deployments in this section as well.

In this section, we will focus on one of the more unique methods we can employ for automated deployments. We can leverage the Jenkins master to control and distribute software to connected slave devices using this methodology. This can be particularly useful when deploying a desktop client application or embedded solution. However, it is not limited to those architecture types specifically.

While writing the deployment automation itself will be left to you, the connectivity to the remote device would be entirely managed by Jenkins. In addition to this, Jenkins can serve as a poor man's monitoring solution for the deployment nodes. The architecture of such a solution is illustrated in *Figure 6-14*.

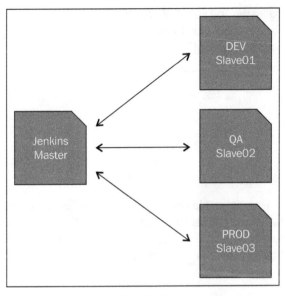

Figure 6-14: Master-slave deployment architecture

When using a master and slave node deployment solution, the implementation would require a number of deploy jobs defined within the Jenkins system to be explicitly tied to target deployment machines or devices (slaves). Tying a job to a specific device is accomplished via the restrict where this job can run option located on the detailed job configuration page for the preferred job. The automation in each deployment job would simply need to fetch a deployment package, verify the checksum, extract the contents, and execute the deployment steps defined within. Jenkins would then report back to the success or failure of the automation. Once implemented, this could eaily be connected as a promotion step using the Promoted Builds plugin.

When setting up a Jenkins slave node deployment system, Jenkins provides a number of useful built-in features to facilitate monitoring of disk space, swap space, CPU load, and more. These can be very handy when the environments require a solid availability schedule.

Tying a Jenkins job to a specific set of slaves is easy and can be accomplished through the **Restrict where this project can be run** option on the job configuration page, as shown in the following screenshot:

Figure 6-15: Tying Jenkins job to slaves

Executing automation on those slaves can also be implemented in a straightforward manner. The **Execute Shell** or **Execute Windows Shell** build steps provide a straightforward mechanism to write and execute automation on a targeted deployment node. You can follow these basic steps when deploying an application onto a slave node:

1. Download the deployment package from the DML (you could use copy the artifacts here if you use Jenkins as your DML).
2. Verify that the CRC checksums for the package are downloaded.
3. Extract the deployment package (unzip, tar, and so on).
4. Execute the deployment scripts embedded in the package.
5. Run application startup sequences.

The preceding list simply provides a basic set of guidelines. Diverse technology stacks and setups will obviously vary. For additional information on passing version information from one job to another, refer to *Chapter 7, Build Pipelines*. For additional information surrounding the Jenkins master and slave setups, see *Chapter 2, Distributed Builds – Master/Slave Mode*.

Summary

Today, there are various methods and means to facilitate automated deployments for a software project. Whatever the technology is, we can learn and innovate creative ways to attach that to Jenkins. By attaching our deployments to Jenkins, we can move Jenkins into the realm of an automation orchestration platform and out of the realm of grandma's build tool. Whichever way you decide to implement automated deployments, be sure to try and facilitate the following best practice features:

- Deploying any version of a software solution should be as easy as a button click

- Rolling forward or backward in time should also be a button click

- Maintaining your environmental configurations in code form (infrastructure as code)

In this chapter of *Mastering Jenkins* we discovered some innovative ways we can approach software delivery and some tricks we can leverage to automate deployments. We learned about packaging, and versioning our tests as well as automation scripts. We covered artifact repositories and how to leverage an artifact repo to facilitate scalable deployment solutions. Finally we learned new ways to leverage the master and slave solution to facilitate additional deployment scenarios.

In the next chapter we will discover build pipelines. Build pipelines in Jenkins provide a scalable way to connect jobs together, and pass data between them. In the next chapter we will begin to understand how to connect build operations, to deployments, and tie them together with automated testing verification. This will be a fun journey, so let's get going.

7
Build Pipelines

Build pipelines were conceived in software engineering in the 2012 book titled *Continuous Delivery* authored by Jez Humble, and David Farley. Since the release of this revolutionary book, there have been numerous technology organizations that have implemented build pipelines, to increase the efficiency of their software delivery process. While the idea of a build pipeline is new in software engineering, it is not an entirely new concept. The principles of build pipelines have been in place in the manufacturing industry for some time now, where they are better known as factory assembly lines. In manufacturing practices, organizations have effectively reduced costs in engineering and delivery, which as a result allowed them to become more competitive. Modern manufacturing processes, coupled with efficient automation, reduces the manpower required to assemble and deliver a product. This, in turn, reduces a company's operating expenses, and increases profit margins.

"Even the palest ink is brighter than the most retentive memory" – Chinese proverb

Implementing build pipelines in Jenkins takes careful architectural planning and strategy coupled with highly efficient automation applied across all engineering disciplines. In order to implement a build pipeline solution, an organization will need to focus its efforts on the following areas:

- Conventions and standards (convention over configuration)
- Automation
- Efficient automated testing
- Defining pipeline conventions and structure

In this chapter, we will discover how to leverage Jenkins and architect highly efficient build pipelines. This is in an effort to facilitate efficient software delivery, and catch software defects prior to release, which can save an organization money.. Build pipelines in Jenkins, when implemented correctly, can help encourage collaboration, increase throughput, and provide rapid feedback on quality. Build pipelines, by nature, transcend *Agile and Waterfall* software development paradigms. For management, this will provide a direct visibility into the development and delivery process, and encourage software assets to be always releasable. For the Jenkins enthusiast, learning how to create build pipelines will provide the teach us new ways to leverage Jenkins as a complete software development lifecycle orchestration tool, and ensure repeatability of our software delivery processes.

In this chapter of *Mastering Jenkins*, we will cover the following high-level topics:

- Business value propositions for build pipelines (to sell to management)
- Architecting a build pipeline
- Implementing build pipelines in Jenkins

Tying business capital into inefficient software assembly lines impedes market viability, reduces working capital, and restricts the business's ability to compete. Replacing unknown or costly development and release paradigms with automation, conventions, and efficiency can help streamline the manual error-prone processes.

The value proposition of build pipelines

For software organizations, defects can be extremely costly. For each defect identified, the amount of time spent by engineering, quality assurance, and related teams to rectify it is equivalent to the amount of time and resources that are distracted from feature development and strategic business initiatives. It is, by nature, a one to one ratio. Identifying and addressing defects earlier in the software development lifecycle by through the use of build pipelines can save multitudes of time, resources and solidify business credibility.

Over the years, there have been a number of independent research studies conducted to better quantify the relative costs associated with software development efforts including bug fixing, software architecture, project management, and so on. The most notable research into defect analysis, specifically, was conducted by Barry Boehm in 2007 and is illustrated in *Figure 7-1*.

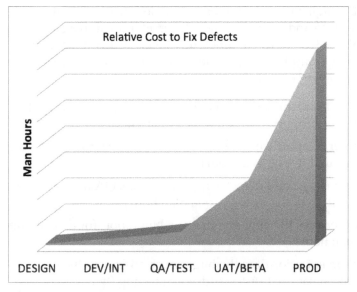

Figure 7-1: Relative cost of bug fixes

His research, derived from related **Defense Advanced Research Projects Agency (DARPA)** investigations, describes the relative costs associated with fixing defects in relation to the software development lifecycle. This research is quite startling for SaaS engineering organizations. It describes the phases within the software development lifecycle where a software defect becomes increasingly expensive to address.

The value proposition of build pipelines is that software development resources, quality assurance personnel, and the related ancillary teams have to collaborate to build, deploy, and test a complete software project in pre-production environments, and then automatically flow the results into well-formed releases. By implementing this type of a solution through automation, the organization will be able to identify defects before they pose a risk to credibility or become a catastrophy. To better understand the chart in the preceding image, let's take a quick look at how an inefficient, risky development practice might impact a business.

Defects identified by end users, customers, or consumers of a software solution are costly and damage the reputation of the business and its products. When multitudes of defects are identified after a software project has been released, the credibility of the business suffers, and acquiring new clientele becomes increasingly difficult.

To highlight the high cost of defect resolution, let's take a minute to identify the associated scope and costs. For each defect identified in a software project post-release, the defect itself will inherently be triaged and managed by numerous stakeholders. For example a single defect identified after a release could potentially navigate the following workflow.

1. The defect is identified by customer(s) who opens a support request with the company's support representative (1 man hour per report)

2. Customer Support works with the customer to either verify the issue, or work around it (one man hour)

3. If the issue is a valid defect, support contacts QA for bug verification and prioritization of the remedy (one man hour)

4. QA reproduces the bug, and opens a bug report for a development resource (one man hour)

5. Development prioritizes the bug report, addresses the issue, and passes the verification back to QA for additional testing (two man hours)

6. Ops deploys the updated software or re-releases it (one man hour)

7. Support verifies that the issue is properly addressed and contacts the customer(s) (one man hour)

In the preceding workflow, we can see how a single defect can add up to many man hours, which can make them expensive to fix. Additionally, we can see approximately how many company resources will be actively engaged in the resolution of a defect. Could it be possible to attach a dollar amount to each bug addressed by the engineering team? Let's take a minute to investigate, and see if we can define (in dollars and cents) the cost associated with addressing a defect in a software project.

The following diagram illustrates an example (with the dollar amounts) attached to each engineering resource segment:

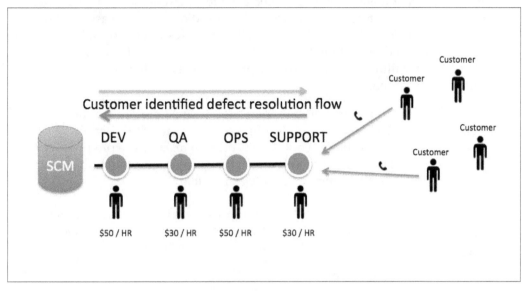

Figure 7-2: Customer-identified defect resolution flow

Based on the preceding data, a single defect could at a minimum amount to **$220.00** (or more) in man-hours alone. To showcase how we derived that figure, let's look at an example of man-hours to dollar conversions for a single defect, and the calculated costs associated with it, as given in *Figure 7-3*.

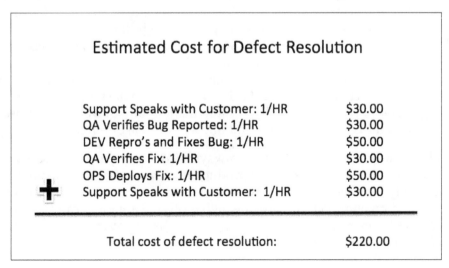

Figure 7-3: Sample bug fix costs

By implementing build pipelines, the idea is to catch defects earlier in the engineering process, know about them sooner, and reduce the amount of manpower invested in rectifying them. A build pipeline aims to solve engineering frustrations by outlining a set of pre-release processes and verification steps that assist in this effort. The earlier these defects are identified, the fewer resources needed to assist in their management and resolution, thus saving the organization effort, time, and money. While failure within a software project is inevitably part of the equation. Costly failures do not need to be.

To assist in identifying software defects earlier, well-defined pre-production environments should be introduced for testing and identifying the potential integration, stress, or production rollout defects prior to release. The pre-production environments that are introduced should match the configuration and implementation of the production or release systems as closely as possible.

It is important to note that the term *production* is loosely described, and may represent a web server, database server, embedded device, or a desktop system. It may even represent manufacturing or a CDN. On the other hand, the term "release" is simply defined as available for customer consumption.

To better grasp the idea of this whole solution, let's take a few minutes to learn how to architect a build pipeline, and what its individual components are.

Architecting a build pipeline

Build pipelines are the progression of logical development, quality and delivery steps; these steps define the way a software project will be built, delivered, and tested. By implementing build pipelines, we are crafting a solution where build packages or containers flow through repeatable delivery processes in a continuous manner. Gates are added to the pipeline to ensure that quality metrics are collected, and integration defects are identified. Each gate defined in the pipeline represents a go/no-go determination. Eventually, the automation solution vets and releases a build through the complete pipeline and into a *production* or released status.

As we hinted earlier, *production* does not always need to apply to cloud-based software or rack-mounted servers. The production or *released* status of a build pipeline simply represents the end goal. For embedded solutions or shrink-wrapped software, build pipelines can still provide high levels of value, and can further the organization's business agenda by providing an *always releasable* software solution, which can then be strategically marketed.

To begin our quest in architecting a build pipeline in Jenkins, let's take a look at the way to organize our delivery solution. We will do this by dividing the build pipeline into segments, each of which represents the deployment and test iterations of the SDLC that we described earlier in *Chapter 5, Advanced Automated Testing*.

The first segment of the build pipeline

The first segment of a build pipeline is a bit unique, as it contains the build process, source code verification, unit tests, static code analysis, packaging, initial integration deployment steps, and a run of automated tests. The maturity of your specific implementation may vary, and it is *OK* if it initially lacks some of the more advanced features such as static code analysis. Let's take a moment to look at an example of the first segment of a build pipeline so we can begin to understand the flow of automation, and integration initiatives and flow. *Figure 7-4* illustrates this in better detail:

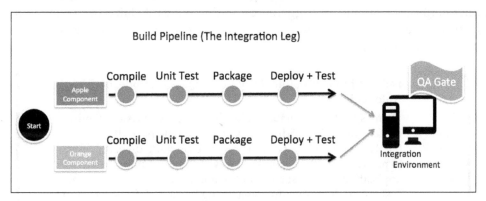

Figure 7-4: First segment of Build Pipeline

In the example provided above, we have illustrated two basic software components that will inevitably interact with each other. As such they each have their own build pipeline which feed into an integration environment. From the two distinct components (apples and oranges) provided in the preceding illustration, we can see clearly that the apple and orange components each flow through their own build processes and subsequently flow into an **Integration Environment**. The Integration Environment is designed to provide a unified pre-production integration environment where the interaction and compatibility of the components can be tested. After the components have been deployed and tested (hopefully via automated testing apparatuses), they are presented with a quality gate.

This initial integration build pipeline segment gives development personnel a chance to review the quality and interaction between the connected components prior to delivering them to quality assurance. Through the implementation of the **Integration Environment**, the development organization can gain insight into the interaction of individual components with the other components installed on the system. By setting up an automated deployment into the integration environment, which closely mirrors production, we can assist development in catching the integration defects, encourage the implementation of better architecture, and avoid exposing bad build artifacts to quality assurance personnel.

To facilitate the quick recovery of any defects identified, the implementation of a build pipeline notification (feedback loop) solution should be implemented after each logical pipeline segment completes. For example after the completion (or failure) of build and unit test procedures, a notification should be triggered to the respective stakeholders. After deployment or testing of the integration environment completes another notification should be triggered providing relevant status of the deployment and pass/fail rate related quality metrics. This practice should continue logically as the pipeline segments progress.

Failures in the pipeline (DEV Code, QA Test Code, or Automation code)

If any specific automation fails, the best practice is to identify the failure, and to address it as an immediate need. It is OK to fail. Failing simply means the pipeline catching defects prior to production. The key is to simply continue to improve the application code, test code, automation code, and notification systems with the eventual goal being to catch defects earlier in the SDLC through automation.

The first segment of the build pipeline will most definitely gain the most foot traffic. As the development, QA, DevOps, and related teams commit the code into the same source control repository mainline, the resulting commits should trigger the execution of the pipeline in Jenkins. Each pipeline segment in Jenkins should include a complete build, deployment, and testing solution. The more frequent the commits, the higher the level of collaboration, and the more intelligent the software architecture will become.

Now that we understand the architecture of the first leg of a build pipeline, we will most definitely want to create additional legs. Logically, each additional leg will position itself to the right of the previous leg. Implementing additional legs in a build pipeline can be accomplished in a fashion similar to the first but with a truncated set of steps. In the next section, we will discover how to implement additional pipeline segments.

Additional pipeline segments

The creation of additional segments is accomplished in a fashion similar to the first minus the build and the unit test portions. Each additional pipeline segment will by nature have an expanded audience and involve additional resources in the delivery process. When adding additional segments to a build pipeline each subsequent segment should have a defined purpose and value proposition. Additional segments of a build pipeline should either aim to expand the user validation scope or provide scalability testing facilities. To better define how to architect additional pipeline segments *Figure 7-5a* describes the basic flow:

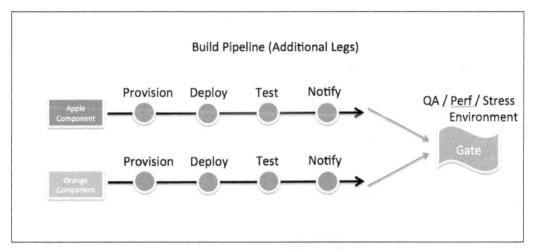

Figure 7-5a: Basic flow of the pipeline

Subsequently, after each leg is executed, additional segments of the pipeline will logically connect to the right of the previous segment. This type of implementation requires a set of common automations that can be leveraged across the various segments without too much customization (except in the areas of testing and deployment location). To clarify this a bit, the following diagram illustrates the 50,00 foot overview of a build pipeline:

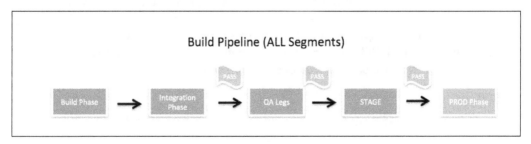

Figure 7-5b: High-level view of a Build pipeline

From the preceding diagram, we can see that the build passes through **Build Phase**, **Integration Phase**, **QA Legs**, **Stage**, and into **Production**.

 When implementing a set of standardized environments, it is considered a best practice to also create a *staging* environment. The staging environment should mimic production completely, and should be kept off-limits by the engineering personnel. The staging environment will represent the last chance to catch deployment automation failures or inconsistencies, and therefore should remain sterile.

Each additional pipeline section that is created should automate, at a minimum, the following:

- Automated continuous AND/OR push button deployments to the environment (any version)

- Automated testing of the environment after the deployment has been completed with an initial set of smoke tests to verify the basic operational status as a precursor

- A complete notification solution (feedback loops) to facilitate the communication of failures and successes to the proper stakeholders of the pipeline segment.

The complete pipeline

The goal of a build pipeline is to allow builds to flow through it continuously in a similar manner to water flowing through a plumbing system; fluid and always available. The end destination is the deployment and/or release of changes contained in the builds into production. Production is an obvious term for web based software, but how about shrink-wrapped solutions or embedded products? These too can be released into production. For software organizations that provide shrink wrapped solutions, or embedded technologies this final destination would represent simply the availability of a releasable package to the business, which could then be selectively released (say to a CDN) when business interests choose to do so. Regardless of weather or not the software project is deployed onto a multi-server cloud installation or released to an embedded manufacturing company, build pipelines provide a set of processes for, automated delivery and validation.

When a software project is shipped the final steps taken that provide general availability of the software represent the beginning of return on investment, in engineering costs. If the software project has numerous defects, regressions, or lacks quality the ROI, and potential profitability of the business will be damaged. By implementing a build pipeline we can facilitate faster process flows, more efficient development patterns, higher quality releases, and scalable automation. The more agility the organization has to outmaneuver the competition in strategic business goals the more likelihood there will be for a profitable business.

Visualizing the final pipeline

Now that we have a better understanding of the architecture of the pre-production automation and how to architect the individual legs let's take a look at a completed build pipeline. The deployment to production of a software project should be architected and implemented in the same fashion as the pre-production deployments, complete with automated (non-destructive) smoke, and functional tests, and validations.

The final leg of the pipeline implementation and definition of our production rollout solution should simply be a logical progression and replica of what was already performed within the pre-production environments.

To illustrate basic deployment workflow let's take a look at an example of a complete build pipeline from beginning to end. *Figure 7-6* illustrates an example of an integrated component based pipeline, which might be logically expanded or contracted based on architecture, technology stack, or development process:

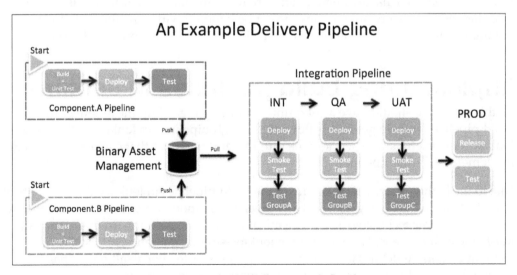

Figure 7-6: Production rollout example flowchart

Alterations for shrink-wrapped and embedded projects

For embedded and shrink-wrapped software projects, obviously a deployment onto a cloud or server infrastructure is not going to be the natural course of action. Instead, the software is released into a business holding area (CDN/DML), or provided to a manufacturer for mass production. Build pipelines continue to have much value in this type of a development ecosphere. Build pipelines allow the business to have an always-releasable build, and not have to depend on engineering for viable release candidates. *Figure 7-7*, depicts a general overview of this type of release activity:

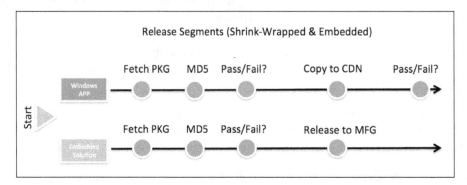

Figure 7-7: Embedded and shrink-wrapped software releases

The process for embedded and shrink-wrapped software will probably be unique to your own specific hardware and software implementation requirements. Having said that, pending software releases should be handled with care and tested via automation just prior to being placed on a CDN or in a DML storage solution.

Implementing build pipelines in Jenkins

At this point, we should have a solid understanding regarding the architecture of a build pipeline. To help get builds flowing through pipelines in Jenkins, let's take a look at some useful strategies, Jenkins plugins, and practices that can assist us when implementing build pipelines.

Due to the highly customizable nature of the build pipelines in Jenkins, there are lots of ways to achieve the same goal. Most low-level automation implementations are highly dependent on the technology stack, organization, and the platform. In this section of *Mastering Jenkins*, we will aim to provide Jenkins-specific guidance, applicable tips, techniques, and guidelines to leverage some plugins instead of an all-encompassing guide which would most certainly miss the mark for many readers.

The following sections are organized by topic and may not be suitable for all implementations of a build pipeline. Although we've tried to select the most applicable solutions, relevant plugins, and valuable techniques, you can take note of the important sections and discard the ones that are of little value to your specific implementation or solution.

Upstream jobs – triggered

The most widely-utilized mechanism for triggering downstream jobs (jobs which execute after the a specified job has completed) is to leverage the default feature provided by Jenkins—the triggering of a job contingent on another job. This solution will allow Jenkins to can automatically trigger a job based on another job's status and execution criteria. This is conveniently available in the detailed job configuration, under the **Build Triggers** section. *Figure 7-8* shows an example of triggering a downstream job based on the completion of another dependent job:

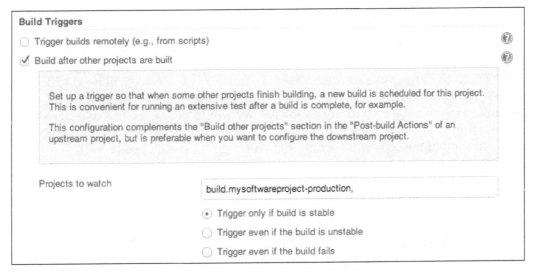

Figure 7-8: Creating a build trigger based on an upstream job

An additional option that this solution provides is the ability to skip triggering based on build stability. The radio buttons shown in the preceding screenshot provide a simple way to skip triggering if the targeted build job does not meet stability requirements.

Once the configuration has been saved, the downstream job will automatically identify the upstream job that it is dependent on, and listen for trigger events. Additionally, the linking of the jobs will now be visible via the job overview page as illustrated in the following screenshot:

Figure 7-9: Linking of jobs

Downstream jobs – via post build actions

The Jenkins system, by default, also provides a linking solution in the post-build phase, of a job's execution. This downstream job solution allows us to trigger another job *AFTER* the current one has completed. To implement this, we will need to define a post-build action in the detailed job configuration page of the current job. For example, if we want job *foo* to trigger job *bar*, we would define the link as a post-build action within the detailed job configuration page for job *foo*. *Figure 7-10* illustrates the configuration of the post-build action that will trigger the bar.project.

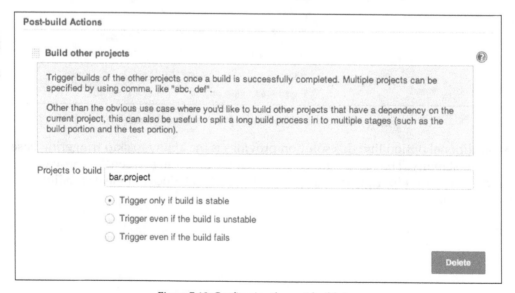

Figure 7-10: Configuring the post-build step

Once the configuration has been saved, Jenkins will begin triggering the downstream job immediately after each execution based on the criteria specified in the post build action.

In a similar manner as upstream jobs, the Jenkins job, which contains a post-build action step to trigger a down-stream job, will provide links to the downstream jobs directly in the job overview page. This is illustrated in *Figure 7-11*.

Downstream Projects

● Sample Maven Project ▾

Permalinks

- Last build (#7), 8.7 sec ago
- Last stable build (#7), 8.7 sec ago
- Last successful build (#7), 8.7 sec ago
- Last failed build (#3), 7 days 23 hr ago
- Last unsuccessful build (#3), 7 days 23 hr ago

Figure 7-11: The Jenkins job providing direct links to downstream jobs

When implementing upstream and downstream jobs, the possibilities are endless. Just make sure to keep the system organized and well-defined to prevent the tangling of dependent jobs.

The Parameterized Trigger plugin

Arguably one of the most valuable plugins that Jenkins offers is the parameterized trigger plugin. This plugin provides a scalable approach for triggering other Jenkins jobs, and passing variable-based parameters to them. This becomes even more useful when we pass the details surrounding the build or deployment packages or the version information to targeted downstream jobs. The home page for this plugin can be found at the following link:

```
https://wiki.jenkins-ci.org/display/JENKINS/
Parameterized+Trigger+Plugin
```

Once this plugin has been installed onto a Jenkins system, it will be accessible via the following detailed job configuration options:

- As a build step in a Jenkins project
- As a post-build action
- As a promotion step via the Promoted Build plugin

The parameterized triggers plugin provides the ability to initiate downstream jobs, pass parameters (in multiple formats), and hinge the success of the calling Jenkins job based on the result of the triggered job. This may sound more complicated than it really is. Let's take a quick look at an example. *Figure 7-12* illustrates a basic configuration of a downstream triggered project:

Figure 7-12: Trigger parameterized job configuration

The configuration options seen in the preceding screenshot showcase only the most basic capabilities of the plugin. One of the more robust features of the parameterized triggers plugin is the ability to pass parameters via the Oracle Java properties files from one job to another.

A Java properties file is simply a basic text file containing equals-delimited variables. Below is an example of a very basic Java properties file:

```
APPNAME=myproject
VERSION=1.0.0.0
DEPLOYSCRIPT=deploy.yml
```

A handy use for a Java properties file is to archive build-related metadata. For example, you may wish to define artifact URLs or the version information in the `build.properties` file and then pass that information from one Jenkins job to another. Leveraging this plugin in conjunction with a properties file creates a robust way of passing variable data from one job to another.

When leveraging a properties file, the downstream job will receive these data points as environment variables that can be automated against. This provides a nice way of aggregating the metadata from one job and passing it to another.

The Promoted build plugin

The Promoted build plugin is also arguably one of the most valuable plugins within the Jenkins plugin ecosystem. Build promotions represent an easy way for the stakeholders to bless a specific build as viable for further testing or release. This process is one of the core aspects of a build pipeline (quality gate). By promoting builds through a build pipeline, continuous delivery practices can be coupled with manual verification processes in an aim to eventually remove the gates and facilitate true continuous delivery.

Builds could flow from one logical group within engineering to another, and dedicated assignees would be assigned the rights to promote builds. This allows for an engineering team to visually inspect a build and act as a verification gate before allowing it to flow to the next logical build pipeline segment. The workflow of a promotion process via the promoted builds plugin might look something like what is described in *Figure 7-13* below:

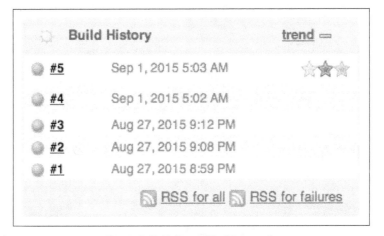

Figure 7-13: Promoted build example

Notice that, in the case of our screenshot, the promoted builds plugin, which is illustrated via the graphical stars in the build history, looks nothing like the build pipeline architecture that we discussed earlier in the chapter. When we drill into a specific Promoted build, we are presented with the relevant detailed information surrounding the promotion. To access the details surrounding the promotion, the **Promoted builds** link should be available to the left of any build IDs that have been promoted. This navigation option is illustrated in *Figure 7-14*.

Figure 7-14: The navigation option

As we drill into a given build, we can expose the additional information surrounding the promotion. *Figure 7-15* illustrates a Promoted build, #234, that has passed the development phase of the build pipeline and is awaiting QA verification:

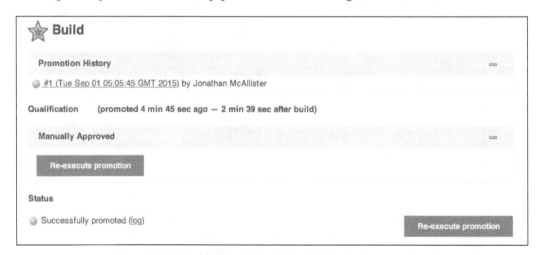

Figure 7-15: A Promoted build that has passed the development phase

Each promotion step provides the option for a colored star that can be used to notate the success of the promotion process in the build history. In reality, the promoted build plugin simply acts as a wrapper for software process and automation and provides a way to gate the execution of the automation on properly authenticated button clicks.

Configuring build promotions in Jenkins via the Promoted build plugin is actually quite easy. The promotion processes are described in the detailed job configuration page, where any number of promotions and sub steps can be defined. Let's take a look at an example configuration:

Figure 7-16: Example of Promotion Pipeline Segment configuration

The preceding example describes a basic promotion (quality gate approval) implementation that triggers a downstream job `deploy.mysoftwareapp.int` as part of the promotion process. In this example configuration, we hinge the execution of the **Promotion Process** on a manual approval step.

Additional segments in the build pipeline can be set up as promotion steps each with required dependencies on the previous promotions defined in the job configuration. This allows us to define a specific ordering of our downstream jobs, and will tell Jenkins to prevent a promotion step from taking place if the pre-requisite promotion steps have not been executed and completed successfully.

To implement this functionality, simply mark the checkbox and specify a definition for the required upstream promotion steps to define the behavior. The following screenshot illustrates an example of the approval configuration and the required upstream promotions as part of the workflow:

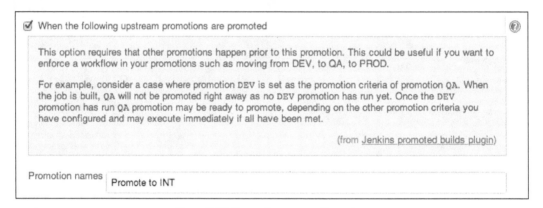

Figure 7-17: Promotion step configuration

The Post-Build Tasks plugin

When implementing feedback loops (automated notification systems to communicate status), often it may be logical to execute a script or to send an e-mail based on the status of a downstream job. In this case, using a post-build action in Jenkins may be a logical solution. But how do we communicate a failed-status e-mail or a successful one? The solution for this lies in the Post-Build Tasks plugin. To implement post-build tasks in Jenkins, we will need to ensure that we have the Post-Build Task plugin installed. This handy plugin can trigger conditional script operations, based on text or a regular expression, matching the job's status in the console log. If you don't have the plugin installed on your Jenkins system, you can procure it at the following URL:

```
https://wiki.jenkins-ci.org/display/JENKINS/Post+build+task
```

Once installed, we can create post-build operational tasks as shown in the following screenshot:

Figure 7-18: Post-build operational tasks

The log regex matching provided by the post build task plugin provides the ability to match regular expressions as well as raw text from the console log. This feature allows us to set up any number of automation sequences or notifications (hint*) based on the downstream job or automation outputs.

The Delivery Pipeline plugin

The *Delivery Pipeline* plugin in Jenkins provides a high-level, real-time overview status of a build pipeline. The plugin includes complete linking information surrounding the upstream and downstream jobs as well as live execution indicators, and more. Historically, in Jenkins the only plugin to provide such details was the build pipeline plugin; however, the improved functionality of the Delivery Pipeline plugin makes this a solution worth looking into when developing build pipelines in Jenkins. The Delivery Pipeline plugin documentation can be found at the following URL:

```
https://wiki.jenkins-ci.org/display/JENKINS/Delivery+Pipeline+Plugin
```

To begin using the delivery pipeline plugin, we will first need to install it from the Jenkins administration UI (plugin manager). Once a build pipeline has been created, we can better visualize it by creating a new **Delivery Pipeline View**. To implement this, we will start by creating a new view in Jenkins and selecting **Delivery Pipeline View** from the available radio selections as shown in *Figure 7-19*.

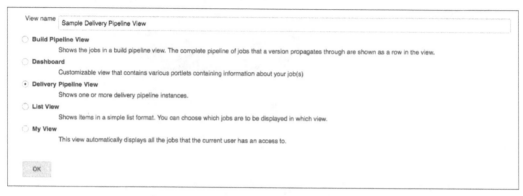

Figure 7-19: Creating the Delivery Pipeline View

Upon creating the pipeline view, we are presented with a number of configuration options. Let's take a look at some of the key options and learn what they do.

The first thing we will need to specify when configuring the **Delivery Pipeline View** is the starting point. This is accomplished by selecting the job name from the initial job dropdown. Once that item has been selected, there may be some additional items you might wish to configure. A complete overview of the configuration options available (including the initial job option) is described in the *Figure 7-20*.

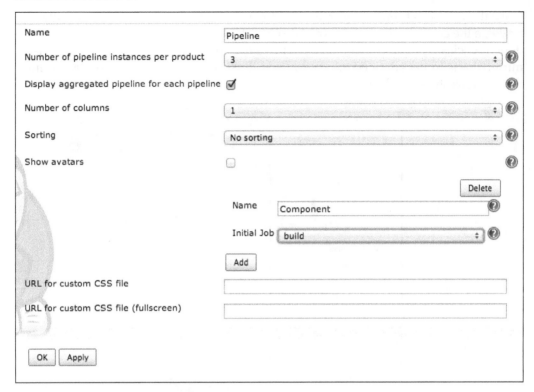

Figure 7-20: Delivery Pipeline configuration

Another useful feature is the **URL for custom CSS file** option. This allows us to customize the look and feel of a pipeline view to fit with any color themes we may wish to support.

The **Enable start of new pipeline build** toggle provides a **Build Now** button directly in the view for the pipeline. This allows direct execution of the pipeline and the sub-automation jobs at the click of a button.

The **Display aggregated pipeline for each pipeline** toggle is a beneficial combined aggregated view of the currently attached downstream jobs in the pipeline. This provides us with the ability to see the most recent executions of these jobs and their associated build numbers.

Once the view has been configured to preference and saved, it will automatically traverse the configuration of the **Initial Job** and identify its downstream dependencies. The plugin will perform this sync operation on a scheduled once-a-minute basis (unless defined otherwise) and illustrate the job and live status within the view, as shown in *Figure 7-21*.

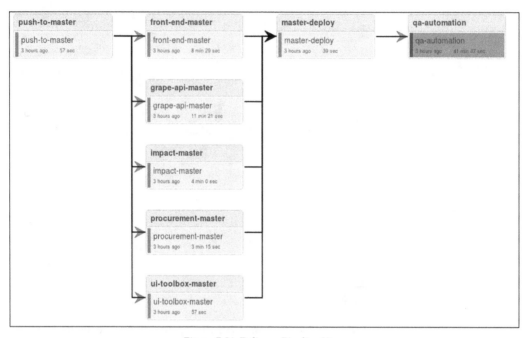

Figure 7-21: Delivery Pipeline View

Once configured, this plugin provides a bird's-eye view of a delivery pipeline for a given software project. Let's spend a few minutes learning how to create a delivery pipeline using this plugin.

The Continuous Delivery plugin in Jenkins allows us to create *views* that will connect build pipeline segments and display them in visual form. After the plugin has been installed and a build pipeline view has been created, we will need to configure two defining characteristics that describe our build pipeline. The two configuration characteristics we will need to input, will identify the beginning and end segments respectively. From the view configuration page (associated with the delivery pipeline) we will need to add a component and configure these two endpoints. *Figure 7-22* shows the basic implementation of a delivery pipeline view, including the name, initial job, and final job.

Figure 7-22: Basic implementation of the pipeline

After the initial configuration has been completed, the plugin will traverse the downstream job dependencies (jobs which are linked together) and automatically create a basic pipeline view. From here, we will want to specify our pipeline segments by name. In each of the identified downstream jobs, there will now be an option to specify a stage and task name, which will define and organize the segments of the build pipeline. To keep the pipeline segments organized it may be wise to categorize jobs by segment name. For example CI, INT, QA, and so on. *Figure 7-23* illustrates the additional options available within the downstream jobs:

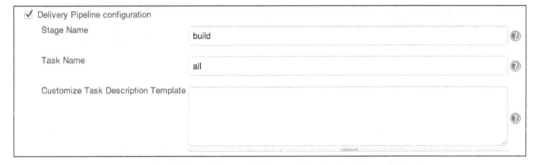

Figure 7-23: The additional options within the downstream jobs

This plugin has a number of handy visualization features that can make the implementation of build pipelines considerably more user-friendly. For additional details surrounding this plugin, consult the *Jenkins-ci.org* plugin wiki page.

Connecting two Jenkins instances – development and production

In some situations, it may be a wise idea to spin up a production Jenkins instance to facilitate production deployments. This will help restrict access to production, and can help segregate production deployments from the earlier segments of the pipeline. Deployments that flow into the production Jenkins instance would be triggered by the development Jenkins instance, remain generally isolated from the engineering personnel, and provide proper connectivity to production from a DMZ firewall area. *Figure 7-24* illustrates an example of such an architecture:

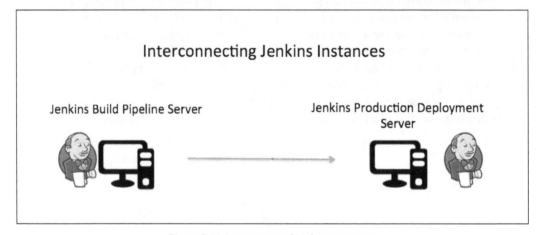

Figure 7-24: Interconnected Jenkins instances

To facilitate automated deployments to a production environment, the production instance of Jenkins will need to have proper connectivity to the production servers and should be configured to use matrix-based authentication be pre-configured with a service account that has access to the appropriate jobs.

To assist in triggering remote Jenkins jobs, there are a couple of methodologies that we can employ. The first is a Jenkins plugin that is aptly titled *Call remote job* and can be found at the following URL:

```
https://wiki.jenkins-ci.org/display/JENKINS/Call+Remote+Job+Plugin
```

This plugin provides a simple build action to **Call remote jenkins job** and facilitates the input of the relevant Jenkins host, job name, and parameters via the configuration UI as shown in *Figure 7-25*.

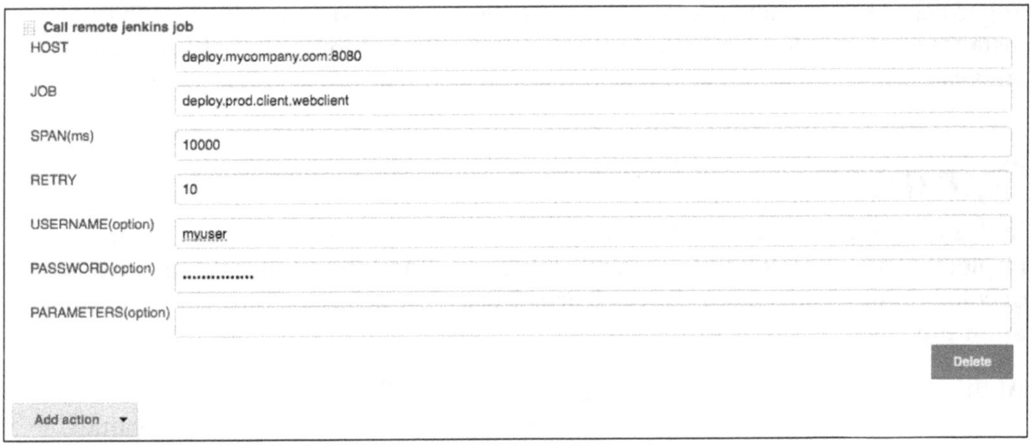

Figure 7-25: Call remote Jenkins job configuration UI

The second option is to use the Jenkins **CLI** (**Command Line Interface**) from a script. Below is an example in Ruby that illustrates how to trigger a remote Jenkins job using the Jenkins CLI (converting this to a language of your choice should be a fairly simple task):

```
# -----------------------------------------------------------
# FUNC: jenkins_triggerRemoteJenkinsJob(sJenkinsURL, sJobName,
sParameters)
# DESC: triggers a remote jenkins job using jenkins cli
# ----------------------------------------------
def jenkins_triggerRemoteJob(sURL, sJobName, sParameters)



puts "Downloading jenkins cli"
  `cd #{ENV['WORKSPACE']} && rm jenkins-cli* && wget http://build.
lifesize.com/jnlpJars/jenkins-cli.jar`

  puts "Executing remote Jenkins Job: #{sJobName}"
  `cd #{ENV['WORKSPACE']} && java -jar 'jenkins-cli.jar' -s #{sURL}
build \"#{sJobName}\" -s --username foouser --password foouser123 -p
VERSION=1.0.0.0 -s
echo The exit code is %errorlevel%`

end
```

The preceding code can be saved in a .rb file and then called inside a shell script or via the Ruby plugin, which allows Jenkins to run Ruby code. It could also be converted, fairly easily, to a programming language of your preference.

Regardless of the option selected, dividing the production-accessible Jenkins instance from development and build systems is a good idea when the resources are available.

Summary

In this chapter, we discovered techniques that we can leverage to architect and implement automated build pipelines. Build pipelines represent the culmination of collaboration and standards. We learned ways to encourage business buy-in for build pipelines, and how to architect and implement build pipelines in Jenkins.

At this point we should now have a good understanding of the concepts surrounding the creation of build-pipelines, automated delivery, and the value proposition of the implementation. During the course of the chapter, we encouraged the development of a mindset favoring an increased release velocity through build pipelines and standardized conventions. The change in mindset will improve quality by reducing the time to market and risk. Continuing to automate your path towards automated validation and delivery will undoubtedly not go unnoticed. The reward lies in the journey.

In the next chapter, we will dive into the underlying principles and practices of continuous integration, continuous improvement processes, continuous delivery, and the cadillac of continuous practices—continuous deployment.

8
Continuous Practices

Hewlett Packard, The Chrysler Corporation, and the United States Department of Defense independently conducted research and analytical studies on continuous practices [including Kaizen (Continuous Improvement), Continuous Integration, Continuous Delivery, and Continuous Deployment]. The results of this research generated a wealth of evidence that substantiate the benefits of low-risk, high-frequency incremental software integrations, which is in stark comparison to isolated engineering paradigms. The most notable benefits include: improved business operational efficiency, reduced risk, a notable decrease in integration defects, and an increase in stability.

Some of the most prominent organizations to adopt and benefit from continuous practices include Etsy, Netflix, Facebook, Amazon, Google, and Flickr. Despite all the accolades surrounding continuous practices, practical implementation strategies using Jenkins, specifically, are a bit sparse. This chapter aims to resolve that scarcity and provides concrete implementation foundations that can be applied at organizations of any size.

> Two monks were arguing about a flag. One said: "The flag is moving"; the other said: "The wind is moving". The sixth patriarch happened to be passing by. He told them: "Not the wind, not the flag; It's the mind that moves." – A Chinese Proverb

In this chapter of *Mastering Jenkins*, we will discover all things continuous. We begin with Kaizen (Continuous Improvement), which can assist in identifying and eliminating inefficient process, unknown standards , and confusing development patterns. From there we will discover Continuous Integration, Continuous Delivery, and Continuous Deployment practices. Together we will learn how to architect and implement strategies for each of these evolutionary software build and delivery approaches. Through our learning, we will identify some tricks and tips in Jenkins that we can leverage to build a complete continuous system, complete with rapid feedback loops, scaled automated no-downtime deployments, and automated test execution.

Together we will learn the components required to deliver software more efficiently by leveraging modern continuous practices. By the end of this chapter, you will have a solid gasp of the steps needed for streamlining engineering efforts and reducing wasted man-hours by increasing efficiency through rapid iterations, and continuous practices. The following topics will be covered in this chapter:

- Kaizen (Continuous Improvement)
- Continuous Integration
- Continuous Delivery
- Continuous Deployment

The aim of this chapter is to provide a foundation level understanding of the necessary culture, processes and mindset advances needed to effectively drive and implement true Continuous Integration, Continuous Delivery, and Continuous Deployment at scale.

 It is important to note that Continuous Integration and subsequent practices are not for everyone. No one specific practice can pretend to represent a universal solution that will be applicable to all business models. The main objective here is to describe these solutions and the value they can provide an organization.

Let's begin our journey into continuous practices by starting with the Kaizen culture. It will be through a Kaizen culture initiative that the other continuous practices will become possible.

Kaizen – Continuous Improvement

In the 1950's, Toyota Motor Corporation began a company-wide endeavor to develop and deliver automotive solutions that could compete against the well-entrenched American auto manufacturers of that era. Upon embarking on this journey, Toyota (the only Japanese auto manufacturer) lacked the manufacturing efficiency required to adequately expand its business to a global audience. To address these deficiencies, Toyota innovated Kaizen culture, and implemented Continuous Improvement initiatives across the organization. This began Toyota's long journey to improve quality and assembly-line throughput at its production plants. These initiatives would eventually vault Toyota into global success.

"Kaizen is the belief that many small changes over time create huge changes in the future." -- Toyota.com

The word Kaizen can be directly translated as, *to change for the better*. Kai is most commonly translated into English as *change*, and Zen translates as *good*. The English translation of this phrase was eventually varied to become *Continuous Improvement*, and the two terms became synonymous. After Kaizen was implemented successfully at Toyota, it grew in recognition. The term was later introduced to a more global audience in the 1980's by Masaaki Imai (the primary thought leader of the Kaizen movement) in his published book *The Key to Japan's Competitive Success* — ISBN-13: 978-0075543329 . Since its initial inception and recognition at Toyota, Kaizen has become a guiding principle not only for manufacturing processes, but also for personal improvement philosophies and engineering development efforts worldwide.

Through the adoption of Continuous Improvement initiatives, Toyota managed to pivot its business model and adapt to an increasingly competitive marketplace. This ushered Toyota into a new era of operational efficiency that reduced manufacturing costs and improved quality. These process improvements eventually guided Toyota into significant financial profit margins over their direct American competitors during one of the most tumultuous times in modern financial history. In March, 2007, just prior to the financial banking disasters, Toyota reported a company-wide profit of *$13.7 billion*, whereas GM and Ford reported combined financial losses of *-$1.97 billion*.

At the time of writing of this book, Continuous Improvement is still touted on Toyota's website as a fundamental culture initiative. Toyota continues to recognize Kaizen as its chosen path to quality and innovation in manufacturing for the foreseeable future.

"Kaizen is the heart of the Toyota Production System. Like all mass-production systems, the Toyota process requires that all tasks, both human and mechanical, be very precisely defined and standardized to ensure maximum quality, eliminate waste and improve efficiency." – Toyota.com

Now that we have some background history of the Continuous Improvement movement, and the successes of Toyota, let's take a minute to cover some high-level concepts of Continuous Improvement. These will help us gain a foundational understanding of this practice. Continuous Improvement is aimed at being an organization-wide culture initiative. It simply encourages employees to identify and address inefficiencies and process pain points. A Kaizen culture is built on six guiding principles. Let's take a look at these in greater detail. The following image shows a Continuous Improvement wheel, which illustrates the guiding principles that will help increase efficiency:

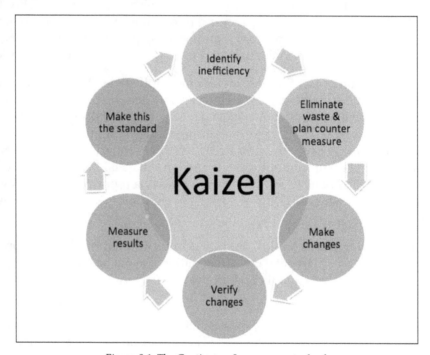

Figure 8-1: The Continuous Improvement wheel

When the Continuous Improvement wheel is put in motion, the culture of the organization will inherently go through a transformation. Continuous Improvement provides the personnel with an empowering responsibility to identify process bottlenecks, propose changes, validate the process changes through hypothesis testing, and effect a tangible change.

Continuous Improvement facilitates a sustained grassroots-based shift in the internal culture, aimed at improving quality and efficiency. It is important to note that Kaizen, by nature, is not intended for the transformation of an incoherent software engineering process overnight. Instead, it simply codifies an initiative to incrementally improve the culture and support a efficiency oriented software development paradigm, with greater emphasis on cross-functional collaboration.

When implementing Kaizen, there are a few key principles that can help guide the initiative. These principles are illustrated in *Figure 8-2*:

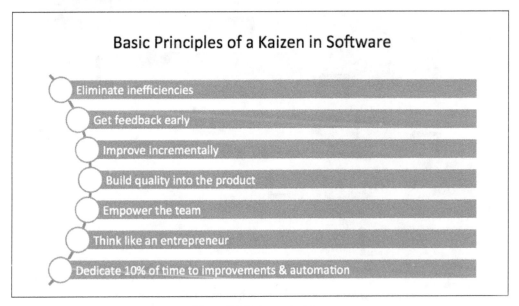

Figure 8-2: Kaizen principles

The tactics illustrated in the preeceding figure aim to identify process inefficiencies and improve them. This will help encourage the development of a business case for automation and standards. This can be manifested in Jenkins by creating increasingly efficient build pipeline solutions. Through a shift in mindset and a fundamental transformation of traditionally isolated software engineering silos, an organization can explicitly drive automation initiatives, determine the viability of a product through experiments (to ensure that engineering resources are not wasted), ensure the product is always releasable through feedback loops, and pivot the business trajectory through analytics.

To begin, we will need to identify existing processes, and analyze the efficiency of each. *Figure 8-3* (A CMMI Diagram) illustrates a basic approach to identifying and maturing an organization's development, quality, and delivery processes:

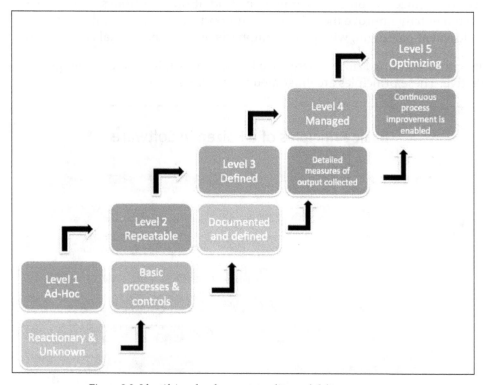

Figure 8-3: Identifying development, quality, and delivery processes

Kanban

Implementing continuous improvement will inevitably touch upon a number of software development methodologies. It would be wise to begin with an agile approach to software development in an effort to introduce the basic development processes and release cadences. Once a consistent cadence has been achieved and the organization's efficiency has improved somewhat, continuous practices will, in practice, transcend waterfall and agile. To support a completely continuous system, we can again look to Toyota's leadership for guidance.

Kanban provides a practical engineering solution for managing an influx of requests and requirements and streamlines development efforts and output to customers. Kanban logically fits into a Continuous Improvement initiative, and supports all levels of continuous practices. In a Kanban approach to software development, work items are identified and prioritized via a defined engineering queue. One by one, the individual work items (cards) are selected for implementation, and they subsequently flow through pre-defined implementation phases and moving closer and closer to released. After completing the release of a work item (card), the work item would be marked as completed.

A Kanban strategy allows for the backlog to be continually updated and populated with new issues or technical debt work items. It allows for proper prioritization of each item and alleviates the need for heavy-handed story points or rushed implementations which can inhibit quality.

Continuous Integration

Continuous Integration (**CI**) as an engineering practice has its roots back to the 1980's and now antiquated CVS glory days. Widespread adoption of Continuous Integration practices didnt really occur until after the introduction of **Extreme Programming** (**XP**) in the year 2000. XP identified Continuous Integration in its doctrine and continues to be evangelized through the tireless work of Kent Beck, Martin Fowler, and Don Wells.

The XP approach to CI specifically advocated for trunk-based development (or very short-lived feature branches), coupled with frequent integrations into a shared mainline (daily), automatically triggered builds, unit testing, and rapid feedback loops. Since its inception, there have been many debates and heated discussions by technologists surrounding best practices, implementation strategies, and branching patterns. ThoughtWorks best describes Continuous Integration on its website via the following definition:

Continuous Integration (**CI**) is a development practice that requires developers to integrate code into a shared repository several times a day. Each check-in is then verified by an automated build, allowing teams to detect problems early.

By implementing Continuous Integration, engineering organizations are striving to improve software quality, reduce merge conflicts, and alleviate integration defects. Integrating code changes frequently, by utilizing the source control mainline to communicate software development changes, can help in increasing communication and identify integration defects earlier in the software development lifecycle.

Prior to the widespread adoption of source control solutions, automated testing, and Continuous Integration, software organizations would often face complex and painful integration phases just prior to release. These integration phases were exacerbated when business units pressured engineering for monetary returns on investment, and software integration efforts hindered the ROI. During this era, the software integration phases were long and arduous due to a lack of coordinated development efforts, isolated engineering development patterns, and conflicting or overlapping code.

During this era the integration phase of the software development lifecycle posed the most risk. It often resulted in delayed or failed software launches. The resulting integration hell cost companies millions of dollars in wasted man-hours, and often put the livelihood of the organization at risk. Continuous Integration and modern source control systems were developed to solve these issues by providing a centralized integration solution, coupled with defined integration processes and communication apparatuses for development engineers.

Continuous Integration stands in stark contrast to the widely-adopted practice of feature branch development and obligatory merge techniques (often occurring just prior to release). By integrating code changes frequently with other developers, and standardizing on a mainline development paradigm, software development organizations were able to effectively alleviate most integration risks. This simple, yet highly effective, strategy also provides predefined input point from which a software project can be built and released.

What Continuous Integration is not

Over the years, Continuous Integration has been misidentified as the implementation of build tools such as Jenkins, **TeamCity**, or **CruiseControl**, connected via automated polling and build execution. This reflects an incomplete representation of CI practices. Jenkins and other similar solutions do offer automated build features including the ability to execute a build based on a detected change to the software source tree. However, these implementations fall short in describing Continuous Integration. The capability of a build system to automatically build based on detected code changes is a key component of Continuous Integration; however, this is Continuous Integration its simply an automated build apparatus. Continuous integration has larger implications.

Software build such as Jenkins were designed to aid in the practice of Continuous Integration, and do not represent Continuous Integration itself. To be more explicit, Continuous Integration is not the implementation of a specific tool or automation solution. Instead, CI represents the act of *Continuously Integrating* code changes across team members in an effort to avoid last-minute, wide-scale merge conflicts and feature defects due to a lack of communication. *Figure 8-4* illustrates a standard mainline development pattern, that is based on continuous integration:

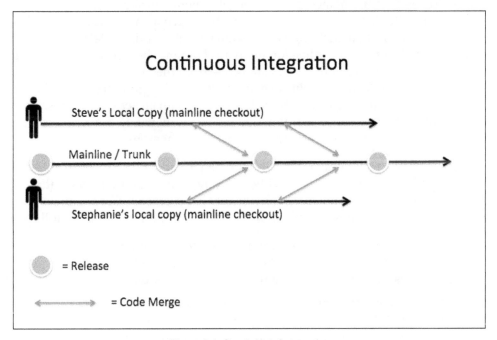

Figure 8-4: Continuous Integration

Thought leaders including Martin Fowler, Jez Humble, and James Shore, have expanded this practice, and helped reshape engineering at many organizations worldwide. While the benefits of CI are quantifiable, the implementation has remained elusive. Let's consider the following quote from the founder of Continuous Delivery, Jez Humble:

> *"Continuous Integration is NOT running Jenkins on your feature branches. Continuous Integration is a practice where every developer integrates their changes to the mainline at least once a day"* – *Jez Humble*

This sounds easy enough, but actually, it is arguably the most challenging aspect of Continuous Integration. Committing to a central mainline development pattern in ALL cases requires a very high level of collaboration, step-by-step planning, and communication. These characteristics represent the key differences between a simple coder and an engineer. The social and communication requirements of Continuous Integration are often difficult for the traditionally introverted developer, as it exposes the code in its early stages. The CI anti-pattern is that it's easier and safer to create code in an isolated feature branch until the development efforts have been completed. The main issue with this culture is in the procrastination of communication and the divergence of the feature branch from other source lines over time. Delaying the integration of code into the mainline for any period of time (by an order of magnitude) compounds the divergence of the segregated code from the mainline and ALL other feature branches. This technical debt created by delaying integration efforts will continue to increase until the feature branch is synced with all active branches. The complexity of the merge will be compounded when additional developers create new feature branches, and the code drift across branches becomes greater.

Now that we have a better grasp of the branching practices required for Continuous Integration, let's take a moment to quickly cover the defining criteria of Continuous Integration, and identify some guiding points of CI. To practice Continuous Integration, the software development group must, at a minimum, do the following:

- Implement a trunk-based development model (or a highly disciplined, short-lived feature branch solution), where each developer commits (or merges) code into the mainline at least once per day
- Automate the detection of commits, and initiate a build for every commit detected
- Automate the execution and reporting of unit tests, which must run as part of the build process and aim to validate the code IO operability
- Create a rapid feedback loop system to notify and flag any potential defects detected by the build process
- Place urgency on addressing or reverting any violating code commits that break the build

Implementing true Continuous Integration in practice can be a difficult undertaking for any organization. Continuous Integration requires a fundamental shift in developer discipline, communication, and the adoption of good software practices. Continuous Integration encourages branching in code instead of branching in source control. By branching in code, long running features can continue to be developed and shared without the need to create extraneous source control based branches.

> **Branching and CI**
>
> Continuous Integration practices are not opposed to feature branches. The important requirement is that any branches that are created should be very short-lived and scoped appropriately. Any branches created must have frequent merges into the mainline and a short lifecycle. The anti-pattern of CI is to allow feature branches to grow uncontrollably into a divergent code base that is so far away from the mainline that it becomes risky to merge it back into the mainline.

To support Continuous Integration, there are a few well-vetted, guiding software architectural techniques that can be employed to assist in reducing the risk of integrating. We will discuss those next.

Code-based branching techniques

To apply Continuous Integration, we will need to learn some development practices that support this Continuous Integration. One such practice involves creating branches in code instead of in a source control repository. The most obvious form of code branching is a simple IF-THEN-ELSE statement. Conditional logic, by nature, allows us to alter the path of execution and ignore code blocks that do not meet a specified criteria. This solution represents one very basic example of branching in code.

Branching by abstraction and feature toggles are two additional software architectural techniques that can be employed to alleviate the need for source control based feature branches. These two architectural variants allow the development group to refactor components, prototype new efforts, and implement new functionality without creating additional development lines in the source control solution. In this section of *Mastering Jenkins*, we will learn some tips and techniques that can be leveraged to reduce risk and keep the mainline stable while providing support for under-construction development implementations.

Branch by abstraction

Branching by abstraction is an architectural technique designed to facilitate refactoring efforts and allow replacement parts to co-exist with living implementations without risk. This architecture allows incomplete efforts to continue without the need to create and manage a new branch in the source control system. This code-based branching solution involves creating an abstraction layer, which can be communicated through. When the development effort on the replacement component has been completed, the older version of the component would then be phased out and replaced with the new one. *Figure 8-5* illustrates a simple architectural diagram of a refactoring effort, managed through the branching by abstraction technique:

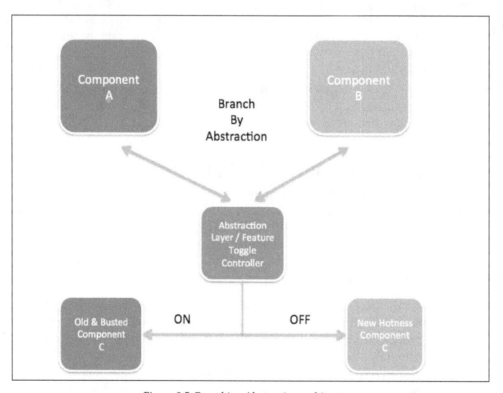

Figure 8-5: Branching Abstraction architecture

The practical implementation of this paradigm could be altered a bit and supported by implementing a component-based folder structure. The following example shows this altered refactoring effort in the simplest form:

```
OLD - /opt/myapplication/component/
NEW - /opt/myapplication/component.v2/
```

To swap the components, simply rename them or create a `symlink`. This solution could also be implemented by using a feature toggle configuration file that pivots the implementation through a switch.

Feature toggles

Feature toggles represent a source code branching technique which, enable or disable functionality based on a condition. By implementing feature toggles, we can hide incomplete development efforts by setting a configuration value or toggling a switch. This allows us to effectively decouple the availability or release of a software feature from the deployment of the software itself.

Most of us use feature toggles all the time, and we don't even realize it. Basic conditional logic lies at the heart of the feature toggle solution. Consider the following code example:

```
If (bToggle == true) {
    ...
} else {
    ...
}
```

This simple if/then conditional block is the most basic feature toggle. It simply identifies if a condition is met, and executes the containing code based on the state of the toggle. A more modern example of a feature toggle solution for an HTML/ Javascript web project might look like the following:

```
<script type="text/javascript">
<!--
    function toggle_feature(id)
    {
        var e = document.getElementById(id);
        if(e.style.display == 'block')
            e.style.display = 'none';
        else
            e.style.display = 'block';
    }
//-->
</script>

<a href="#" onclick="toggle_feature('PrototypeFeature');">Click here
to view the prototype effort</a>

<div id="PrototypeFeature">This feature is hidden from view until its
toggled on</div>
```

Feature toggle branching techniques are not limited to HTML and web-based development projects. Currently, there are a number of pre-fabricated feature toggle solutions available for a wide variety of platforms and development languages. Let's take a look some of the numerous feature toggle frameworks available that can help us jump-start a branching-in-code initiative:

- Feature toggles in Java:
    - ° Togglz: `http://www.togglz.org`
    - ° FF4J: `http://www.ff4j.org`
    - ° Fitchy: `https://code.google.com/p/fitchy/`

- Feature toggles in Python:
    - ° Gargoyle: `https://pypi.python.org/pypi/gargoyle`
    - ° Gutter: `https://github.com/disqus/gutter`

- Feature toggles in .NET, C#:
    - ° FeatureSwitcher: `https://github.com/mexx/FeatureSwitcher`
    - ° NFeature: `https://www.nuget.org/packages/NFeature/`
    - ° FlipIt: `https://github.com/timscott/flipit`
    - ° FeatureToggleNET: `https://github.com/jason-roberts/FeatureToggle`
    - ° FeatureBee: `http://www.nuget.org/packages/FeatureBee/`

- Feature toggles in Ruby and Ruby on Rails:
    - ° Rollout - `https://github.com/FetLife/rollout`
    - ° Feature_flipper - `https://github.com/jnunemaker/flipper`
    - ° Flip - `https://github.com/pda/flip`
    - ° Setler - `https://github.com/ckdake/setler`

- Feature Toggles in Embedded/C/C++ (Constructs) (coding techniques):
    - ° Ifdef
    - ° Make targets

Fail fast and recover even faster

Through failure and the experience that comes with it, the human race learns to adapt and evolve (or at least some of us do). What's important is not how many times we fail; it's how fast we manage to recover and learn from our failures. Failures in software systems are also a part of the industry. No software project can purport to be completely free of defects. While failure is inevitable, it does not have to be expensive. We can fail in a visible and catastrophic manner, or we can fail quietly with minimal customer impact. These ideas are the cornerstone of continuous practices. Our aim should be to identify the failures earlier (where possible), hide failures (where possible) from our customers, and continually improve.

Failures in software manifest themselves in a number of ways, including compilation errors, failures in viability or user acceptance, failures in processes, or failures in deployments. There are generally two viable options to consider when presented with a failure. Fix it, or roll it back.

Identifying failures earlier in the SDLC by continuously integrating, creating build pipelines for delivery, and limiting commit sizes can provide numerous benefits. These solutions all provide an apparatus that works to identify failures earlier in the software development lifecycle, thus saving us from failing in production. By adopting these practices, we gain significant strides in quality and efficiency. Some of the notable benefits include the following:

- Less time spent debugging and locating the defective code segments due to smaller commit sizes

- Increased levels of collaboration

- Quicker recovery times when outages do occur or failures are detected

Distributed Version Control

Distributed Version Control Systems (**DVCS**) such as Git and Mercurial have become very popular. These solutions provide a number of welcome features including lightweight branching, pull-requests for code-review, and distributed repositories. They are in stark contrast to the traditionally centralized source control solutions such as SVN or Perforce, as they allow each developer to maintain a uniquely independent copy of the entire source control repository on their local machine. Distributed source control systems also create a number of potential pitfalls and trouble areas that can easily lead to integration problems when not implemented properly.

DVCS indeed creates an interesting quasi anti-pattern related to continuous practices. The anti-pattern becomes apparent when DVCS is used as a means to isolate feature work for extended periods of time. This is because DVCS provides a set of tools that can be leveraged by development to either *Continuously Integrate* or *Continuously Isolate*. Developers have the option to isolate/hide their work from the mainline IF they choose to do so OR push and pull with a frequency to reduce the risk of integration problems and collaborate more. It entirely depends on how the tool is leveraged.

 One possible solution to this anti-pattern is to break development work into manageable sprints that are modularly defined, leverage feature toggles, and utilize the short-lived feature branches. By implementing this type of solution, the development organization can connect logically defined sprint efforts to feature toggles, and integrate the completed work continuously with the mainline. The completed work would then go-live via a feature toggle switch when the implementation is complete.

When implementing a branching pattern within an organization (preferably CI based) it is important to keep it simple and well defined. When no patterns are implemented or communicated, problems will lie ahead. These problems are exacerbated when employees quit and take the branching pattern knowledge with them. Undoubtedly, the more simplistic the approach, the more uniform the outcome.

Continuous Integration in Jenkins

To initiate the execution of a Jenkins job, Jenkins leverages build triggers. Build triggers are defined for each job within Jenkins through the detailed job configuration page (SCM polling, GIT pushes, and so on). Each source control solution operates a bit differently, but the general implementation of build triggers is similar for each. Jenkins can either watch for changes, or the source control solution can be configured to notify (push) Jenkins of a completed commit.

SCM polling

Polling a source control solution for changes can be configured in the job configuration page. This solution provides a way for Jenkins to reach out to the source control system and check if there have been any changes since the last poll execution based on the criteria specified in the job configuration page. To configure SCM polling, toggle the **Poll SCM** checkbox. Jenkins will then display the polling configuration text area, which will allow us to specify our CRON-based polling criteria as shown in *Figure 8-6*:

```
url = jenkins + "crumbIssuer/api/xml?xpath=concat(//
crumbRequestField,"":"",//crumb)"
Set http = CreateObject("Microsoft.XMLHTTP")
http.open "GET", url, False
http.setRequestHeader "Content-Type", "text/plain;charset=UTF-8"
http.send
crumb = null
if http.status = 200 then
  crumb = split(http.responseText,":")
end if


url = jenkins + "subversion/" + uuid + "/notifyCommit?rev=" + rev
Wscript.Echo url

Set http = CreateObject("Microsoft.XMLHTTP")
http.open "POST", url, False
http.setRequestHeader "Content-Type", "text/plain;charset=UTF-8"
if not isnull(crumb) then
  http.setRequestHeader crumb(0),crumb(1)
  http.send changed
  if http.status <> 200 then
    Wscript.Echo "Error. HTTP Status: " & http.status & ". Body: " &
http.responseText
  end if
end if
```

*Nix–Bash

```
#!/bin/sh
REPOS="$1"
REV="$2"


# No environment  is passed to svn hook scripts; set paths to external
tools explicitly:
WGET=/usr/bin/wget
SVNLOOK=/usr/bin/svnlook


# If your server requires authentication, it is recommended that you
set up a .netrc file to store your username and password
# Better yet, since Jenkins v. 1.426, use the generated API Token in
place of the password
# See https://wiki.jenkins-ci.org/display/JENKINS/
Authenticating+scripted+clients
```

```
# Since no environment is passed to hook scripts, you need to set
$HOME (where your .netrc lives)
# By convention, this should be the home dir of whichever user is
running the svn process (i.e. apache)
HOME=/var/www/

UUID=`$SVNLOOK uuid $REPOS`
NOTIFY_URL="subversion/${UUID}/notifyCommit?rev=${REV}"
CRUMB_ISSUER_URL='crumbIssuer/api/xml?xpath=concat(//
crumbRequestField,":",//crumb)'

function notifyCI {
  # URL to Hudson/Jenkins server application (with protocol, hostname,
port and deployment descriptor if needed)
  CISERVER=$1

  # Check if "[X] Prevent Cross Site Request Forgery exploits" is
activated
  # so we can present a valid crumb or a proper header
  HEADER="Content-Type:text/plain;charset=UTF-8"
  CRUMB=`$WGET --auth-no-challenge --output-document -
${CISERVER}/${CRUMB_ISSUER_URL}`
  if [ "$CRUMB" != "" ]; then HEADER=$CRUMB; fi

  $WGET \
    --auth-no-challenge \
    --header $HEADER \
    --post-data "`$SVNLOOK changed --revision $REV $REPOS`" \
    --output-document "-"\
    --timeout=2 \
    ${CISERVER}/${NOTIFY_URL}
}


# The code above was placed in a function so you can easily notify
multiple Jenkins/Hudson servers:
notifyCI "http://myPC.company.local:8080"
notifyCI "http://jenkins.company.com:8080/jenkins"
```

Triggering a Jenkins job via GitHub push

With the recent trends in GitHub-based solutions, SCM Polling via Jenkins is no longer needed (and is strongly advised against). GitHub and other similar GIT solutions provide direct integration with Jenkins via the API, and can be configured to push change notifications to the Jenkins subsystems (thus triggering a build). Let's learn how to connect Jenkins to GitHub and set up an automatic build trigger solution.

 To configure this, we will need to ensure that we have the appropriate access levels in GitHub, and have the right access to configure a repository's settings.

Jenkins configurations

To begin, let's start on the Jenkins side of the fence. In Jenkins, we will need to install the GitHub Jenkins plugin. Details of this plugin can be found at the following URL:

`https://wiki.jenkins-ci.org/display/JENKINS/GitHub+Plugin`

Once the Jenkins GitHub plugin has been installed, we will need to configure our job in Jenkins and allow GitHub to notify it after each successful push. This can be implemented in the detailed job configuration page (for a specified job) by configuring the Jenkins job to Build when a change is pushed to GitHub. To get started, tick the checkbox located in the job configuration page as illustrated in *Figure 8-7*.

Figure 8-7: Job configuration options

Now that we have our Jenkins job configured to listen for GitHub push notifications, we will need to specify the GitHub repository that Jenkins will accept such requests from. This field is also located in the Jenkins detailed job configuration page and is illustrated in *Figure 8-8*:

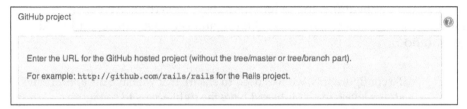

Figure 8-8: Specifying the GitHub repository during configuration

GitHub configurations:

Now that we have our Jenkins job configured, let's turn our attention to GitHub. To begin, log in to `https://www.github.com` with a repository administrator account, and navigate to the target repository. Once there, click the **Settings** link on the right and choose **WebHooks & Services** from the **Options** menu on the left-hand side. Now click **Add Service**, and select the **Jenkins (GitHub plugin)** option from the available services dropdown. The breadcrumb navigation we just described is illustrated as follows:

MyRepository->Settings->WebHooks & Services->Add Service

After the **Jenkins (GitHub plugin)** option has been selected, we will see a configuration page similar to *Figure 8-9*:

Figure 8-9: GitHub plugin configuration

After completing the configuration form that is seen in the preceding screenshot, specify the appropriate URL for Jenkins (this must be accessible through the Internet). Once this has been configured, click **Add service** to complete the GitHub integration, and enable GitHub to begin pushing the changes to Jenkins.

To verify that Jenkins is properly communicating with GitHub, simply try to make a commit to the repository and verify that Jenkins triggers the appropriate job. Once completed, we will have successfully integrated Jenkins with GitHub-implemented automated push notifications.

Continuous Delivery

Continuous Delivery represents a logical extension to Continuous Integration practices. It expands the automation defined in continuous integration beyond simply using a shared mainline, building the software project and executing unit tests. Continuous Delivery adds automated deployments and acceptance test verification automation to the solution and ensures the software project is in an always-releasable state. To better describe this process, let's take a look at some basic characteristics of Continuous Delivery:

- The development resources use Continuous Integration to commit changes to the mainline of the source control solution multiple times per day, and the automation system initiates a complete build, deploy, and test validation for each commit

- Automated tests should execute against every change deployed, and help ensure that the software remains in an always-releasable state.

- Every committed change is treated as potentially releasable, and extra care is taken to ensure that incomplete development work is hidden and does not impact the readiness of the software

- Feedback loops are developed to facilitate notifications of failures. This includes build results, test execution reports, delivery status, and user acceptance verification

- Iterations are short and feedback is rapid, allowing business interests to weigh in on software development efforts and propose alterations along the way

- Business interests, instead of engineering, will decide when to physically release the software project; as such, the software automation should facilitate this goal

As described previously, **Continuous Delivery (CD)** represents the expansion of Continuous Integration practices. At the time of writing of this book, Continuous Delivery approaches have been successfully implemented at scale across numerous organizations including as Amazon, Wells Fargo, and others. The value of CD derives from the ability to tie software releases to business interests, collect feedback rapidly, and course correct efficiently. *Figure 8-10* illustrates the basic automation flow for Continuous Delivery:

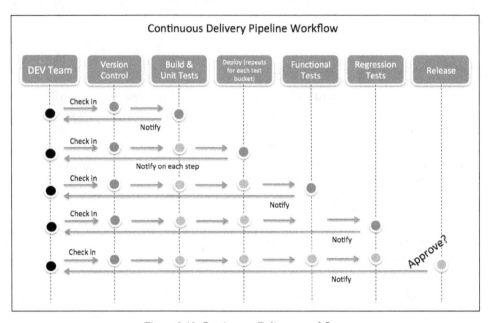

Figure 8-10: Continuous Delivery workflow

As we can see in the preceding diagram, this practice allows businesses to rapidly develop, strategically market, and release software based on pivoting market demands instead of engineering time frames.

When implementing a continuous delivery solution, there are a few key points that we should keep in mind:

- Keep the build fast
- Illuminate the failures, and recover immediately
- Make deployments push-button, for any version to any environment
- Automate testing and validation operations with defined buckets for each logical test group (unit, smoke, functional, and regression)
- Use feature toggles to avoid branching
- Get feedback early and often (automation feedback, test feedback, build feedback, and UAT feedback)

The principles of Continuous Delivery

Continuous Delivery was founded on the premise of standardized and automated release processes, build pipelines, and logical quality gates with rapid feedback loops. In a Continuous Delivery paradigm, builds flow from development to QA and beyond like water in a pipe. The practical application of the Continuous Delivery principles lies in frequent commits to the mainline, which, in turn, execute the build pipeline automation suite, pass through automated quality gates for verification, and are individually signed off by business interests in a completely automated fashion. The idea of incrementally exposing risk can be better illustrated through a *Circle of Trust* diagram, as shown in *Figure 8-11*:

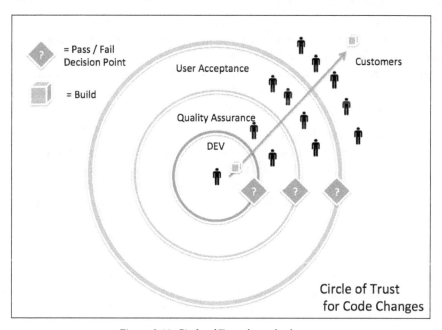

Figure 8-11: Circle of Trust for code changes

As illustrated in the preceding trust diagram, the number of people exposed to a build expands incrementally as the build passes from one logical development or business group to another. This model places emphasis on verification and attempts to remove waste (time) by exposing the build output only to groups that have a vested interest in the build at that phase.

Continuous Delivery in Jenkins

Applying the Continuous Delivery principles in Jenkins can be accomplished in a number of ways. That said, there are some definite tips and tricks that can be leveraged to make the implementation easier. In this section, we will discuss and illustrate some easier. Continuous Delivery tactics and learn how to apply them in Jenkins. Your specific implementation of Continuous Delivery will most definitely be unique to your organization; so, from this section, take what is useful, research anything that is missing, and disregard what is useless. Let's get started.

Rapid feedback loops

Rapid feedback loops are a baseline implementation requirement for Continuous Delivery. Applying this with Jenkins can be accomplished in a pretty slick manner using a combination of the **Email-Ext** plugin and some HTML template magic. In large-scale Jenkins implementations, it is not wise to manage many e-mail templates, and creating a single transformable one can help save time and effort. Let's take a look how to do this in Jenkins.

The Email-Ext plugin provides Jenkins with the capabilities of completely customizable e-mail notifications. It allows the Jenkins system to customize just about every aspect of notifications and can be leveraged as an easy-to-implement, template-based e-mail solution. To begin with, we will need to install the plugin into our Jenkins system. The details for this plugin can be found at the following web address:

```
https://wiki.jenkins-ci.org/display/JENKINS/Email-ext+plugin
```

Once the plug-in has been installed into a Jenkins system, we will need to configure the basic connection details and optional settings. To begin, navigate to the Jenkins administration area and locate the **Extended Email Notification** section.

Jenkins->Manage Jenkins->Configure System

On this page, we will need to specify, at a minimum, the following details:

- SMTP Server
- SMTP Authentication details (User Name + Password)
- Reply-to List (nobody@domain.com)
- System Admin Email Address (located earlier on the page)

The completed form should look something like *Figure 8-12*:

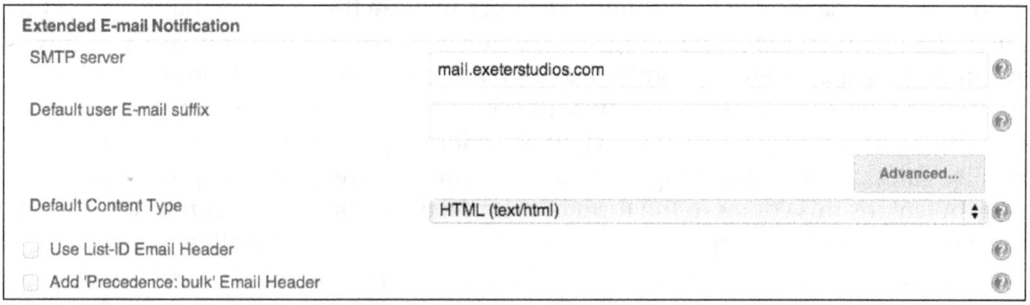

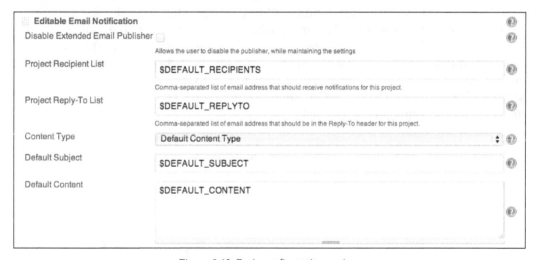

Figure 8-12: Completed form

Once the basic SMTP configuration details have been specified, we can then add the **Editable Email Notification** post build step to our jobs (in the detailed job configuration page), and configure the e-mail contents appropriately. The following screenshot illustrates the basic configuration options required for the build step to operate:

Figure 8-13: Basic configuration options

As we can see from the preceding screenshot, environment variables can be piped into the plugin via the job's automation to define the e-mail contents, recipient list, and other related details. Through this plugin we can also specify triggers for a given email template, customize the recipient list, and much more. This plugin makes for a highly effective feedback loop solution.

Quality gates and approvals

Two of the key aspects of Continuous Delivery include the implementation of end to end automation and implementing an assembly line approach to software delivery. As an organization begins a continuous delivery initiative manual intervention will be required, until automated deployments and testing apparatuses are implemented and up to par. To help move in the right direction implementing approval based quality gates can help encourage the adoption and ensure quality requirements are met. In Jenkins this comes in the form of promoted builds. This requires individuals to signoff on a given change or release as it flows through the pipeline. Back in the day, this used to be managed through a *Release Signoff* sheet, which would often be maintained manually on paper. In the modern digital age, this is managed through the Promoted Build plugin in Jenkins, whereby we can add LDAP or Active Directory integration to ensure that only properly authorized users have the access to promote builds. We discussed the implementation of the Promoted build plugin in an earlier chapter. However, there is room to expand this concept and learn some additional tips and tricks to ensure that we have a solid and secure implementation.

Integrating Jenkins with **Lightweight Directory Access Protocol (LDAP)** is generally a straightforward exercise. This solution allows a corporate authentication system to be tied directly into Jenkins. This means that, once the security integration is configured in Jenkins, we will be able to login to the Jenkins system (UI) by using our corporate account credentials. To connect Jenkins to a corporate authentication engine, we will first need to configure Jenkins to talk to the corporate security servers. This is configured in the **Global Security** administration area of the Jenkins user interface as shown in *Figure 8-14*:

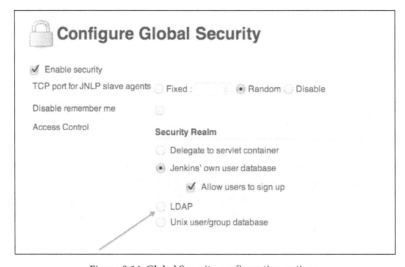

Figure 8-14: Global Security configuration options

The global security area of Jenkins allows us to specify the type of authentication that Jenkins will use for users who wish to access the Jenkins system. By default, Jenkins provides a built-in internal database for managing users; we will have to alter this to support LDAP. To configure this system to utilize LDAP, click the **LDAP** radio button, and enter your LDAP server details as illustrated in the following screenshot:

⦿ LDAP	
	ldap://hs.some1.com:389
	⊖ Syntax of server field is SERVER or SERVER:PORT or ldaps://SERVER[:PORT]
root DN	
	☐ Allow blank rootDN
User search base	
User search filter	
Group search base	
Manager DN	
	⊖ Syntax of server field is SERVER or SERVER:PORT or ldaps://SERVER[:PORT]
Manager Password	
	⊖ Syntax of server field is SERVER or SERVER:PORT or ldaps://SERVER[:PORT]

Figure 8-15: LDAP server details

Fill out the form with your company's LDAP specifics, and click **Save**. If you happen to get stuck on this configuration, the Jenkins community has graciously provided additional in-depth documentation. This documentation can be found at the following URL:

```
https://wiki.jenkins-ci.org/display/JENKINS/LDAP+Plugin
```

For users who wish to leverage Active Directory, there is a Jenkins plugin which can facilitate this type of integrated security solution. For more details on this plugin, please consult the plugin page at the following URL:

```
https://wiki.jenkins-ci.org/display/JENKINS/
Active+Directory+plugin
```

Once the authentication solution has successfully been configured, we can utilize it to set approvers in the promoted builds plugin. To configure a promotion approver, we will need to edit the desired Jenkins project, and specify the users who should have the promote permissions. *Figure 8-16* shows an example of this configuration:

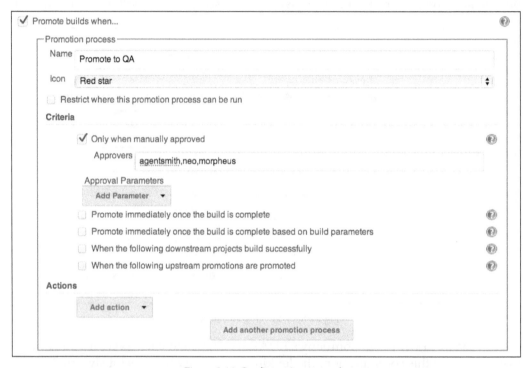

Figure 8-16: Configuration example

As we can see, the Promoted build plugin provides an excellent signoff sheet solution. It is complete with access security controls, promotion criteria, and a robust build step implementation solution.

Build pipeline workflow and visualization

When build pipelines are created initially, the most common practice is to simply daisy-chain the jobs together. This is a perfectly reasonable initial-implementation approach but, in the long term, this may get confusing and it may become difficult to track the workflow of daisy-chained jobs. To assist with this issue, Jenkins offers a plugin to help visualize build pipelines, appropriately named the Build Pipelines plugin. Details of this plugin can be found at the following web URL:

```
https://wiki.jenkins-ci.org/display/JENKINS/Build+Pipeline+Plugin
```

This plugin provides an additional view option, populated by specifying an entry point to the pipeline, detecting upstream and downstream jobs, and creating a visual representation of the pipeline. Upon the initial installation of the plugin, we can see an additional option available to us when we create a new dashboard view. This is illustrated in the *Figure 8-17*:

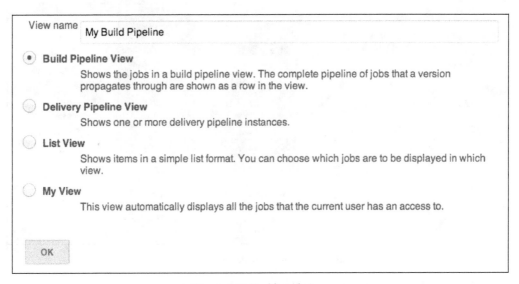

Figure 8-17: Dashboard view

After we have created a pipeline view using the build pipeline plugin, Jenkins will present us with a number of configuration options. The most basic configuration options required are the name of the view and the initial job dropdown selection option, as seen *Figure 8-18*:

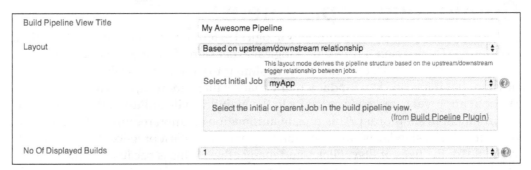

Figure 8-18: Pipeline view configuration options

Once the basic configurations have been defined, click the **OK** button to save the view. This will prompt the plugin to perform an initial scan of the linked jobs and generate the pipeline view. An example of a completely developed pipeline is illustrated in *Figure 8-19*:

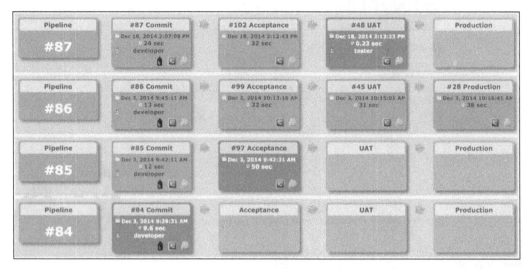

Figure 8-19: Completely developed pipeline

Once the view has been created; it till give us an excellent visual representation of our build pipeline. There are a number of features and customizations that we could apply to the pipeline view, but we will let you explore those and tweak the solution to your own specific needs.

Continuous Deployment

Just as Continuous Delivery represents a logical extension of Continuous Integration, Continuous Deployment represents a logical expansion of Continuous Delivery practices. Continuous Deployment is very similar to Continuous Delivery in a lot of ways, but it has one key fundamental variance: there are no approval gates. Without approval gates, code commits to the mainline will end up in the production environment in short order. This type of automation solution requires a high-level of discipline, strict standards, and rock solid automation. It is a practice that has proven valuable for the likes of Etsy, Flickr, and many others. This is because Continuous Deployment dramatically increases deployment velocity. *Figure 8-20* describes both Continuous Delivery and Continuous Deployment, to better showcase the fundamental difference between, them:

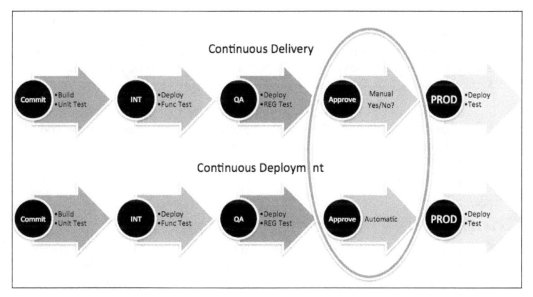

Figure 8-20: Differentiation between Continuous Delivery and Continuous Deployment

It is important to understand that Continuous Deployment is not for everyone, and is a solution that may not be feasible for some software architectures or product types. For example, in embedded software or Desktop application software, Continuous Deployment will only be a viable solution with properly architected background upgrade mechanisms, as we don't want to alienate users due to the frequency of the upgrades. On the other hand, it's something that could be applied, with excellent results, to a simple API web service or a SaaS-based web application.

If the business unit indeed desires to migrate towards a Continuous Deployment solution, tight controls on quality will be required to facilitate stability and avoid outages. These controls may include any of the following:

- The required unit testing with code coverage metrics
- The required a/b testing or experiment-driven development
- Paired programming
- Automated rollbacks
- Code reviews and static code analysis implementations
- Behavior-driven development (BDD)
- Test-driven development (TDD)
- Automated smoke tests in production

Additionally, it is important to note that, since a Continuous Deployment solution is a significant evolutionary step forward, the implementation of the Continuous Delivery practices will be a prerequisite. This solution will need to be proven stable and trusted prior to the removal of the approval gates. Once removed, though, the deployment velocity will significantly increase as a result.

The quantifiable value of Continuous Deployment is well advertised by companies such as Amazon who realized a 78 percent reduction in production outages, and a 60% reduction in downtime minutes due to catastrophic defects. That said, implementing Continuous Deployment will require a buy-in from the stakeholders and business interests alike.

Continuous Deployment in Jenkins

Applying Continuous Deployment practices in Jenkins is actually a simple exercise once Continuous Integration and Continuous Delivery have been completed. It's simply a matter of removing the *approve* criteria and allowing builds to flow freely through the environments, and eventually to production. *Figure 8-21* illustrates a basic continuous deployment implementation using the Promoted build plugin described earlier in the *Continuous Delivery* section:

Figure 8-21: Promoted build plugin implementation

Once the promotions become automatic, the build automation solutions will continuously deploy for every commit to the mainline (given that all the automated tests have been passed).

Summary

In this chapter of *Mastering Jenkins*, we discovered all things continuous. We learned the history and background of Kaizen, Continuous Integration, and related disciplines. We should now have a solid understanding of how to advocate for and develop Kaizen, Continuous Integration, Continuous Delivery, and Continuous Deployment practices at an organization. We also learned how to connect Jenkins into SVN and GitHub to facilitate automated, push-based builds. We discovered examples for maintaining a stable mainline using feature toggles, branching by abstraction, and automation. From our examples of each, we should be able to build upon and drive best practice implementations in Jenkins. We also learned some key differences between each of the Continuous Practices and learned how to differentiate these in Jenkins.

In the next chapter of *Mastering Jenkins*, we will learn how to integrate Jenkins into Selenium, Ansible, Docker, and other highly-valued DevOps solutions. Our journey will lead us on an adventure in creating a Selenium grid, implementing Jenkins via Docker containers, and adapting Jenkins to execute scaled deployments using Ansible. Let's continue forward.

9
Integrating Jenkins with Other Technologies

Jenkins has come a long way since its initial introduction as a unified Java build tool. It has matured significantly and evolved into a robust automation system and project orchestration solution. Jenkins has been extended significantly by the open source community and is now capable of communicating and integrating with numerous technologies, and platforms. With the advent of these integration capabilities, Jenkins has seen widespread growth and adoption by organizations worldwide. As Jenkins enthusiasts, we get to navigate this complex technical landscape and gain experience in evaluating and integrating Jenkins with a multitude of new technologies. Dabbling in new technology arenas and innovation is what makes developing pipelines in Jenkins so exciting.

> *"When the winds of change blow, some people build walls while others build windmills"* – *Chinese proverb*

In this chapter of *Mastering Jenkins* we will discover some creative ways to integrate Jenkins with newer technologies, while learning about innovative engineering trends. We will discover some of the latest technologies to hit the market, and see how to integrate them into Jenkins. Below are the objectives we will cover in this chapter:

- Docker containers
- Jenkins and Ansible
- Jenkins and Artifactory
- Jenkins and Selenium
- Jenkins and Jira

After completing this chapter of *Mastering Jenkins* we should have a fundamental understanding of how to integrate Jenkins into a number of technology solutions. Let's begin our journey.

Jenkins and Docker – Linux guide

Docker is a hot trend amongst technology enthusiasts, DevOps teams, and software engineers. It offers a new and innovative lightweight containerized approach to building and hosting virtualized software solutions. The Docker container technology allows us to create and deliver completely virtualized *containers* that can house a single application, a suite of software services, or a full release. Docker features source control-like functionality that allows container developers to track incremental changes, revert changes (if necessary), and share their solutions. The advantage of this technology over traditional virtualization solutions is that it offers a less resource-intensive solution for hosting and delivering an application or environment regardless of the physical server infrastructures.

The Docker technology stack ensures that a container will operate in a predictable manner regardless of its origin or destination hardware. To accomplish this feat Docker provides a complete Linux file-system foundation in its base. It then makes the base level solution available for all containers hosted within. This base includes tools, network devices, libraries, and related operating system level features that may be required by any of the attached containers. Docker also provides a lightweight Linux kernel, shared across all containers on the Docker system. This kernel was developed to explicitly utilize less memory and fewer system resources.

To better illustrate the architecture of Docker containers, the figure below shows a high-level overview of the virtualization architecture Docker provides:

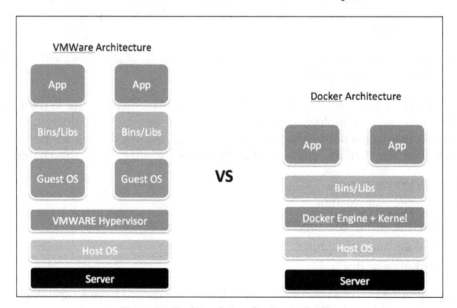

Figure 9-1: Traditional virtualization vs Docker

As we can see, Docker offers an easily transportable way to develop and deploy a completely operable solution and define the environment requirements prior to use. This solution mitigates the infamous *it works on my machine* straw man argument. If your team is focusing on a more DevOps-style approach to software delivery, containers can flow through build pipelines, get validated for quality (bake), ensure lower risks surrounding infrastructure, and reduce environment variances upon reaching production.

Docker offers a number of highly valuable features for engineering organizations. Lets take a moment to look at a few:

- Low-risk portable deployments based on baked pre-production testing of the same content
- Clear definitions of Docker container contents
- Collaborative sharing (public registry), which allows containers to be shared easily
- Shared kernel and OS solution that eliminates the duplication of OS files
- Source control-like functionality and version tracking
- A highly extendable tool ecosystem created from the published Docker API

Now that we have a pretty good picture of the Docker virtualization architecture, and the advantages this technology provides, lets take a few minutes to look at some use cases and see how we can leverage container-based solutions.

The practical use cases for Docker containers are potentially endless. It can be used for delivery pipelines, developer programming environments, software debugging, bug reproduction, build environment hosting, Jenkins master and slave scalability, low-risk tests of new software solutions, and so much more.

Since Dockers use cases are virtually endless, let's focus on some Jenkins-specific use cases. More specifically we will focus on tutorials for the following use cases:

- Running Jenkins itself inside a Docker container (Linux)
- Spinning up Jenkins slave nodes through Docker containers (setup and teardown automatically)

> One of the most beneficial ways Docker can be implemented is for DevOps deployments. This solution allows Docker containers to flow with a pre-installed solution from one logical group to another in a DevOps build pipeline. This is a notable and generally accepted way to make use of Docker and it is worth researching further as your development and delivery process matures.

Running Jenkins inside a Docker container – Linux

Our friendly Jenkins master instance can directly run inside a Docker Container. In this section we will look at implementing a master Jenkins instance that resides inside a Docker container. This solution provides a high-level of flexibility for the Jenkins (master) in the sense that it can be easily backed-up, shared, tested, and version controlled. It can even be migrated from one location to another with minimal effort, and provides assured operability. To implement this solution we can utilize one of the registry provided containers created by the Jenkins community and available on Docker's central registry. How cool is that!

If you have not taken the opportunity to install Docker, there are a few options available. The first is to head over to `http://www.docker.com` and grab it (Windows and Mac users). For Linux users, the Docker organization has graciously provided `aptitude` and `yum` packages that can be installed from a traditional package management system. Below are the commands needed to get Docker installed under CentOS and Ubuntu Linux:

CentOS:

```
#> Yum install docker
```

Ubuntu/Debian:

```
#>apt-get upgrade
#>apt-get install docker
```

Once Docker has been installed we will need to verify it is functioning properly. To begin let's open a command line terminal session, and type the following command into the terminal:

```
#> Docker info
```

Once executed Docker should output something like the following to the terminal display:

```
Containers: 0
Images: 0
Storage Driver: aufs
 Root Dir: /mnt/sda1/var/lib/docker/aufs
 Backing Filesystem: extfs
 Dirs: 0
 Dirperm1 Supported: true
Execution Driver: native-0.2
Kernel Version: 4.0.5-boot2docker
```

```
Operating System: Boot2Docker 1.7.0 (TCL 6.3); master : 7960f90 - Thu
Jun 18 18:31:45 UTC 2015
CPUs: 8
...
```

Once Docker has been verified to be working properly, we can begin checking out the features that Docker offers. The Docker registry provides a number of pre-made containers, which can make our lives significantly easier and assist us in getting started without too much hassle. To make matters even better the Jenkins LTS release line we discussed earlier in *Chapter 1*, *Setup and Configuration of Jenkins*, has been converted into an official Docker solution. The Jenkins LTS container is also available directly through the Docker registry. The details are provided below:

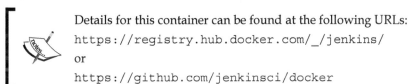

> Details for this container can be found at the following URLs:
> https://registry.hub.docker.com/_/jenkins/
> or
> https://github.com/jenkinsci/docker

To obtain this pre-made Jenkins container simply type the following into the command line terminal:

```
#> docker pull jenkins
```

Once fetched, the output of the console terminal should reflect something like the following:

```
Pulling repository jenkins
f509350ab0be: Pull complete
b0b7b9978dda: Pull complete
6a0b67c37920: Downloading 171.9 MB/199.1 MB
1f80eb0f8128: Download complete
1d1aa175e120: Download complete
1fd02545bba6: Download complete
52b8ae4dbae9: Download complete
...
Status: jenkins:latest: The image you are pulling has been verified.
Important: image verification is a tech preview feature and should not
be relied on to provide security.
Digest: sha256:9ac333ae3271cf19497fd3abd170c42d50c4d2e0c84eca17fa23db
18c455922a
Status: Downloaded newer image for jenkins:latest
```

Once the container has been downloaded, we will want to fire it up and enable a persistent file system volume. This will ensure that any changes we make don't get automatically wiped upon shutdown. The command to start the Jenkins container is provided below:

```
#> docker run --name myjenkins -p 8080:8080 -v /var/jenkins_home jenkins
```

Once the container has fired up we should be able to access our Jenkins container via our web browser (`http://localhost:8080`) as illustrated in *Figure 9-2*:

Figure 9-2: Jenkins running in a Docker container

Dynamic Jenkins slave nodes using Docker

In addition to being able to host a Jenkins master instance, Docker can be implemented to provide scalable Jenkins slave nodes. This tutorial aims to facilitate Docker containers that are automatically provisioned as Jenkins slave nodes, utilized by a Jenkins master to run an automation routine (build), and then removed one the build has completed. This type of solution becomes very valuable when there is a need for a highly scalable build solution that leverages many concurrent builds, based on a templated OS.

To implement Jenkins slave nodes using Docker containers there are a few pre-requisite requirements. These are provided in the following section.

Pre-requisite requirements

In this section we will discuss the pre-requisite requirements for our Docker slave node solution. Obviously Docker will need to be installed and functioning prior to being available for Jenkins use. Beyond the base level Docker installation requirement we will need to install a couple of Jenkins plugins. The Jenkins plugins can each be installed from the Jenkins user interface via the plugin management system.

- The Jenkins Docker plugin(http://wiki.jenkins-ci.org/display/ JENKINS/Docker+Plugin)

- Jenkins JClouds plugin (http://wiki.jenkins-ci.org/display/JENKINS/ JClouds+Plugin)

Implementation tutorial

Once the pre-requisite requirements have been taken care of, we will want to grab the ready-made everga/Jenkins-slave Docker image, which can be found at (https://index.docker.io/u/evarga/jenkins-slave/). To do this via the command line enter the following input into the terminal:

```
#> docker pull evarga/jenkins-slave
```

Once the `evarga` container has been fetched, we should see the following output on the terminal from Docker:

```
Pulling repository evarga/jenkins-slave
8880612971b0: Pulling dependent layers
511136ea3c5a: Download complete
c7b7c6419568: Download complete
70c8faa62a44: Download complete
d735006ad9c1: Download complete
04c5d3b7b065: Download complete
...
Status: Downloaded newer image for evarga/jenkins-slave:latest
```

Once the Docker image has been fetched and installed properly let's verify the status via the following command:

```
#> docker images
```

Our command's output should look similar to the following.

```
REPOSITORY              TAG             IMAGE ID            CREATED
VIRTUAL SIZE
evarga/jenkins-slave    latest          8880612971b0        6 months
ago         610.8 MB
```

Now that we have obtained the `evarga/jenkins-slave` Docker container, let's fire up our Docker container. To accomplish this, enter the following command into the terminal:

```
#> docker run -i -t evarga/jenkins-slave /bin/bash
root@dd9372b1ec2d:/#
```

The next step will be to get our freshly obtained Docker image to operate as a Jenkins slave group. To do this we will need to implement some basic authentication changes. These changes include the following:

- Create SSH Keys for ROOT (required for the Docker Jenkins Plugin)
- Add path to the SSH Keys to /etc/ssh/sshd_config and /etc/ssh/ssh_config
- Create authorized_keys file

To create an SSH ROOT key we will need to input the following commands into our Docker container via the command line:

```
#> ssh-keygen -t rsa  # This will guide us through the generation of SSH keys located in /root/.ssh
```

Next we will need to alter the ssh_config, and sshd_config files to point to the authorized_keys file location. To accomplish input the following into the terminal:

```
#> echo "AuthorizedKeysFile /etc/ssh/authorized_keys" >> /etc/ssh/sshd_config
```

Next we will want to add a simple pointer in our ssh_config file to the RSA key we generated a moment ago. To do this type the following in the Docker container's command line terminal:

```
#> echo "IdentityFile /root/.ssh/id_rsa" >> /etc/ssh/ssh_config
```

Finally we will want to commit the changes we just made to our Docker container so that they don't vanish upon restart. To do this we will use the Docker commit command, which is illustrated below:

```
#> Docker commit
```

Many of these changes could also be accomplished via a Docker file. Creating and managing docker files is outside the scope of this book, however details regarding docker files can be found on Docker's website.

Now that we have the authentication alterations out of the way we can focus on the Jenkins Docker plugin, and configure it to utilize our Docker container as a slave node.

 The details of the Jenkins Docker plugin can be found at the following URL:

`https://wiki.jenkins-ci.org/display/JENKINS/`
`Docker+Plugin`

Once the plugin has been installed into Jenkins, Jenkins will provide us with the ability to create a Docker *cloud* in the Jenkins configuration area. Navigate to this configuration section by following the below described navigation steps:

```
Jenkins->Manage Jenkins->Configure System-> Cloud->'Add New Cloud'-
>'Docker'
```

In the configuration area Jenkins will provide us with the ability to add a Docker cloud, which will subsequently display a configuration section similar to the one in the figure below:

Figure 9-3: The configuration screen

Once the cloud has been added to the Jenkins configuration, Jenkins will present us with a number of configuration options. We will need to specify at a minimum a name for our Docker cloud. Once these changes have been made, click the **Add Template** button and proceed to configure the form with the details provided in *Figure 9-4*:

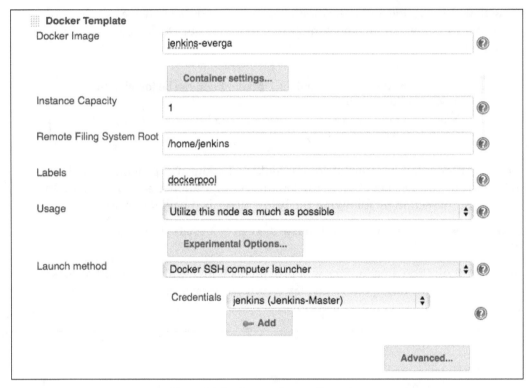

Figure 9-4: Docker template configuration

In the **Docker Template** configuration section we will also want to configure a *label* that will be applied to the Docker slave nodes. This is identical in nature to the slave labels we discussed in *Chapter 2, Distributed Builds – Master/Slave Mode*. In our example we set this to dockerpool. We will also want to make sure we specify jenkins-everga as the ID for the Docker image. Once the configuration details are in place click the **SAVE** button to save the Mode configuration changes to disk.

The final step necessary to implement dynamic Docker containers as slave-nodes is to restrict selected Jenkins jobs to execute builds only on the pre-configured *docker-jenkins* label. This configuration will need to be performed for each targeted Jenkins job in the detailed job configuration page. The implementation should look similar to *Figure 9-5*:

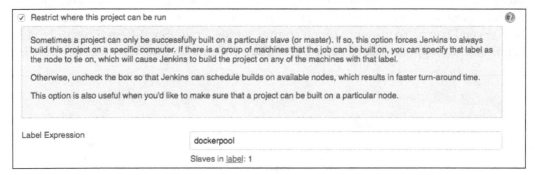

Figure 9-5: Additional job configuration by setting label expression

It is now time to verify that our setup was successful. Save the job configuration, and run the Jenkins job we just configured. If it's functioning properly it should automatically spin up a new instance of the Docker container for every build executed, and then tear it down once completed.

Integrating Jenkins with Ansible – Linux and Windows

Ansible is a relatively recent addition to the DevOps landscape. Ansible provides as an easy to use alternative to traditional configuration management tools such as Puppet and Chef. Ansible offers a hybrid solution for automating deployments, executing provisioning automation, and managing the configuration state of infrastructure through **Infrastructure as Code (IaC)**. Ansible is well known for its ease of use, powerful technology platform, and a vast array of module-based technology integrations. Integrating Ansible into Jenkins can provide a number of additional benefits including push button deployment capabilities, push button environment server provisioning, and integrated configuration management solutions. A low learning curve and powerful technology platform make Ansible a wise choice for any SCM team or DevOps group.

To properly integrate Ansible with Jenkins we need to first understand the basic technology architecture, and general capabilities of Ansible itself. Ansible can be used in two distinct ways. The first is a push model in which Ansible utilizes SSH (Linux), or native PowerShell-Remoting (Windows) communication apparatuses to reach out to a target configuration item (server), install the Ansible service, execute a playbook (automation script), and delete the service. The second is a pull model where an Ansible playbook is executed locally on a target configuration item (server) and has no requirement for a control server, PowerShell-Remoting, or SSH communication apparatus. *Figure 9-6* illustrates the pull architecture in better detail:

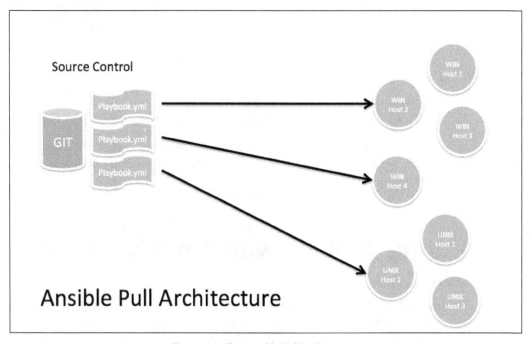

Figure 9-6: The Ansible Pull architecture

Through the pull based architecture Ansible will retrieve its playbooks and execution information from source control. This allows each node to act independently, and provides a level of autonomy across the solution. An Ansible pull solution is in stark contrast to the alternative push based architecture, which is described in *Figure 9-7*:

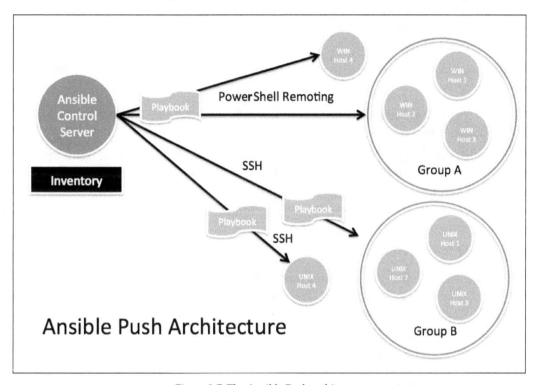

Figure 9-7: The Ansible Push architecture

As we can see from the push architecture diagram, Ansible will instruct any targeted hosts to install Ansible as a temporary executor, pass it the necessary playbook, wait for it to finish execution, and then remove the temporary executor from each of the given deployment nodes.

Now that we have a basic understanding of the architecture that Ansible utilizes, let's take a look at integrating Ansible playbooks with Jenkins. There are probably any number of ways to accomplish the execution of Ansible playbooks via Jenkins, but for the purpose of brevity we will discuss one specific approach in an effort to learn the basics.

In the following example we will discover how to create a Jenkins job, which will *provision* a target machine (remote IP address) to contain a set of basic compilers and linker's using an Ansible playbook. While this implementation illustrates a provisioning, it could be leveraged to execute any playbook on a target system. This type of solution can be especially handy for creating or enforcing build environment prerequisite configurations or spinning up a new developer environment from a fresh OS installation.

To begin we will assume that we have a basic Ubuntu Linux setup and the following pre-requisites:

- An Ansible installation (`http://www.ansible.com`) installed on our Jenkins master server (`apt-get install Ansible`)

- A target Debian/Ubuntu @ `http://www.ubuntu.com`) machine spun up (with an IP address `192.168.1.5`)

- A standard `sudo` account configured on 192.168.1.5 and available for us to use to login to the machine via the following username/password credentials:

    ° BUILD/BUILD123

Now that we have the pre-requisites out of the way, let's take a look at how to integrate Ansible into the Jenkins UI by creating a job that will execute a playbook against a target machine (`192.168.1.5`) via a button click.

To begin, create a freestyle Jenkins job. For our example we will call it `scm.execute.ansible.playbook` as shown in *Figure 9-8*:

Jenkins -> New Item -> Freestyle project -> `scm.execute.ansible.playbook`

Figure 9-8: A freestyle Jenkins job example

After naming the job, click the **OK** button to proceed to the detailed job configuration page. From there we will define the input parameters of the job, create the shell execution build steps to call Ansible, and define how Ansible will be called.

From the detailed job configuration page in Jenkins we will want to configure a Jenkins job effectively execute an Ansible playbook against a target server. Ansible manages authentication credentials (access to target servers) through SSH keys and individual server IP addresses in a centralized host file. To make our implementation dynamic we will need to configure our Jenkins job to alter these inputs. To accomplish this we will need to add a few configurations to our Jenkins job. First lets add a **Execute Shell** build step, and fill it in with the following bash code:

```
############ Remove then Create Temp.Hosts file with target IP.
file="$WORKSPACE/temp.hosts"
[[ -f "$file" ]] && rm -f "$file"
echo "[all]" >> $WORKSPACE/temp.host
echo "$ANSIBLETARGETIP" >> $WORKSPACE/temp.host
############ Execute the Ansible Playbook.
export PYTHONUNBUFFERED=1
ansible-playbook -i /$WORKSPACE/temp.hosts /$WORKSPACE/infrastructure/
ansible-playbooks/$ANSIBLEPLAYBOOK.yml --user root --verbose
```

Now that the build step has been added lets take a minute to review what it does. The above bash shell script and automation will effectively perform the following actions as a build step:

1. Remove an existing `temp.host` file that exists in the `$WORKSPACE` location.

2. Create a new `temp.host` file and concatenate it with the contents of the variable `$ANSIBLETARGETIP` (we will define this in a moment).

3. Enable Ansible real-time logging (Python buffer).

4. Trigger the execution of an Ansible playbook, whose filename will be dynamically set via the variable `$ANSIBLEPLAYBOOK`.

Now that we have our bash build step, let's get Jenkins to pass the playbook name and target IP address dynamically to the shell script. This is accomplished by adding build parameters to the Jenkins job as shown in *Figure 9-9*:

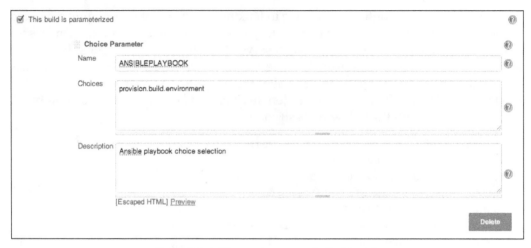

Figure 9-9: Adding parameters to the Jenkins job

The above screenshot shows the addition of a simple choice parameter in Jenkins. This will appear as a dropdown input requirement when we attempt to run the job. The choice selected is then passed into our automation through the $ANSIBLEPLAYBOOK environment variable. When we add playbooks to the system we will need to update the choices appropriately. Each choice represents an Ansible playbook filename (minus the .YML extension).

Figure 9-10: Adding input for ANSIBLETARGETIP (String)

In the preceeding figure we illustrate the addition of an $ANSIBLETARGETIP parameter. This parameter will allow us to input the target IP address when running the Jenkins job. After creating the proper build input parameters, implement a source control checkout solution in the Jenkins job. This will ensure the job fetches any YML playbooks from source control and will make them available to our automation.

This implementation method is not the only way to tie Ansible into Jenkins. In recent months the Jenkins community has made a Jenkins plugin for Ansible available within the plugin ecosystem. It provides a build step option to execute a playbook against a machine IP. More details surrounding the new Jenkins Ansible plugin can be found at `https://wiki.jenkins-ci.org/display/JENKINS/Ansible+Plugin`.

Now that we have the basic Jenkins Job defined, to execute our playbooks we will need to provide an automated way for the Ansible control server (also our Jenkins master) to *authenticate* with the target machine, and execute the playbook against it (even if it has never accessed the server before). Typically this is done via the Ansible inventory file, which manages a hard-coded list of servers and groups. However in the case of developer build machines, making the inventory dynamic can provide an easy way to provision a build environment or deployment servers alike.

To accomplish this we can leverage the previously defined Jenkins job parameters, and a simple `expect` script as shown below:

```
#!/usr/bin/expect -f

# Get the Target IP address (to connect to)
set nodehostname [lindex $argv 0];

# First attempt to use ssh-copy-id to connect to the target without
the need for a password
spawn ssh-copy-id BUILD@$nodehostname
expect {
    ")?"    {send "yes\n";     exp_continue}
    word:   {send "BUILD123\n"; exp_continue}
    eof
}


# Next attempt to ssh to the target as user and alter the root
password
spawn ssh BUILD@$nodehostname -t "sudo passwd root"
expect {
  BUILD: { send "BUILD\n";

            expect {
             password: {send "BUILD123\n";
```

```
                    exp_continue
             }}

   }
}

# Finally attempt to ssh-copy-id for root so no password is needed
spawn ssh-copy-id root@$nodehostname
expect {
    ")?"    {send "yes\n";      exp_continue}
    word:   {send "BUILD123\n"; exp_continue}
    eof
}
```

To make the expect script available to Jenkins, we will need to save it to the Ansible control (also our Jenkins master) server (in our example we chose to save it to /var/lib/scripts/ansibleprovision.sh), and have it run as an **Execute shell** build step in our build job. *Figure 9-11* illustrates the Jenkins job build step required to tie all of this together:

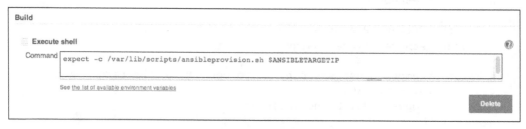

Figure 9-11: Jenkins job build step

Now that we have the Jenkins playbook execution job created, let's take a look at an example Ansible playbook. Playbooks in Ansible simply provide automated content in human-readable YAML form. The following YAML code segment is a simple Ansible playbook that installs a gcc compiler and git onto an Ubuntu Linux host.

```
---
- hosts: apache
  sudo: yes
  tasks:
    - name: Install required system packages.
      apt: pkg={{ item }} state=installed update-cache=yes
      with_items:
        - gcc
        - git-core
```

Once the playbook has been created, commit it to source control and configure the Jenkins job to fetch it when the job runs. In our example job we titled the provided playbook `provision.build.environment.yml`. Once everything has been saved click the **Build with Parameters** button to test it out. If everything works as expected you should be able to quickly point this job at an IP address and run the playbook.

In the above example we learned some of the basics of the Ansible architecture and discovered an unconventional way to mix it with Jenkins to provide a new level of automation and configuration management. As you build out your automation and build pipelines, it may be wise to tie this into you build server provisioning so that enforcing the build environment of Jenkins slaves is as simple as executing a playbook against the target system prior to executing the build. This can provide a pretty handy way of ensuring build environments are always up-to-date before running the build automation and any compilation steps.

Jenkins and Artifactory

Jfrog's Artifactory (and Sonatype Nexus) have been pivotal advocates for Continuous Delivery implementations for some time now. Artifactory provides a set of centrally configurable repositories, which can be leveraged to facilitate uploading, storing, downloading, and fetching build packages, Docker containers (Docker registries through Artifactory requires the Pro version), and binary assets. Implementing an Artifactory based solution (or similar tool) can assist in maturing SCM processes by ensuring that binary outputs of build processes are backed up, managed, and available across diverse development teams, sales representatives, or ancillary staff.

In addition to Artifactory acting as a DML and organizing a binary asset collection, an Artifact repository solution provides an easily automated central source of truth for all things binary (including dependencies). This allows Artifactory to effectively manage dependencies, and makes them automatable (via Maven, IVY, or Gradle), and transparent.

To better understand the basic architecture of Artifactory in conjunction with Jenkins, the figure below provides a basic architecture illustration:

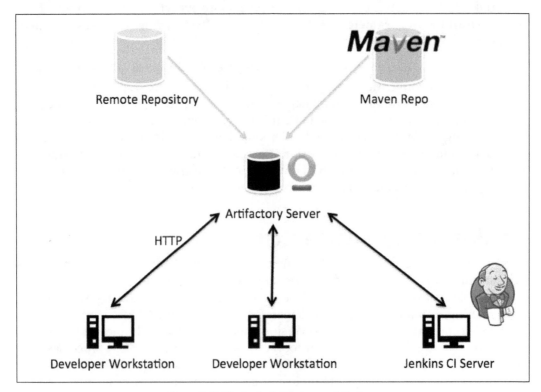

Figure 9-12: The basic Artifactory architecture

Uploading binary assets from Jenkins is easily accomplished through the Jenkins Artfiactory plugin, which is freely available at `https://wiki.jenkins-ci.org/display/JENKINS/Artifactory+Plugin`.

Once the Artifactory plugin has been installed we will need to be configure it to point to our Artifactory installation URL and provide the proper credentials necessary to *deploy* artifacts into a given repository. These configuration steps will need to be performed in the main Jenkins configuration area. The navigation steps necessary to get to the configuration area are as follows:

Jenkins->Manage Jenkins->Configure System->Artifactory

An screenshot of the **Artifactory** configuration section is provided below:

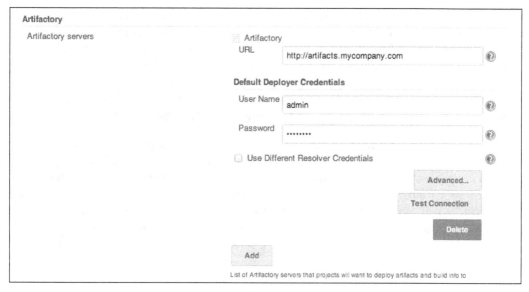

Figure 9-13: The Artifactory configuration section

Once the plugin has been properly set up we can begin to implement Artifactory actions within Jenkins jobs. These are defined within the detailed Jenkins job configuration area in the build environment section, which is illustrated in *Figure 9-14*:

Figure 9-14: The build environment section

Each of the earlier-illustrated checkboxes expands to a detailed configuration section with a number of options available. For a complete set of documentation details regarding each of these checkboxes, the plugin overview page can be consulted. A link to this page is provided below:

```
https://wiki.jenkins-ci.org/display/JENKINS/Artifactory+Plugin
```

Jenkins and Selenium Grid

If your organization is developing SaaS or web applications and has not been leveraging a Selenium Grid for automated testing you're really missing out on something special. A Selenium Grid provides a distributed automated testing solution that executes test cases in parallel. In this section of *Mastering Jenking* we will learn how to spin up a Selenium Grid, write basic unit tests, and capture the results in Jenkins. By learning this we can begin harnessing a Selenium Grid and help advocate for a scalable automated testing solution within Jenkins.

The architecture of a Selenium Grid is a single hub and multiple connected nodes, which is very similar in nature to a Jenkins master and slave node solution. The hub receives a testing manifest and distributes the tests for execution across the attached nodes. This distributed test architecture allows for multiple tests to execute in parallel, which reduces test execution time dramatically. To illustrate a Selenium Grid's architecture, *Figure 9-15* describes the basic configuration of a Selenium Grid and a few connected test nodes of varying operating systems:

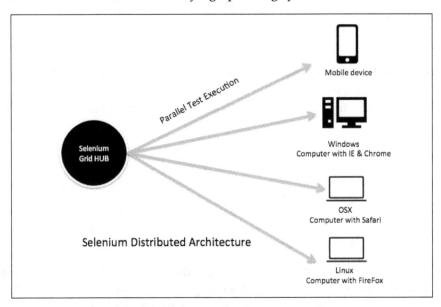

Figure 9-15: Selenium distributed architecture

The **Selenium Grid Hub** can be summarily described as a test case dealer. It simply manages a suite of test cases and hands individual test case executions to available nodes matching the necessary OS and web browser criteria in parallel on the grid. The hub will then collate the results and manage the feedback to the calling source. A **Selenium Grid Hub** could be described as having the following characteristics:

- The hub represents the only entry point into the grid, facilitates the assignment of tests for execution by the connected nodes, and collates reporting details

- The hub is responsible for maintaining an active connection with any nodes and manages the distribution of tests to the grid nodes

- The hub will typically be an isolated VM or server and should not be dual-purposed as a node

Selenium Grid nodes could be VMs, computers, available servers, or Docker containers. Any nodes that have been connected to the Selenium Grid hub are then leveraged for the execution of automated test cases. Selenium Grid nodes can physically be any combination of operating systems, web browsers, and platforms so long as they have the Selenium node service installed. Selenium Grid nodes by nature are not intelligent and do not represent a usable selenium service by themselves. To better describe how Selenium Grid nodes operate, lets look at their characteristics:

- A Selenium node does not necessarily need to be of the same architecture or OS as the hub

- There can be one or more selenium nodes connected to a Selenium Grid hub

- Selenium nodes have the roll of `webdriver` defined when launching the selenium service from the command line

Spinning up a Selenium Grid

In this section we will learn how to spin up a simple Selenium Grid. This involves ensuring you have the following pre-requisites:

- A machine to act as the **Selenium Grid HUB** (for our example it will be on IP `192.168.1.2`)

- A machine to act as a Selenium Grid node (for our example it will be on IP `192.168.1.100`)

- Java v1.6 or higher on both the Grid HUB, and Grid Node described above

To begin the build-out of our mini Selenium Grid we will first want to configure the hub to run the Selenium application and assume the role of a grid hub. To accomplish this we will need to download Selenium onto the server from the following URL:

```
http://docs.seleniumhq.org/download/
```

Once Selenium has been downloaded to the hub server navigate to the download directory on the hub on the command line and execute the following command:

```
#> Java –jar selenium-server-standalone-2.4.6.jar –role hub
```

Once enabled the hub should respond with the following output:

```
Jun 25, 2015 4:05:00 AM org.openqa.grid.selenium.GridLauncher main
INFO: Launching a selenium grid server
2015-06-25 04:05:13.063:INFO:osjs.Server:jetty-7.x.y-SNAPSHOT
...
```

Let's make sure that our Selenium Grid is accessible via the grid hub UI. Open a web browser session and navigate to the following URL:

```
http://192.168.1.2:4444/
```

If the grid is up and running it should display a graphical grid status page. Now let's turn our attention to connecting up a node to the hub we just spun up. To begin the build-out, start by logging into to the node server and download the *Selenium Grid Java application* onto it.

Open a command line terminal, navigate to the folder Selenium was downloaded to, and type the following into the command line terminal:

```
#> Java –jar selenium-server-standalone-2.46.0.jar –role webdriver –hub
http://192.168.1.2:4444/grid/register -port 5566
```

 IP Address note: In our example we used `192.168.1.2` for the hub, and `192.168.1.100` as the `webdriver` node. In your example these will probably be different. Be sure to modify the commands to reflect your local settings as you implement this.

Once the hub and the node are spun up and connected we are ready to create and execute some Selenium tests on our new mini-grid.

Writing tests and integrating them into Jenkins

Now that we have a basic Selenium Grid created we can dig into learning how to write automated tests, and wire them into Jenkins. Selenium tests can be written in any number of programming languages such as Ruby, Python, Java, C#, and more. Selenium itself supports a multitude of platforms and web browsers. In the upcoming example we will learn how to create a simple Ruby test suite that attaches to a Selenium Grid, loads a web page, and reports the results. Individual implementations of Selenium test suites in various programming languages will be similar and can be researched independently.

Before we begin writing automated tests that connect to Selenium through a Ruby test suite we will need to install a few Ruby gems. Ruby gems are simply extensions and provide additional capabilities to the Ruby programming language. Installing a gem can be accomplished quite easily through the gem command, which will typically be available alongside Ruby itself. For our example we will need the Selenium WebDriver, yarjuf, and RSpec gems. These Ruby gems will need to be added to both our local development environment, and the Jenkins automation environment respectively. Below are the commands we will need to execute to install our selenium-webdriver gem, yarjuf gem, and rspec gem.

```
#> gem install selenium-webdriver
#> gem install rspec
#> gem install yarjuf
```

The Selenium WebDriver gem provides API level support for the Selenium Grid, and will allow us to create automated test cases that run on our grid. More information (including the source code) for this gem can be found at the following URL:

```
https://github.com/seleniumhq/selenium
```

The rspec gem offers TDD and BDD testing capabilities to Ruby. It is open-source and free. Further information on rspec can be found at the following URL:

```
http://rspec.info
```

The RSpec JUnit formatter (yarjuf) gem provides JUnit formatted output support for RSpec tests. This helps make the output Jenkins-friendly and consumable by the JUnit Test Jenkins plugin. Additional information on this gem can be found at:

```
https://github.com/sj26/rspec_junit_formatter
```

After installing these gems, the output of the gem install commands should reflect something similar to the following:

Selenium-webdriver:

```
Parsing documentation for selenium-webdriver-2.46.2

Installing ri documentation for selenium-webdriver-2.46.2

Done installing documentation for websocket, ffi, childprocess, rubyzip, selenium-webdriver after 56 seconds

5 gems installed
```

RSpec:

```
...

Fetching: rspec-3.3.0.gem (100%)

Successfully installed rspec-3.3.0

Parsing documentation for rspec-support-3.3.0

Installing ri documentation for rspec-support-3.3.0

Parsing documentation for rspec-core-3.3.1

Installing ri documentation for rspec-core-3.3.1

6 gems installed
```

RSpec JUnit Formatter:

```
Fetching: rspec_junit_formatter-0.2.3.gem (100%)

Successfully installed rspec_junit_formatter-0.2.3

Parsing documentation for rspec_junit_formatter-0.2.3

Installing ri documentation for rspec_junit_formatter-0.2.3

Done installing documentation for rspec_junit_formatter after 0 seconds

1 gem installed
```

Now that we have the Ruby gems installed, let's look at some Ruby test code. Our test suite example is provided below.

```
# -- Define required GEMS
require 'rubygems'
require 'selenium-webdriver'
require 'rspec'

# ----------------------
# Test Suite Definition
# --------------------
```

```ruby
describe "ExampleSeleniuTestSuite" do

    # --------------------
    # Test Suite Setup (ALL)
    # ---------------
    attr_reader :selenium_driver
    before(:all) do

        # -- Defines the Selenium WebDriver details
        @selenium_driver = Selenium::WebDriver.for(
          :remote,
          url: 'http://10.10.33.231:4444/wd/hub',
          desired_capabilities: :chrome) # you can also use :chrome,
:safari, etc.

    end

    # --------------------
    # Test Case Setup
    # ---------------
    before(:each) do

        # -- Setup browser session (a safe url to start from)
        @selenium_driver.get "http://example.com"

    end

    # --------------------
    # Test Suite TearDown
    # ---------------
    after(:all) do

        # -- Close our Selenium Instance
        @selenium_driver.close

    end

    # --------------------
    # Test Case 1
    # ---------------
    it "can find the right title" do

        @selenium_driver.get "http://www.google.com"
```

```
        expect(@selenium_driver.title).to eq('Google')

    end

  end
```

Once you have reviewed the above provided ruby test suite, save it as [`gridtest.rb`], commit it to source control, and then test locally by executing the following command via the command line terminal:

```
#> rspec gridtest.rb
```

If everything worked as expected we should see the following output in the command line terminal:

```
Finished in 6.02 seconds (files took 1.08 seconds to load)

1 example, 0 failures
```

Now that we have a basic automated test suite written (and hopefully working), we can shift focus over to running the tests through Jenkins.

Connecting the above Ruby test suite to Jenkins can be accomplished fairly easily. To start we will want to make sure the JUnit test report plugin is installed in Jenkins. More details surrounding this plugin can be found at the URL below:

```
https://wiki.jenkins-ci.org/display/JENKINS/JUnit+Plugin
```

First create a freestyle Jenkins job and configure it to pull the source code for the test suite we just created by adding the appropriate SCM steps to a new freestyle build job. The SCM step will need to specify the location in your source control system that the Ruby script was committed to. For the purposes of our tutorial we will refer to our Jenkins job as `test.selenium.grid`.

Next we will need to add a build step to execute the Ruby script we created earlier and execute our tests. Adding an Execute Shell build step and defining the `rspec` command are documented below:

```
#> rspec --format RspecJunitFormatter  --out rspec.xml gridtest.rb
```

Once we have the tests running through Jenkins, we will want to configure our Jenkins job to search for the XML results after the grid tests have been executed. This will provide the nice test trend graphs that Jenkins is so famous for. This is accomplished by adding a **Publish JUnit test result report** post build action to the Jenkins job. The configuration details are described in the figure below:

Post-build Actions

 Publish JUnit test result report

Test report XMLs

/rspec.xml

Fileset 'includes' setting that specifies the generated raw XML report files, such as 'myproject/target/test-reports/*.xml'. Basedir of the fileset is the workspace root.

☐ Retain long standard output/error

Health report amplification factor

1.0

1% failing tests scores as 99% health. 5% failing tests scores as 95% health

Delete

Figure 9-16: Adding a post-build action to the Jenkins job

Finally we can save the Jenkins job, and execute our Selenium Grid tests by clicking the **Build-Now** button. If everything went correctly we should see the following output from the Jenkins console logs and collated test report in Jenkins:

```
Finished in 6.36 seconds (files took 0.91697 seconds to load)

1 example, 0 failures
```

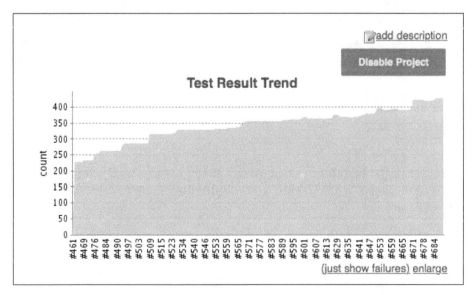

Figure 9-17: Jenkins console log output

Jenkins and Jira

Atlassian's Jira (http://www.atlassian.com) has quickly become an industry-wide powerhouse for tracking Agile efforts, managing development implementation queues, and providing project management solutions for software teams. In more recent releases of Jira and Jenkins have been bridged, and Jira now supports a tight coupling of Jenkins jobs and Jira tickets.

In this section of *Mastering Jenkins* we will discover how to implement Jenkins jobs with Jira projects in an effort to increase efficiency and support traceability throughout our pipelines and engineering landscape.

To begin we will need to have a few pre-requisites in place. Specifically we will need the following items:

- A Jira installation that is web-accessible by Jenkins
- Administrative access to Jira and Jenkins
- A Jenkins installation which is web-accessible by Jira
- Any number of projects in Jenkins, and Jira

To begin our integration efforts lets start by installing the Atlassian marketplace Jenkins plugin into Jira. This can be done via the **Addons** tab, which is available within the administration area of Jira. A screenshot of this plugin and its Install button is provided below:

Figure 9-18: The Jenkins plugin for JIRA

To continue click the **Install** button shown in the figure above. Once the installation process has completed, we will want to configure the plugin to communicate properly with Jenkins.

The plugin creates an administration-accessible **Jenkins Configuration** menu option, which will be available in the addons area of Jira after the installation has completed. To configure the plugin we will need to navigate into the Jenkins configuration in Jira. A screenshot of this menu link is provided below:

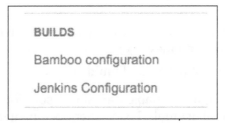

Figure 9-19: The menu link in the Jenkins configuration menu

When we click on the **Jenkins Configuration** link Jira will navigate us to a tutorial that we will need to follow in order to get the plugin properly working in conjunction with Jenkins. The tutorial page for configuring the application links is illustrated below in *Figure 9-20*:

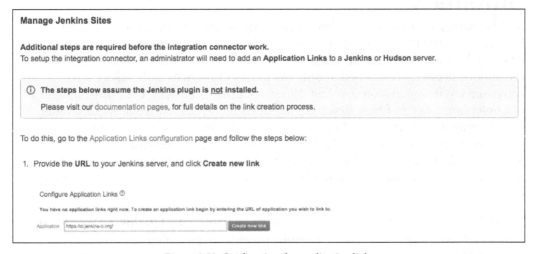

Figure 9-20: Configuring the application links

Once the tutorial has been followed, Jenkins should be completely integrated into Jira. Jira itself will provide a number of new features that will allow us to track Jenkins builds directly. Lets take a look at a few of these features:

- Per project CI builds tab (provides an aggregated view of recent builds for the project)

- Per issue/ticket CI builds tab (shows which builds have a given ticket identified in the commit message)

- Real-time updating of tickets and builds in Jira

This solution provides a highly valuable traceability solution for Jira and Jenkins and integrates these two robust tools. For further documentation on Jenkins and Jira integrations you can consult the plugin documentation at the following URL:

```
https://marvelution.atlassian.net/wiki/display/JJI/
Advanced+Application+Links
```

Summary

In this chapter we discovered some interesting technology stacks and learned how we can integrate them into Jenkins. We learned about Docker and how to leverage its scalable container solutions as Jenkins slave nodes, and how to house the Jenkins master. We learned about Ansible and how we can leverage it to provision environments on demand. We spent time discussing the implementation of a Selenium Grid and how to write some tests using it. Finally we spent time in Jira learning how to integrate Jenkins into this widely adopted Agile bug tracking solution. When evaluating new technologies we can make Jenkins accomplish just about anything but the emphasis should be placed on keeping the system stable and scalable. From here you should be able to research other new technologies and evaluate them.

In the final chapter of *Mastering Jenkins* we will discover the Jenkins API, and learn how to setup a plugin development environment, create a plugin, and install it into our Jenkins system. This will provide us with much greater control over the implementation of our Jenkins system. Let's proceed.

10
Extending Jenkins

Jenkins has gained a lot of notoriety is summarily due its highly extensible architecture, and widely developed plugin ecosystem. The open-source community to-date has developed hundreds of centrally available plugins, in an effort to maximize the capabilities of Jenkins, integrate it with other technologies, and provide tighter coupling with other development-related tooling. The popular catch phrase surrounding the Jenkins plugin ecosystem is *There's a plugin for that*, and indeed there probably is.

> *"If I have seen further it is by standing on the shoulders of giants."* – *Sir Issac Newton*

The Jenkins open source development community in conjunction with enterprise software organizations have introduced a vast collection of ready-made plugins that can tailor Jenkins to meet almost any organizations' specific tools and processes. Even with all of the ready-made plugins it may be necessary to implement a custom plugin for a specific need or solution. Creating plugins for Jenkins provides us with the ability to customize almost every aspect of the Jenkins system and even extend plugins that already exist. Developing plugins for Jenkins may sound like a daunting task at first but with a little effort, research and perseverance we will learn how to create and deploy custom functionality for the Jenkins system through the Jenkins plugin architecture.

In this final chapter, we will learn about Jenkins plugin development and the ins-and outs of the Jenkins plugin architecture. This will help us gain a better understanding of the Jenkins subsystems and discover some of the available tools we can leverage to extend Jenkins and integrate it with unique development processes and tools.

The primary objectives for this chapter will include:

- Setting up the development environment (IntelliJ IDEA)
- The Plugin skeleton
- Importing a Maven-generated skeleton into IntelliJ
- Understanding the Architecture of a Jenkins Plugin
- Working with Jelly Tags and files

Plug-in development tip

While creating plugins for Jenkins can be fun and intellectually stimulating, it is important to avoid duplicating the efforts of the Jenkins open source development community. Be sure to check the plugin development page to make sure that a given plugin or idea does not already exist prior to beginning the hard work of implementing a new one. For a complete list of plugins, please refer to the following URL: `https://wiki.jenkins-ci.org/display/JENKINS/Plugins`.

Setting up the development environment

Jenkins, **Hudson Plug-in Interface** (**HPI**) plugins are developed primarily using the **Java Development Kit** (**JDK**) in concert with Apache Maven. This set of tutorials and subsequent sections focuses on using IntelliJ for the plugin development IDE. However, plugins can in fact be developed using many other IDE's and languages (JRuby, Eclipse, Groovy, and so on). Since the vast majority of Jenkins plugins available today have been crafted using the Java JDK and Maven, we will focus on that particular technology stack.

To get started we will need to configure a basic Jenkins plugin development environment, including compilers, linkers, and project lifecycle tools. The majority of this can be accomplished by installing the following items onto the target plugin development machine:

- Maven 3 (`http://maven.apache.org/install.html`)
- Oracle Java JDK 1.7 [`http://www.oracle.com/technetwork/java/javase/downloads/index.html`]

Once the Java JDK (1.7+) and Maven automation tools have been installed on the local machine, we will need to replace the primary Maven settings file, and enable communication with the Jenkins CI artifact repositories, which will allow Maven to fetch dependencies and enable HPI goals from the command line.

The Apache Maven settings file that we will need to modify can be located in one of the following locations (depending on your OS):

- Windows — `C:\<PATHTOUSERPROFILE>\.m2\settings.xml`

- Mac OS X / `*NIX` - `~/.m2/settings.xml`

To update the Maven settings file you can use your favorite text editor (VI, nano, emacs, Notepad etc.) The contents of the Apache Maven `settings.xml` file should reflect the following example, which was taken from `https://wiki.jenkins-ci.org/display/JENKINS/Plugin+tutorial`.

```
<settings>
  <pluginGroups>
    <pluginGroup>org.jenkins-ci.tools</pluginGroup>
  </pluginGroups>

  <profiles>
    <!-- Give access to Jenkins plugins -->
    <profile>
      <id>jenkins</id>
      <activation>
        <activeByDefault>true</activeByDefault>
      </activation>
      <repositories>
        <repository>
          <id>repo.jenkins-ci.org</id>
          <url>http://repo.jenkins-ci.org/public/</url>
        </repository>
      </repositories>
      <pluginRepositories>
        <pluginRepository>
          <id>repo.jenkins-ci.org</id>
          <url>http://repo.jenkins-ci.org/public/</url>
        </pluginRepository>
      </pluginRepositories>
    </profile>
  </profiles>
  <mirrors>
    <mirror>
      <id>repo.jenkins-ci.org</id>
      <url>http://repo.jenkins-ci.org/public/</url>
      <mirrorOf>m.g.o-public</mirrorOf>
    </mirror>
  </mirrors>
</settings>
```

Once the changes to the XML file have been made, save the file and overwrite your existing local copy. As we mentioned earlier, the configuration file changes will enable HPI shorthand support in Maven for command line goals, enable artifact downloads, and allow us to create Jenkins plugin skeleton structures.

Let's take a minute to verify everything is configured properly. From the command line, change to a suitable test (something you can get to easily and that isn't critical for later) directory, and enter the following command into the terminal.

```
#> mvn hpi:help
```

 As Jenkins plugin developers we will further leverage the HPI goals to create, compile, debug, and release Jenkins plugins. Later in this chapter we will learn to use these goals directly inside the IntelliJ IDEA for proper GUI development.

Once Maven has executed the `hpi:help` goal Maven will display a detailed help output for the available HPI goals. Each of these is described next:

```
[INFO] Scanning for projects...
[INFO]
[INFO] ------------------------------------------------------------
[INFO] Building Maven Stub Project (No POM) 1
[INFO] ------------------------------------------------------------
[INFO]
[INFO] --- maven-hpi-plugin:1.114-cloudbees-1:help (default-cli) @
standalone-pom ---
[INFO] Maven Jenkins Plugin 1.114-cloudbees-1
  Maven2 plugin for developing Jenkins plugins
```

This plugin has 14 goals:

- `hpi:assemble-dependencies`
    - Used to assemble transitive dependencies of plugins into one location
    - Unlike other similar mojos in this plugin, this one traverses dependencies through its graph

- `hpi:bundle-plugins`
    - Takes the current project, lists all the transitive dependencies, then copies them into a specified directory
    - Used to assemble `jenkins.war` by bundling all the necessary plugins

- `hpi:create`
  - ○ Builds a new plugin template. Most of this is really just a rip-off from the `archetype:create` goal, but since Maven doesn't really let one Mojo calls another Mojo, this turns out to be the easiest.

- `hpi:custom-war`
  - ○ Builds a custom Jenkins war that includes all the additional plugins referenced in this POM

- `hpi:generate-taglib-interface`
  - ○ Generates the strongly-typed Java interfaces for Groovy taglibs

- `hpi:help`
  - ○ Displays help information on the maven-hpi-plugin
  - ○ Calls `mvn hpi:help -Ddetail=true -Dgoal=<goal-name>` to display parameter details

- `hpi:hpi`
  - ○ Builds a war/webapp

- `hpi:hpl`
  - ○ Generates `.hpl` file

- `hpi:insert-test`
  - ○ Inserts default test suite

- `hpi:list-plugin-dependencies`
  - ○ Lists all the plugin dependencies

- `hpi:resolve-test-dependencies`
  - ○ Places test-dependency plugins into somewhere the test harness can pick them up
  - ○ See `TestPluginManager.loadBundledPlugins()` where the test harness uses it

- `hpi:run`
  - ○ Runs Jenkins with the current plugin project
  - ○ This only needs the source files to be compiled, so run in the compile phase
  - ○ To specify the HTTP port, use `Djetty.port=PORT`

- `hpi:test-hpl`

  ○ Generate a .hpl file in the test class directory so that test harness can locate the plugin

- `hpi:validate`

  ```
  Make sure that we are running in the right environment
  [INFO] ---------------------------------------------------------
  [INFO] BUILD SUCCESS
  [INFO] ---------------------------------------------------------
  [INFO] Total time: 10.453s
  [INFO] Finished at: Mon Jul 27 11:12:46 CDT 2015
  [INFO] Final Memory: 9M/124M
  [INFO] ---------------------------------------------------------
  ```

From the above command line output we should be able to gain a basic grasp of how to manage plugins through the Maven command line, and a pretty good idea of the available HPI goals (details for each HPI goal were provided earlier). As we mentioned previously, these HPI-specific goals help us create, debug, and develop Jenkins plugins. What is important to understand here is that the HPI goals we executed on the command line are the same set of tasks the IDE will make available. From here we will shift the focus over to integrating Maven and HPI with a proper plugin development IDE.

One of the more popular JAVA development IDE's available is IntelliJ IDEA solution. In this section, we will learn how to create and import a Jenkins plugin into this popular Java development IDE. Let's take a minute to install it onto the target development machine.

The IntelliJ IDEA installer can be located at the following URL:

- JetBrains ItelliJ IDEA (`https://www.jetbrains.com/idea/`)

As you may have noticed from the JetBrains website there are two versions of the IntelliJ IDEA development IDE available. One is the community edition (free), and the other is the ultimate edition (paid). For the purposes of cost and availability, we will be continuing this chapter using the free community edition. To proceed, download the appropriate version of the IDE for your operating system and use the installation wizard to configure the basic installation.

Once the IDE is installed let's fire it up. Upon initial launch we are presented with a screen that looks similar to the one illustrated in *Figure 10-1* [depending on the version of IntelliJ installed]:

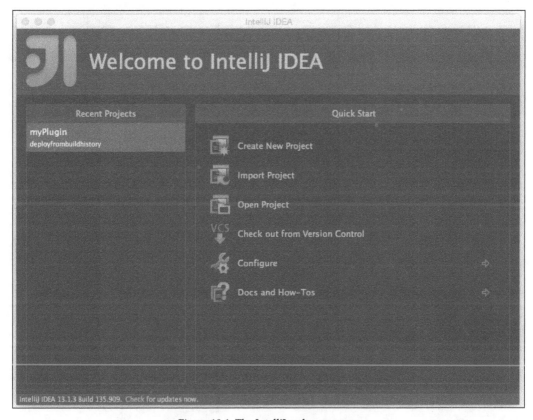

Figure 10-1: The IntelliJ welcome screen

The IntelliJ development environment has a robust and highly configurable feature set. It supports many development systems and coding scenarios. To proceed with Jenkins plugin development we will need to configure the IntelliJ IDE to support Maven and integrate with our JDK. To begin, though, let's install the *Stapler* plugin, which supports Jenkins. To accomplish this, navigate from the splash screen to the install plugins configuration area by completing the following flow:

Configure->Plugins->Browse Repositories

Upon completion of the above steps, we are presented with a fairly large list of available plugins. We can use the search field to find our Stapler plugin. This is illustrated in *Figure 10-2*:

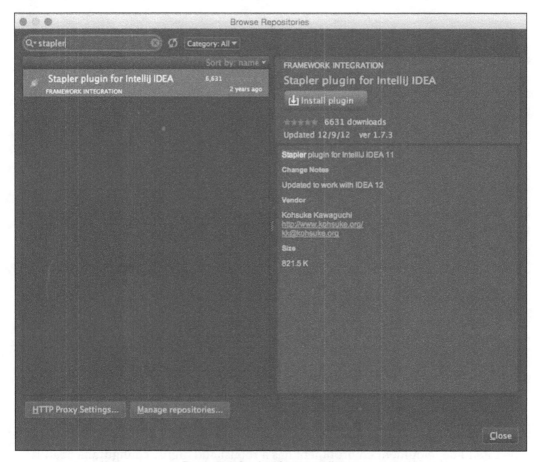

Figure 10-2: Stapler plugin installation

To proceed with the installation of the Stapler plugin, click the **Install plugin** button, and then click **Close**. This will prompt the IDE to install the Stapler plugin into its plugin cache. Upon clicking the **Close** button, IntelliJ IDEA will prompt us to restart it, which will finalize the installation of the plugin and make it available for use.

After IntelliJ has restarted we will need to configure the *Maven Home* environment within the IntelliJ configuration area. IntelliJ provides a pretty comprehensive set of configuration options, accessible directly from the splash screen. To get to the Maven options area perform the following navigation steps from the UI.

Configure -> Preferences -> Maven -> Maven home directory

Maven home directory:	/usr/local/Cellar/maven30/3.0.5/libexec	...	☑ Override
	M2_HOME is used by default		
User settings file:	/Users/admin/.m2/settings.xml	...	☐ Override
Local repository:	/Users/admin/.m2/repository	...	☐ Override

Figure 10-3: Configuring the Maven home directory

In *Figure 10-3,* we can see a screen that allows us to update the Maven home directory field, and specify a user settings file. These are unique to your specific Maven installation. Update the field with the appropriate value for your specific Maven home location and click the **OK** button to persist these settings.

Once saved IntelliJ should now be configured to support Jenkins plugin development via an IDE. In the next sections we will learn about creating Jenkins plugin skeletons, and how to tie the Maven command line implementation into our IntelliJ IDE.

Creating a Jenkins plugin skeleton

Prior to launching the IntelliJ IDE and beginning our plugin development, we will need to generate a plugin skeleton. The Jenkins development community has graciously provided this skeleton framework as a way to encourage developers to extend the Jenkins subsystems. The skeleton provides a foundational development structure for developing Jenkins plugins.

 The skeleton framework is simply a set of files, and folders, that contain the source code for a basic *hello world* plugin. When developing a plugin from scratch this handy framework gives us a great foundational layer that we can start from.

To generate the Jenkins plugin skeleton we will need to command Maven to create it.. The creation of the skeleton structure is accomplished through the `hpi:create` goal on the command line. Let's begin by creating our obligatory *Hello Jenkins* plugin. To do this we will need to execute the command shown below:

```
#>mvn hpi:create
```

Once the command has been inputted we should be prompted by Stapler to define the groupID for the plugin.

Enter the groupId of your plugin [org.jenkins-ci.plugins]:

To proceed input the following and press *ENTER*:

```
com.hellojenkins.jenkins.plugins
```

In Maven a groupID uniquely identifies a project being created and is typically unique across all projects. The conformity requirements of Java would normally require us to enter a domain name (in reverse format) that is uniquely owned or controlled. Since we are performing this exercise merely as an example, this input parameter has a little less significance than it normally would. If we were to develop a plugin that was to be distributed within the Jenkins plugin community (within the available plugins page in Jenkins) it would be in our best interests to come up with a completely unique domain name.

After the groupID has been entered, Maven should prompt us for the artifactID. This configuration item is simply the name of the binary file we will be creating (final distributed filename) minus the version number. To proceed with our plugin creation tutorial, input the following text and press *ENTER*:

```
hellojenkins
```

Once the basic plugin details have been specified, Maven will proceed to build out the skeleton framework structures necessary for Jenkins plugin development. The complete output from Maven is provided below:

```
[INFO] Defaulting package to group ID + artifact ID: com.hellojenkins.
jenkins.plugins.hellojenkins

[INFO] --------------------------------------------------------

[INFO] Using following parameters for creating Archetype: maven-hpi-
plugin:1.114-cloudbees-1

[INFO] --------------------------------------------------------

[INFO] Parameter: basedir, Value: /Users/admin/Desktop/PlugIns/test

[INFO] Parameter: package, Value: com.hellojenkins.jenkins.plugins.
hellojenkins

[INFO] Parameter: groupId, Value: com.hellojenkins.jenkins.plugins

[INFO] Parameter: artifactId, Value: hellojenkins

[INFO] Parameter: version, Value: 1.0-SNAPSHOT

[INFO] ********************* End of debug info from resources from
generated POM **********************

[INFO] Archetype created in dir: /Users/admin/Desktop/PlugIns/test/
```

```
hellojenkins
[INFO] -----------------------------------------------------------
[INFO] BUILD SUCCESS
[INFO] -----------------------------------------------------------
[INFO] Total time: 11:05.586s
[INFO] Finished at: Mon Jul 27 11:08:42 CDT 2015
[INFO] Final Memory: 14M/124M
[INFO] -----------------------------------------------------------
```

Once Maven has completed the skeleton creation process, we can take a look at the plugin folder and file structures it created. Enter either DIR or ls into the command line terminal and verify there is a folder named hellojenkins.

Once the folder has been verified we can launch the development instance of Jenkins and see our plugin in action. To accomplish this we will execute the hpi:run goal from the command line as shown below:

#>mvn hpi:run

If everything fires up as expected Maven will build the plugin, and launch Jenkins with the helloJenkins plugin pre-installed. The URL to access the development instance should be http://localhost:8080/jenkins/.

As the development instance of Jenkins fires up, the command line output from the Maven should look like the following:

```
[INFO] Scanning for projects...
[INFO]
[INFO] -----------------------------------------------------------
[INFO] Building TODO Plugin 1.0-SNAPSHOT
[INFO] -----------------------------------------------------------
[INFO]
[INFO] >>> maven-hpi-plugin:1.106:run (default-cli) > compile @
helloJenkins >>>
[INFO]
[INFO] --- maven-hpi-plugin:1.106:validate (default-validate) @
helloJenkins ---
[INFO]
[INFO] --- maven-enforcer-plugin:1.0.1:enforce (enforce-maven) @
helloJenkins ---
[INFO]
```

```
[INFO] --- maven-enforcer-plugin:1.0.1:display-info (display-info) @
helloJenkins ---

[INFO] Maven Version: 3.3.3

[INFO] JDK Version: 1.8.0_20-ea normalized as: 1.8.0-20

[INFO] OS Info: Arch: x86_64 Family: mac Name: mac os x Version: 10.8.5

[INFO]

[INFO] --- maven-localizer-plugin:1.14:generate (default) @ helloJenkins
---

[INFO]

[INFO] --- maven-resources-plugin:2.5:resources (default-resources) @
helloJenkins ---

[debug] execute contextualize

[INFO] Using 'UTF-8' encoding to copy filtered resources.

[INFO] Copying 5 resources

[INFO]

[INFO] --- maven-compiler-plugin:2.5:compile (default-compile) @
helloJenkins ---

[INFO] Nothing to compile - all classes are up to date

[INFO]

[INFO] <<< maven-hpi-plugin:1.106:run (default-cli) < compile @
helloJenkins <<<

[INFO]

[INFO] --- maven-hpi-plugin:1.106:run (default-cli) @ helloJenkins ---

[INFO] Generating ./work/plugins/helloJenkins.hpl

 [INFO] Context path = /jenkins

[INFO] Tmp directory = /Users/Jonathan/Desktop/test/helloJenkins/target/
work

[INFO] Web defaults =  jetty default

[INFO] Starting jetty 6.1.1 ...

[INFO] jetty-6.1.1

Jenkins home directory: /Users/Jonathan/Desktop/test/helloJenkins/./work
found at: System.getProperty("HUDSON_HOME")

[INFO] Started SelectChannelConnector @ 0.0.0.0:8080

[INFO] Started Jetty Server

[INFO]: Jenkins is fully up and running

...
```

Once Jenkins is up and running we should see our plugin installed. This can be
verified within the plugin management area under the **Installed** tab.

When launching the plugin using `hpi:run`, consider executing Maven with the debugger enabled. This option can help us see the action going on inside the Maven processes. To turn on the debugger simply add `Dhudson.maven.debugPort=5001` to the Maven command line arguments.

The plugin skeleton

In the previous section we commanded Maven to generate a basic plugin skeleton (`hpi:create`) structure, and then launched our plugin in a local development sandbox by executing the `hpi:run` goal. Now that the skeleton structure has been created, let's take a look at the contents of the skeleton structure, and learn about the roles that each of these folders will play in our quest for plugin development:

- `./src`
- `./target`
- `./work`
- `./pom.xml`

From the folder structure described above we can see there are a number of sub-folders, and a POM file. Lets take a minute to examine each of these in greater detail:

- `./src`: This folder contains the source code for the plugin.
- `./target`: This folder contains the compiled binary output (`*.hpi`) and test execution results output.
- `./work`: This folder is created when the plugin is installed into the sandbox and contains the extracted Java classes and respective temporary working files.
- `pom.xml`: This file is the top-level Maven project file, which describes our plugin and build definitions. For more details on Maven POM files the following web URL provides detailed documentation.`https://maven.apache.org/guides/introduction/introduction-to-the-pom.html`.

When we take a closer look at the `src/main` folder, our Jenkins plugin architecture takes on a new level of clarity. Inside this folder we can see the underlying code, graphic resources (if any), jelly files, and general conventions that make up a Jenkins plugin.

Let's take a quick look at the conventions of the skeleton. Java provides a pre-defined folder structure to organize source code (code behind) and user interface elements (resources folder) into logical groupings. This organization methodology can be seen in *Figure 10-4* below:

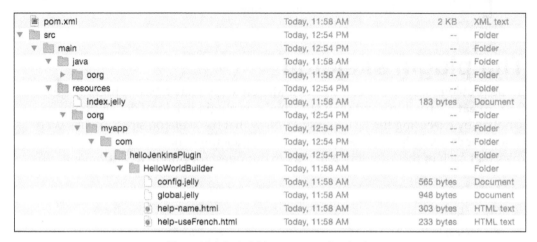

Figure 10-4: Basic folder structure of a plugin

When a plugin is first generated, the main entry point into the plugin architecture is described in the `<pluginname>.java` file generated by the Maven `hpi:create` goal. This file contains the class definitions for our plugin, which initially extends only the Builder extension point. We will discuss extension points and the development architecture of the plugins in the coming sections. Before we get to development architecture let's take a few minutes to look at how to import the plugin into our IntelliJ development IDE.

Importing a Maven-generated skeleton into IntelliJ

Importing a plugin into the IntelliJ IDEA IDE will provide us with a comprehensive set of development tools and will streamline the development of our plugin. To get up-and-running we will need to import an already created plugin (either checked out from GitHub OR created using the mvn hpi:create command). In this section we will discuss how to import a Maven project (the Jenkins hpi plugin) into a new project in IntelliJ IDEA and learn how to use the IDE to actively develop it.

Let's learn how to import our helloJenkins plugin into our development IDE. To accomplish this, first fire up IntelliJIDEA IDE on your local machine. Once fired up, click the **Import Project** navigation icon from the **Quick Start** panel, and navigate to the **helloJenkins** project we created earlier using hpi:create command. This flow is shown in *Figure 10-5*:

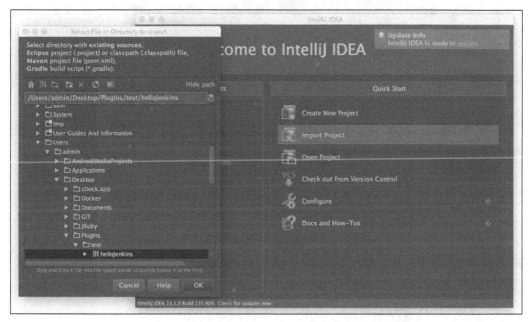

Figure 10-5: Importing a POM from IntelliJ IDEA

Upon clicking the **OK** button shown in the previous dialog, IntelliJ will ask if we want to import an existing Maven or Gradle project, or create a new one from another existing source. In our case we will want to select **Import project from external model** and select **Maven** as our project type. Once this has been completed click **Next** to proceed to the detailed project configuration screen as shown in *Figure 10-6*:

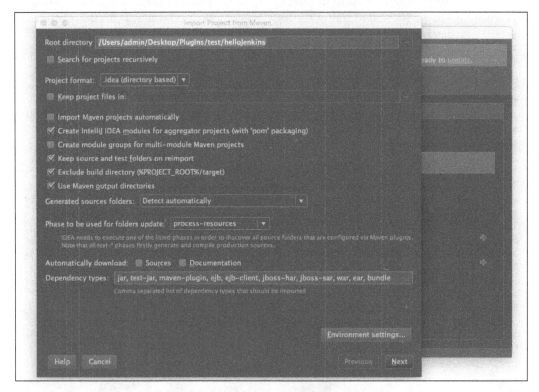

Figure 10-6: A detailed import configuration screen

From the detailed configuration screen there are a few configuration options we will want to set. They are as follows:

- **Root Directory** (path to the Jenkins HPI skeleton folder)
- **Automatically download**: **Sources** [checked]
- **Automatically download**: **Documentation** [checked]
- **Environment settings...** [Maven home directory] [Override checked]

Once the above configurations have been made, click the **Next** button to proceed to the next configuration screen, which will simply prompt us for any profiles we will want to include when importing. For the profile configuration option, specify **jenkins** and click **Next**. Once the import of the profile has completed, IntelliJ will ask us to **Select Maven projects to import**. We should see our plugin already checked (as we described its home location earlier), and will want to additionally tick the box **Open Project Structure after import**. Once this step has been completed, click **Next** to proceed to the Project SDK specification screen.

From the project SDK configuration screen we should be prompted to select a target JDK for our IntelliJ project. *Figure 10-7* illustrates Java JDK 1.8 installed and selected:

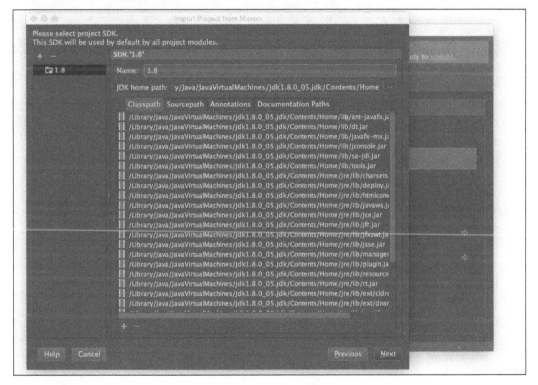

Figure 10-7: Select a JDK

Once this screen has been configured, click **Next** to proceed to the final project import configuration screen, as shown in *Figure 10-8*:

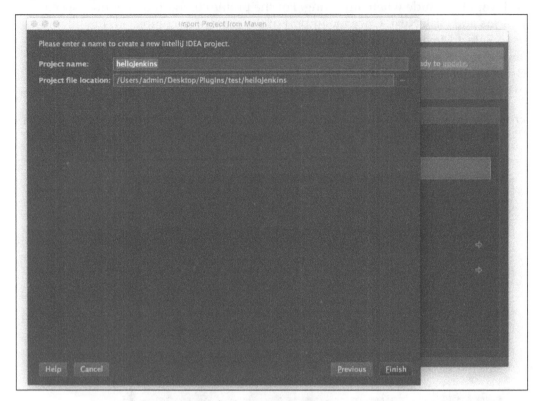

Figure 10-8: The final project import configuration screen

Finally we can click the **Finish** button to finalize the import procedures for our Maven Jenkins plugin project.

IntelliJ at this point will prompt us to do some final processing on the import, and then navigate to us the project editor screen (shown in *Figure 10-9*):

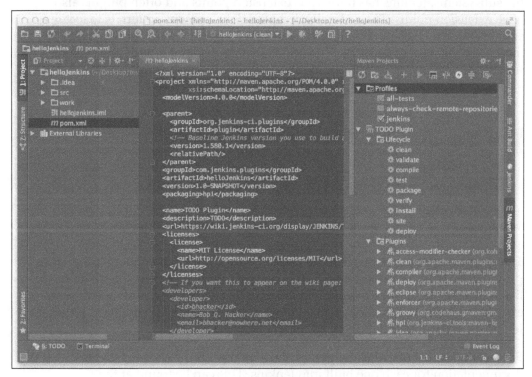

Figure 10-9: Project editor screen

At this point, if you see a screen similar to the one above take a moment to congratulate yourself on achieving the goal of configuring a basic Jenkins plugin development environment with a unified IDE. It's now time to begin coding and building our Jenkins plugin.

The architecture of Jenkins plugins

The Jenkins plugin architecture leverages *extension points*, which essentially provide implementation hooks for plug-in developers to extend the functionality of a given Jenkins subsystem, or plugin. Jenkins itself has hundreds of extension points. Extension points are automatically detected by Jenkins during the loading of the system.

The extension point architecture offers an easy way to extend or alter the inner functionality of an abstract Java class or interface without the need to recompile the subsystems. Jenkins has numerous extension points and often plugins also have extension points. The generally accepted development pattern is to locate a suitable extension point to manipulate, and then extend Jenkins (or a plugin) by implementing a set of classes and methods that override or modify the existing functionality. Some of the more common extension points include:

- SecurityRealm
- Builder
- BuildStep
- Publisher
- Trigger
- Recorder
- ManagementLink

The extension points we just listed represent only a few of the more popular ones provided by Jenkins; these are just a few of many. In reality there are too many to list in this chapter. As we briefly mentioned earlier some plugins define their own extension points, which allow a given plugin to be extended by another. To say Jenkins is extensible is definitely an understatement.

For a complete list of extension points, the Jenkins-ci.org web site provides documentation for each one built into Jenkins. This can be found at the following URL:

```
https://wiki.jenkins-ci.org/display/JENKINS/Extension+points
```

If the idea of extension points seems a bit confusing, it doesn't need to be. Let's take a quick look at a diagramed model, which should help illustrate the concepts of the **Extension Point Architecture** (*Figure 10-10*):

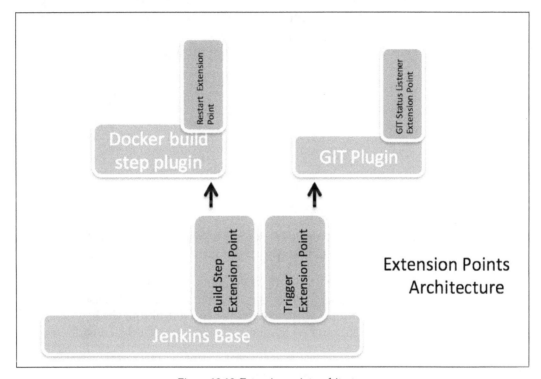

Figure 10-10: Extension point architecture

As we mentioned earlier, extension points in Jenkins are implemented by marking a Java class with the *implements ExtensionPoint* marker. This tells Java that the specified class and its methods can be *Extended* via the Extends annotation marker. We will discuss this concept in further detail by showing some code examples in just a minute. First let's take a moment to understand the basic job lifecycle. This can help us locate a suitable extension point for plugin development.

 It is a general best practice to only extend an existing extension point, and not wise to override non-extension point class types. This will help the system remain in a stable state and help alleviate unknown repercussions.

Understanding the Jenkins job lifecycle

When learning about creating Jenkins plugins, it's important to fully understand the Jenkins project lifecycle; that is to say, the phases a job will go through during execution. By understanding the project's lifecycle we can better identify extension points that can be leveraged to create a plugin that executes in the right phase. When a Jenkins job is executed, it transitions through the following steps in synchronous order:

1. Polling.
2. Pre SCM.
3. SCM.
4. Pre Build.
5. Build (Builder Extension point).
6. Post Build (RecorderNotifier extension point).

Each of the above phases in the lifecycle represents a logical extension point and can be extended by Jenkins plugins and manipulated to provide additional functionality.

Now that we have a general understanding of the lifecycle, let's look at some code fragments that extend various extension points within the lifecycle. Classes that have been extended via a Jenkins plugin will contain the class definition, the extension point inner class descriptor, and any overrides. To better clarify this, consider the following code snippet:

```
public class HelloWorldBuilder extends Builder {

    @Extension // This indicates to Jenkins that this is an
implementation of an extension point. (inner class descriptor)

    public static final class DescriptorImpl extends
BuildStepDescriptor<Builder> {
    }
}
```

In the above example, we can see that we have a simple class `HelloWorldBuilder`, which *extends* the Jenkins `Builder` class. Let's take a look at the `Builder` class source code for Jenkins provided at:

https://github.com/kohsuke/hudson/blob/7a64e030a38561c98954c4c51c4438
c97469dfd6/core/src/main/java/hudson/tasks/Builder.java

We can see that the source code contains a class definition as follows:

```
public abstract class Builder extends BuildStepCompatibilityLayer
implements
Describable<Builder>, ExtensionPoint {
}
```

This shows the connection between our plugin's extension class and its logical parent. The important thing to note here is the `ExtensionPoint` annotation in the class definition.

Based on what we have seen, we can just as easily create our own extension points within our plugin. This will allow other plugin developers to create plugins that will extend ours. To do this we simply need to notate `@Extension` point above the class definition as shown below.

```
@Extension
public class foo extends Bar { ... }
```

From the above class definition we would be providing an extension point for class `foo`, which already extends class `Bar`. This is very much like stapling one extension point onto another.

Using overrides

As we briefly mentioned earlier, overrides define replacement methods. Overrides are simple in nature; they specify a method within a class that will override the originating definition. Overrides in Jenkins allow the plugin developer to completely replace an existing method with one of their own. To help clarify this implementation, consider the following code snippet:

```
@Override
public boolean perform(AbstractBuild build, Launcher launcher,
BuildListener listener) {
    // This is where you 'build' the project.
    // Since this is a dummy, we just say 'hello world' and call
that a build.

    // This also shows how you can consult the global
configuration of the builder
    if (getDescriptor().getUseFrench())
        listener.getLogger().println("Bonjour, "+name+"!");
    else
        listener.getLogger().println("Hello, "+name+"!");
    return true;
}
```

Working with describables and descriptors

When implementing user interface elements in a Jenkins plugin that requires the persistence of information (say a job configuration or form). Jenkins needs a way to render the UI, capture, and then persist any data inputted. The development pattern to facilitate this type of behavior is to use the describable and descriptor annotations, along with a data-bound object.

To help us grok this pattern, we can consider it very much like a cyclic propagation of information. When data is inputted into a configuration form, it's persisted as an instantiated descriptor object, which belongs to our plugin's defining class (eventually this is bound to an XML file on the disk). This implementation is very similar in nature to a class and object instance relationship. The main thing to remember here is that a class is *Describable* and a *Descriptor* is the instantiation of the persisted data.

Let's take a look at some code examples to further explain this:

```
@Extension // This indicates to Jenkins that this is an implementation
of an extension point.
    public static final class DescriptorImpl extends
BuildStepDescriptor<Builder> {


        public DescriptorImpl() {
            load();
        }


}
```

As we can tell from the code above, the implementation of a Descriptor in the plugin is simply an extension of the `BuildStepDescriptor` class. Let's look at a class declaration and see how it was created:

```
public abstract class BuildStepDescriptor<T extends BuildStep &
Describable<T>> extends Descriptor<T> {
    protected BuildStepDescriptor(Class<? extends T> clazz) {
        super(clazz);
    }
}
```

From the above code segment it is apparent that the Jenkins `BuildStepDescriptor` (the originating class) class is `Describable` and our plugin instantiates this using the `DescriptorImpl` method. This is in a lot of ways a similar approach that was used for UI configuration persistence and fits neatly into the plugin architecture.

Jelly tags and files

As our Jenkins development experience progresses, we will need to incorporate user interface elements into our plugins. User interface interaction is implemented in Jenkins plugins through the use of jelly files. Jelly is a tag based UI implementation solution created by Apache, and provides a UI data-binding solution in Jenkins for plugin developers.

The core documentation for Jelly tags can be located on the Apache web site at:

```
http://commons.apache.org/proper/commons-jelly/tags.html
```

The implementation of the Jelly solution in Jenkins adds a couple of conventions. The first is the entry field, which provides automatic data binding connections for the jelly entry field and the instance. The second is the implementation of data binding through the constructor. When the constructor is called it's automatically populated with data submitted from the form. To provide an example of this consider the following code snippets provided by the example Jenkins skeleton:

```
Config.jelly
<?jelly escape-by-default='true'?>
<j:jelly xmlns:j="jelly:core" xmlns:st="jelly:stapler"
xmlns:d="jelly:define" xmlns:l="/lib/layout" xmlns:t="/lib/hudson"
xmlns:f="/lib/form">
  <!--
    This jelly script is used for per-project configuration.

    See global.jelly for a general discussion about jelly script.
  -->

  <!--
    Creates a text field that shows the value of the "name" property.
    When submitted, it will be passed to the corresponding constructor
parameter.
  -->
  <f:entry title="Name" field="name">
    <f:textbox />
  </f:entry>
</j:jelly>

HelloWorldBuilder.java
/ Fields in config.jelly must match the parameter names in the
"DataBoundConstructor"
    @DataBoundConstructor
    public HelloWorldBuilder(String name) {
        this.name = name;
    }
```

As the code purports, the instance of the name variable in our class is automatically populated when the `databoundconstructor` is initialized.

As you may have assumed already, the Jelly file implementation is not limited to simple field-based Web forms. The UI can be populated with any number of Web-based controls. For a complete set of examples, Jenkins provides an open source project on GitHub that helps describe each of the available controls in detail.

```
https://github.com/jenkinsci/jenkins/tree/master/core/src/main/
resources/lib/form
```

Compiling and installing an HPI plugin

So far we have learned how to set up the IntelliJ IDE, develop a basic plugin via extension points, and extend Jenkins. We learned about the project lifecycle and discovered new ways to extend Jenkins. In this section we will see how to build our final `.HPI` and install it onto the Jenkins system. To do this we will want to compile the plugin using Maven with the `install` target specified, and then load it into the Jenkins system. Let's get started.

To generate the final HPI package, open a command line window, navigate to your plugin directory, and enter the following command into the terminal:

```
#> mvn package
```

The compilation and packaging of the plugin take a few minutes to execute and complete. Once completed our terminal window will contain a set of final output that should look something like the following:

```
[INFO] ------------------------------------------------------------
[INFO] BUILD SUCCESS
[INFO] ------------------------------------------------------------
[INFO] Total time: 04:28 min
[INFO] Finished at: 2015-09-28T12:02:49-05:00
[INFO] Final Memory: 52M/488M
[INFO] ------------------------------------------------------------
```

We should now see a new `target` folder listed alongside our `POM.XML` file. This folder will house the final .HPI file we will need to install onto the Jenkins system.

To install this plugin onto a Jenkins system log on to the Jenkins system as an administrator and navigate to the plugin installation page via the following navigational steps:

Manage Jenkins -> Manage Plugins -> Advanced (tab)

From here we should be able to upload the plugin to the Jenkins system and install it in shot via the Upload plugin form presented on the page.

Once the plugin has been uploaded and installed it should be properly listed in the **Installed** plugins tab.

Summary

In this chapter of *Mastering Jenkins* we discovered the details of plugin development in Jenkins. We learned some of the core concepts required for plugin development, and learned how to leverage Maven and IntelliJ to build out a robust development environment.

As our journey into Jenkins comes to an end, we wish you adieu and hope that this book has provided various useful tidbits that will help better define how to achieve continuous practices using Jenkins. When implementing build pipelines, start small grow them organically through proper planning and implementation strategy. Then innovate them. From here we will part ways with one final quote of wisdom.

> *"There are only two mistakes one can make along the road to truth; not going all the way, and not starting."*
>
> *– Buddah*

Index

A

Active Directory
  URL 231
Ansible
  Jenkins, integrating 249-257
  URL 252
Apache reverse proxy
  Jenkins, executing 13-15
Apache web server
  URL 14
Archiva
  URL 150
Artifactory
  Jenkins, integrating 257-259
  URL 258
artifacts
  fetching, archive artifacts used 160, 161
  fetching, from Artifactory 161-163
  fetching, via Maven 163, 164
  retrieving 160
automated tests
  A/B testing 119
  architecture 124-126
  black box tests 118
  capacity tests 117
  executing, via MSTest 135
  functional tests 117
  implementing 114, 115
  in Jenkins 127-133
  product code, connecting 122, 123
  quality, implementing 124
  regression tests 117
  smoke / BVT (Build Verification) tests 116
  unit tests 116
  white box tests 118

B

Behavior Driven Development (BDD) 127
black box tests 118
branch by abstraction 214
Build History panel 105-107
build notification programs
  reference link 67
build pipelines
  additional segments 183, 184
  architecting 180
  Delivery Pipeline plugin 195-199
  downstream jobs, triggering 187
  first segment 181, 182
  Jenkins instances, connecting 200-202
  other projects, building 189
  Parameterized Trigger plugin 189-191
  Post Build Tasks plugin 194, 195
  production pipeline segments 185, 186
  Promoted build plugin 191-194
  release management 184
  release pipeline segments 185, 186
  upstream jobs, triggering 187
  value proposition 176-180
build pipelines, Continuous Delivery (CD)
  URL 233
  visualization 232, 233
  workflow 232, 233
build process
  about 145
  flow 145
  packaging scheme, architecting 146-148
  standardizing 145, 146
build queue panel 67

C

Call remote job plugin
URL 200
capacity tests 117
Categorized View plugin
about 139
URL 139
code based branching techniques
about 213
branch by abstraction 214
command line options
used, for launching headless slave
agents 41
used, for launching Java Web Start
(JavaWS) framework 40
Common Internet File System (CIFS)
about 43
errors, troubleshooting 46
Configuration panel
about 63, 104
options 104
console output 110, 111
Continuous Delivery (CD)
about 225
approvals 230-232
build pipelines 232, 233
characteristics 225
implementing 226
in Jenkins 228
principles 227
quality gates 230-232
rapid feedback loops 228, 229
Continuous Deployment
about 234, 235
in Jenkins 236
Continuous Integration (CI)
about 209, 210
and branches 213
code based branching techniques 213
Distributed Version Control Systems
(DVCS) 217
failures, fixing 217
feature toggles 215, 216

implementing 213
in Jenkins 218
Jenkins job, executing via SVN post-commit
hooks 220
Jenkins job, triggering via GitHub push 223
misconception 210-212
SCM polling 218, 219
CRON-based polling 219
CruiseControl 210

D

DCOM
about 42
errors, troubleshooting 46
slave node, launching on Windows 42-46
**Defense Advanced Research Projects
Agency (DARPA) 177**
Definitive Media Library. *See* **DML**
Delivery Pipeline plugin
configuring 195-199
URL 195
deployment automation
about 158
build artifacts, retrieving 160
executing 168-170
Jenkins slave nodes, leveraging for
deployment 170-172
packages, retrieving 160
describables
implementing 294
descriptors
implementing 294
disaster recovery
about 16
Jenkins mirror, setting up 18-21
snapshot backups 16, 17
distributed builds, Jenkins plugins 58
distributed testing solutions
about 139
parallel down stream jobs 141, 142
Selenium Grid 140
**Distributed Version Control Systems
(DVCS) 217**

DML
about 149
Artifactory, publishing to 153, 154
Docker container, pushing 156-158
Jenkins Artifactory plugin 153, 154
Jenkins artifacts, archiving 151
Maven, publishing via 155

Docker
Jenkins, integrating 240, 241
URL 242
used, for implementing dynamic Jenkins
slave nodes 244

Docker container
Jenkins, running 242-244
URL 243

downstream jobs
other projects, building 188, 189

dynamic Jenkins slave nodes
implementation tutorial 245-249
implementing, Docker used 244
prerequisites 244

E

Email-Ext plugin
about 228
URL 228

evarga/jenkins-slave
URL 245

executor status panel 67

extension points, Jenkins plugins
about 290
URL 290

Extreme Programming (XP) 209

F

failed jobs
disabling 111

feature toggles
about 215
in C# 216
in Embedded / C / C++ 216
in Java 216
in .NET 216
in Python 216

in Ruby 216
in Ruby on Rails 216
reference link 216

freestyle project
about 69
Advanced project options 76
build parameters, defining 74, 75
build steps 80
build triggers 79
creating 70-72
options 73
post-build actions 81
source code management 77

functional tests 117

G

Git
additional behaviors buttons 79
for source control 78
options 78

GitHub
URL 224

GitHub push
GitHub configurations 224
Jenkins configurations 223
Jenkins job, triggering 223
URL 223

Green Balls plugin 66

groups
about 54
creating, for slave node 56, 57

H

headless slave agents
launching, via command line 41

HPI plugin
compiling 296, 297
installing 296, 297

I

Infrastructure as Code (IaC) 249

IntelliJ IDEA
Maven-generated plugin,
importing 285-289
setting up 272-279

J

Java Development Kit (JDK) 272
Java Runtime Environment (JRE) 4
Java Web Start (JavaWS) framework
  headless slave agents, launching via
      command line 41
  launching, via command line 40
  launching, via web browser 39, 40
  launch page 38
  prerequisites 37
  slave node, launching 36
  URL 37
Jelly files 295, 296
Jelly tags
  about 295, 296
  example 295
  URL 295
Jenkins
  architecture 3
  automated tests 127-133
  configuration techniques 3
  executing, behind Apache reverse
      proxy 13-15
  executing, behind NGinX reverse
      proxy 11, 12
  integrating, with Ansible 249-257
  integrating, with Artifactory 257, 259
  integrating, with Docker 240, 241
  integrating, with Jira 268-270
  integrating, with Selenium Grid 260, 261
  MSTest results, publishing 138
  MSTest results, reporting 136, 137
  running, inside Docker container 242-244
  Selenium Grid, integrating 263-267
  URL 11
Jenkins Ansible plugin
  URL 255
Jenkins Artifactory plugin 153, 154
Jenkins Docker plugin
  URL 245
Jenkins fingerprints 164
Jenkins instances
  connecting 200-202
Jenkins JClouds plugin
  URL 245

Jenkins LTS release
  installing 24, 25
  URL 24
Jenkins mirror
  setting up, with rsync 18-21
Jenkins, on Linux and Unix
  installation 9
  Java JVM, configuring 9, 10
Jenkins, on Mac OS X
  installation 22, 23
  Jenkins LTS release, using 23-25
  XML configuration files 25-28
Jenkins, on Microsoft Windows
  installation 4-6
  Java arguments, configuring 7, 8
  JVM, configuring 7, 8
Jenkins plugins
  architecture 289-291
  creating 272
  describables, implementing 294
  descriptors, implementing 294
  extension points 290
  folder structure 283, 284
  job lifecycle 292, 293
  overrides, using 293
  reference link 273
  skeleton, creating 279-283
  URL 17
Jenkins slave nodes
  leveraging, for deployment 170-172
JetBrains ItelliJ IDEA
  URL 276
Jira
  Jenkins, integrating 268-270
  reference link 270
  URL 268
job execution 108
Job Execution Configuration panel 109
jobs
  about 68, 69
  existing job, copying 69
  external job 69
  external jobs, monitoring 85, 86
  filtering, by regular expression 92, 93
  freestyle project 69-72
  Maven project 69, 81, 82

T

TeamCity 210
Test Driven Development (TDD) 122
troubleshooting, DCOM errors
  access denied 46-48
  no more data available 48, 49
  reference link 48, 49

U

Ubuntu
  URL 252
unit tests
  about 116
  performing, through MSTest 133
upstream jobs
  triggering 187
user interface
  about 60
  build queue panel 67
  configuration panel 63
  executor status panel 67
  job table 64, 65
  main header 61, 62
  RSS feeds 66

V

Views
  advanced customization,
      of content 100, 102
  basic content, customizing 98, 99
  creating 90-92
  default view, altering 96-98
  jobs, filtering by regular expression 92, 93
  managing 96

W

white box tests 118
WMI 42

Thank you for buying
Mastering Jenkins

About Packt Publishing

Packt, pronounced 'packed', published its first book, *Mastering phpMyAdmin for Effective MySQL Management*, in April 2004, and subsequently continued to specialize in publishing highly focused books on specific technologies and solutions.

Our books and publications share the experiences of your fellow IT professionals in adapting and customizing today's systems, applications, and frameworks. Our solution-based books give you the knowledge and power to customize the software and technologies you're using to get the job done. Packt books are more specific and less general than the IT books you have seen in the past. Our unique business model allows us to bring you more focused information, giving you more of what you need to know, and less of what you don't.

Packt is a modern yet unique publishing company that focuses on producing quality, cutting-edge books for communities of developers, administrators, and newbies alike. For more information, please visit our website at www.packtpub.com.

About Packt Open Source

In 2010, Packt launched two new brands, Packt Open Source and Packt Enterprise, in order to continue its focus on specialization. This book is part of the Packt Open Source brand, home to books published on software built around open source licenses, and offering information to anybody from advanced developers to budding web designers. The Open Source brand also runs Packt's Open Source Royalty Scheme, by which Packt gives a royalty to each open source project about whose software a book is sold.

Writing for Packt

We welcome all inquiries from people who are interested in authoring. Book proposals should be sent to author@packtpub.com. If your book idea is still at an early stage and you would like to discuss it first before writing a formal book proposal, then please contact us; one of our commissioning editors will get in touch with you.

We're not just looking for published authors; if you have strong technical skills but no writing experience, our experienced editors can help you develop a writing career, or simply get some additional reward for your expertise.

Jenkins Continuous Integration Cookbook
Second Edition

ISBN: 978-1-78439-008-2 Paperback: 408 pages

Over 90 recipes to produce great results from Jenkins using pro-level practices, techniques, and solutions

1. Explore the use of more than 40 best-of-breed plug-ins for improving efficiency.

2. Secure and maintain Jenkins by integrating it with LDAP and CAS, which is a Single Sign-on solution.

3. Step-by-step, easy-to-use instructions to optimize the existing features of Jenkins using the complete set of plug-ins that Jenkins offers.

Apache Flume: Distributed Log Collection for Hadoop
Second Edition

ISBN: 978-1-78439-217-8 Paperback: 178 pages

Design and implement a series of Flume agents to send streamed data into Hadoop

1. Construct a series of Flume agents using the Apache Flume service to efficiently collect, aggregate, and move large amounts of event data.

2. Configure failover paths and load balancing to remove single points of failure.

3. Use this step-by-step guide to stream logs from application servers to Hadoop's HDFS.

Please check **www.PacktPub.com** for information on our titles

Apache Maven Cookbook

ISBN: 978-1-78528-612-4   Paperback: 272 pages

Over 90 hands-on recipes to successfully build and automate development life cycle tasks following Maven conventions and best practices

1. Understand the features of Apache Maven that makes it a powerful tool for build automation.

2. Full of real-world scenarios covering multi-module builds and best practices to make the most out of Maven projects.

3. A step-by-step tutorial guide full of pragmatic examples.

Learning Force.com Application Development

ISBN: 978-1-78217-279-6   Paperback: 406 pages

Use the Force.com platform to design and develop real-world, cutting-edge cloud applications

1. Design, build, and customize real-world applications on the Force.com platform.

2. Reach out to users through public websites and ensure that your Force.com application becomes popular.

3. Discover the tools that will help you develop and deploy your application.

Printed in the USA
CPSIA information can be obtained
at www.ICGtesting.com
LVHW082301041023
760194LV00012B/471

9 781784 390891